Hiking Waterfalls Montana

Help Us Keep This Guide Up to Date

Every effort has been made by the author and editors to make this guide as accurate and useful as possible. However, many things can change after a guide is published—trails are rerouted, techniques evolve, regulations change, facilities come under new management, and so on.

We would appreciate hearing from you concerning your experiences with this guide and how you feel it could be improved and kept up to date. While we may not be able to respond to all comments and suggestions, we'll take them to heart, and we'll also make certain to share them with the author. Please send your comments and suggestions to the following address:

FalconGuides
Reader Response/Editorial Department
246 Goose Lane, Suite 200
Guilford, CT 06437

Thanks for your input, and happy trails!

Hiking Waterfalls Montana

A Guide to the State's Best Waterfall Hikes

Second Edition

John Kratz

FALCONGUIDES

GUILFORD, CONNECTICUT

An imprint of Globe Pequot, the trade division of The Rowman & Littlefield Publishing Group, Inc.
4501 Forbes Blvd., Ste. 200
Lanham, MD 20706
www.rowman.com

Falcon and FalconGuides are registered trademarks and Make Adventure Your Story is a trademark of The Rowman & Littlefield Publishing Group, Inc.

Distributed by NATIONAL BOOK NETWORK

All photos by John Kratz unless otherwise noted
Maps by The Rowman & Littlefield Publishing Group, Inc.

British Library Cataloguing in Publication Information available

Library of Congress Cataloging-in-Publication Data
Name: Kratz, John (John Lawrence), author.
Title: Hiking waterfalls Montana : a guide to the state's best waterfall hikes / John Kratz.
Other titles: Hiking Waterfalls in Montana
Description: Second edition. | Guilford, Connecticut : Globe Pequot, 2022. | Revised edition of: Hiking Waterfalls in Montana, 2017. | Summary: "Fully revised and updated, Hiking Waterfalls Montana, Second Edition includes detailed hike descriptions, maps, and color photos for 100 of the state's most scenic waterfall hikes"—Provided by publisher.
Identifiers: LCCN 2021043659 (print) | LCCN 2021043660 (ebook) | ISBN 9781493061075 (paperback) | ISBN 9781493061082 (epub)
Subjects: LCSH: Hiking—Montana—Guidebooks. | Waterfalls—Montana—Guidebooks. | Trails—Montana—Guidebooks. | Montana—Guidebooks.
Classification: LCC GV199.42.M9 K73 2022 (print) | LCC GV199.42.M9 (ebook) | DDC 796.5109786—dc23
LC record available at https://lccn.loc.gov/2021043659
LC ebook record available at https://lccn.loc.gov/2021043660

∞™ The paper used in this publication meets the minimum requirements of American National Standard for Information Sciences—Permanence of Paper for Printed Library Materials, ANSI/NISO Z39.48-1992.

As long as I live, I'll hear waterfalls and birds and winds sing.
—John Muir, founder, Sierra Club

Contents

Overview

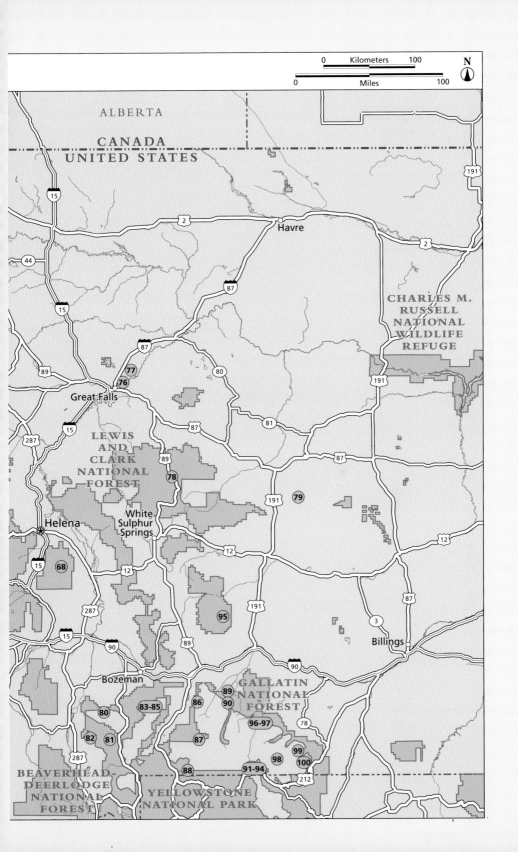

Acknowledgments

I would like to thank many people for the tremendous support and assistance I received during the creation of this book.

First and foremost, I'm grateful for the critical role my parents, Cathy and Larry, played since the beginning. You were the first to lace up my boots and put me on the trail as soon as I learned to walk in this world. In this way, you helped instill in me a deep respect for God's creation and a fervent desire to explore it.

I also want to express gratitude to the many hiking companions who discovered these destinations with me. Much appreciation for bringing the spirit of adventure to the trailheads, for sharing valuable insights along the routes, and for giving strength in numbers while venturing into the wild. Thank you, dear friends and family, for walking these paths with me: Martha Gunsalam, Anne Kratz, Joshua Keeley, Luke Kratz, Lawrence Kratz, Jeff Winmill, Juan Hudorovich, Matt Bell, Ted Muhs, Javier Astaiza, Carlos Villegas, Christian Baker, Brendan Knowles, Eric Forde, Erin Valenti, Maddison Nagle, and William Knight.

A sincere thank-you also goes out to the photographers who helped capture the beauty of the waterfalls and bring colorful images to the pages of this book: Martha Gunsalam, Luke Kratz, Christian Baker, Juan Hudorovich, and Brendan Knowles.

Indeed, I'm very thankful to the folks at Rowman & Littlefield and FalconGuides for the opportunity to create this book and for bringing it to the hiking public. To the readers of FalconGuides, thank you for putting the knowledge of these hikes to practice. The waterfall adventures you enjoy are the fruit of this labor, and they make it all very worthwhile.

Meet Your Guide

John Kratz grew up in Pocatello, Idaho, exploring the mountains that surround his small western hometown. He was first introduced to hiking by his parents, who took him and his three siblings on frequent trips to Yellowstone Park and central Idaho. At these locations, John's first hiking memories were made, and they left a lasting impression.

Beyond the borders of the state of Idaho, the author continued to make hiking one of his greatest passions. Trips into the mountains of Alaska, Wyoming, New York, Oregon, Costa Rica, Argentina, Chile, Peru, Spain, Morocco, Malaysia, and Indonesia further fueled his desire to put trail miles under his belt and spend time in the outdoors. After moving to Missoula, Montana, in 2011 to work as a musician and Spanish teacher, the author immediately began to hit the trails in Big Sky Country.

Photo by Martha Gunsalam.

Hiking Waterfalls in Montana is John's first published hiking guide.

Introduction

Looking back on the adventures I have had while walking over 550 miles of Montana trails, I realize how lucky I am to live in a place like this. All over the state, there are hundreds of trails for accessing mountains and streams in pristine settings. In exploring the state's one hundred best waterfall hikes, I had the special opportunity to travel to many places I never would have thought of visiting. It is now my privilege to share this information with you, so that you and your family may enjoy these places for years to come.

A friend exploring the base of Lower Cedar Falls.

While my purpose for writing this book is to connect people to wildlands, I also sincerely hope to connect people to each other. As Shakespeare once wrote, "One touch of nature makes the whole world kin." So, never take for granted the social aspect of your time in the outdoors. Take your friends and family with you and make memories together. And, with each new hike, renew your appreciation for each other and for the landscape.

The fact is, hiking is incredibly good for us in every way, and there are many reasons to play outdoors. For some hikers, taking a walk in the woods offers a time to relax and find relief from stress. For others, hiking is a time for reflection, inspiration, and renewal. Many hikers enjoy testing their physical limits, and they thrive off the challenges they must overcome on the trail. Others head out in the spirit of adventure and seek beautiful new horizons with each mile. Whatever your motivations may be, I encourage you to hike, and hike often.

How to Use This Guide

This book highlights one hundred of Montana's best waterfall hikes. There are literally hundreds if not thousands of waterfalls of varying size and popularity around the state, and they are found in almost every mountain range. In selecting which waterfalls to feature in this hiking guide, the following criteria were taken into consideration:

Trail Accessibility: This book profiles hikes that are accessible by way of some length of nonmotorized footpath. Therefore, waterfalls like Skalkaho Falls and Oberlin Falls that you can literally drive up to are not included. Since this guide is specifically for hikers, waterfalls that don't have any kind of trail approach, such as Bird

Woman Falls and the tallest waterfall in the state, Sperry Glacier Falls, aren't featured either. Waterfalls like Hole-in-the-Wall Falls, Lake Frances Falls, and Needle Falls that take more than 3 days to reach on foot aren't part of the book either, although they may appear in future editions.

Geographic Distribution: Trails to falls were also chosen to offer hikers opportunities in as many different regions of western Montana as possible where waterfalls exist.

Variety of Ability Levels: You will find hikes that suit every skill level—from wheelchair-accessible nature trails like Lost Creek Falls and Running Eagle Falls, to multiday backpacking trips like the routes to Impasse Falls, Cedar Falls, Pyramid Falls, and Big Salmon Falls.

The table of contents, trail finder, overview map, and hike profiles are tools you can use to select the hike that's best for every occasion.

Table of Contents: The hikes are organized by the mountain ranges in which they are located.

Trail Finder: To assist you in selecting a hike, the trail finder is a handy table that outlines some general aspects: hikes to the tallest waterfalls, hikes to the most secluded waterfalls, family hikes, hikes for swimming or wading, hikes with a chance to view wildlife, hikes with mountain views, hikes with lake views, hikes to waterfalls located a short distance from the trailhead, hikes for backpackers, and hikes to waterfalls with a challenging final approach.

Overview Map: To help you plan where to go, the statewide overview map shows all one hundred destinations spread over Montana. The numbers on the map correspond to the hike numbers.

Hike Profiles: The individual profiles are where you next delve into specific information that will help you finalize your destination decision and plan your hike. Start by reading the brief introduction that describes the highlights, specific challenges, and other general considerations for each hike. Next, review the hike specs section to get more useful, at-a-glance details.

Stream: This tells you the name of the river or creek in which the waterfall is located.

Height: Here you'll find the best estimation of each fall's stature in feet.

Distance: This tells you roughly how many total miles you will walk and whether it is an out-and-back hike, loop trail, or lollipop-shaped route. This is the most important piece of information that determines the overall difficulty of the hike. Please note that mileages in the book were measured on a Recreational Grade GPS device and therefore you should expect some variation from the actual mileage.

Elevation Gain: Another significant factor in assessing the difficulty of the hike is this approximation of the ascent and descent, in feet, required to complete the hike.

Difficulty: Here is the author's overall assessment of the difficulty level based on distance, elevation gain, trail conditions, and other aspects of the hike.

Trail Surface: This tells you what you'll be walking on. For the most part, you'll travel over trails made of dirt and rock, but in a few cases, the path is made of asphalt and is easily accessible by wheelchair.

Hiking Time: Here you'll get a range of how much time in minutes, hours, or days the hike will take so that you can plan accordingly for each adventure. Don't forget to figure in your own estimation of the driving time to and from the trailhead to calculate the overall trip length.

Canine Compatibility: This tells you whether dogs are allowed on the trail. You won't be able to hike with your pet on Yellowstone Park or Glacier Park trails, but most other places allow canine companions.

Seasons: Here you'll get a sense of what months are best to take the hike. This is mostly determined by when certain trails are free of snowpack. This recommendation also takes into account stream fords that are safest after spring-runoff season.

County: This is the name of the county where the hike is located.

Land Status: All the hikes in this guidebook cross public land. Here, you'll learn whether it is a national park, national forest, state park, or tribal land and if it is located in a designated wilderness area. In a few cases, trails cross private easements to access public land, so be mindful of landowner rights and stay on the path.

Fees and Permits: This tells you in which cases you'll need to pay a fee or get a permit to access the trail. When obtaining a permit, be sure to get informed of any specific regulations for hiking and camping in different locations.

Trail Contact: Since the trail descriptions in this guidebook are general, you can contact the various agencies that manage the lands to request up-to-date road and trail conditions. Consult the agencies' websites as well to learn more about the trails, regulations, wildfire closures, and other types of recreation that are available in each area.

Maps: In addition to using the trail maps included in this book, other helpful map resources are listed in this section. The *DeLorme Atlas and Gazetteer Montana* is ideal for driving on back roads around the state. Especially in the case of longer hikes, you should always plan to pack along a more detailed USGS Quad topographical map for the area you will be hiking in. Some hikers carry printed topo maps and others download them to their electronic devices.

Camping: Since hiking and camping often go hand in hand, this final part of the hike specs gives you a tip or two on developed campgrounds or primitive sites in the vicinity of each hike.

Finding the Trailhead: Following the hike specs section, each profile has a short description that specifically guides you in finding the trailhead by way of highways and back roads. The driving directions start from the nearest Montana town. You should compare the mileage listed for each stretch of roadway with your vehicle's odometer readings, so as not to miss a turn. GPS coordinates and elevation details are provided for each trailhead as well.

The Hike: The next part of the hike profile is similar to the introduction in providing you with a narrative about the hike. However, this second description aims to go into more depth on the natural history and topography of the area with facts about the sights along the way. Although not every detail here is essential for you to know to complete the hike, pay special attention at least to the specific directions on trail junctions, stream fords, and how to locate less obvious waterfalls. Keep in mind that the character of waterfalls can change drastically from season to season and from year to year. Therefore, the descriptions of falls in this section and the accompanying photographs may differ from your particular experience. In many cases, this section also provides suggestions for ways to extend the hike beyond the falls.

Trail Map: In addition to the text and photographs, each hike contains a trail map that visually shows geographic features such as roads, trails, trailheads, campgrounds, waterways, mountain passes, and peaks. When two or more hikes are located in the same general area, they often share a map. Some maps maintain a good amount of detail and can help you navigate the route, while others are zoomed out considerably and should be accompanied by a detailed topographical map.

Miles and Directions: The last portion of the hike profile gives you the approximate miles and directions specific to each hike. This lists the mileage from the trailhead to major features along the route such as bridges, fords, junctions, passes, wilderness boundaries, and, of course, waterfalls. Read the descriptions of trail junctions closely because they indicate important turns to make to ensure you find your way. GPS coordinates and elevations are also included here for junctions and waterfalls.

A final word on using this guide—it is important to keep in mind that this book won't prepare you for every circumstance and decision you'll need to make along the way to these waterfalls. Always err on the side of caution and common sense, and whenever possible, use additional resources beyond this book to further prepare you for the adventure.

Safety in the Backcountry

Taking a walk in the wild is always a do-at-your-own-risk activity, and there is no way to completely avoid unforeseen predicaments. However, many easy steps can help you significantly reduce the risk while in the outdoors and make your trip as pleasurable as possible.

As a general rule of thumb, always let someone know your travel plans before departure and try to hike in groups. Be prepared by carrying bear spray, first aid kits, and survival kits. Here are a few potential hazards to be aware of and suggestions on ways to steer clear of trouble:

Drowning: Drowning and water-related accidents are the historic number one cause of death in Glacier National Park and have claimed the lives of hikers all over the state. Always use great care when approaching waterfalls. If you get too close, you may slip on loose rock or wet surfaces and fall into the aggressive torrents of the stream. When crossing rivers or creeks, find the widest spot available and avoid deep water and fast current. Keep in mind that it is often the smaller creeks swollen by spring runoff that are the most dangerous for hikers. Do not make a crossing if it does not appear safe. You can always return and complete the hike when conditions improve.

Hypothermia: Hypothermia occurs when the body's core temperature reaches dangerously low levels after prolonged exposure to cold weather. This can happen at any time of year in Montana. Avoid getting your clothes wet by always carrying a good rain jacket or poncho and using extreme caution when crossing streams. If you begin to experience hypothermic symptoms, change into dry clothes immediately, wrap yourself in a warm blanket or sleeping bag, drink warm liquids, and when possible, do some type of physical activity to increase your core temperature. In the case of more severe symptoms, seek medical help as soon as possible.

Dehydration: Drink plenty of water before, during, and after your hike to avoid dehydration. Exposure to hot environments will increase the amount of water you'll need to take in to stay hydrated.

Giardia: These bacteria are found in streams all over Montana and can cause sickness if ingested. To avoid infection, use a filter to purify water from streams or pack in all the water you plan to drink during the hike. Boiling water for at least a minute is another way to remove giardia from the water. Never drink water directly from rivers or creeks.

Falling: The risk of falling in canyon terrain is definitely something to consider when exploring waterfalls. Be smart and never approach a canyon rim or the top of a headwall. Also, be on the alert for sudden gusts of wind when hiking in steep, mountainous country.

Avalanches: With temperatures warming up and deep snowpack in the high country, avalanches are a significant hazard to backcountry travelers in the spring. Don't walk along or under steep slopes of snowpack in the early season. Use your judgment to stay clear of potential snow slides. If you do decide to venture near steep snowpack, hike in groups and be prepared with beacons, shovels, and other avalanche equipment.

Lightning Storms: Pay attention to the changing weather and avoid open areas and tall objects if a thunderstorm appears to be moving in. Retreat to the vehicle if possible, or take shelter away from mountaintops, lone trees, or streams. Stay in a protected area until at least 30 minutes after the last sound of thunder.

Wildlife Encounters

Bears: Montana is home to healthy populations of both black bears and grizzly bears, and you have a chance of encountering both species in most of the mountain ranges featured in this book. Bears' natural instinct, however, is to avoid interactions with humans. Consider yourself lucky if you do manage to see one—the presence of these magnificent creatures and other large predators in Montana is an indication that our wilderness is still intact.

Many people consider bears to be a bigger threat to hiking safety than they really are and needlessly suffer from "bearanoia." Compared to other hazards like hypothermia, drowning, and falling, the instances of injury or death due to bear attacks are very few. Nonetheless, there are essential practices that will help you avoid unwanted conflict with bruins.

Bears typically only charge humans when they feel threatened, and for this reason, it is important to avoid surprising a bear. Some hikers prefer to travel in groups and maintain active conversation that alerts bears of their approach. Others sing or use bells or whistles while hiking in the wild. It is important to make some kind of noise, especially when entering thick brush or other areas of low visibility.

In the event of a bear encounter, never approach the bear. Stand tall and begin to retreat slowly. Do not look the bear in the eyes as this can be perceived as an act of aggression. If you are charged by a distressed bear, use your bear spray. This has been

A young cinnamon black bear.

proven to be the most effective way to deter a bear attack. If you don't have bear spray and are attacked, fall onto the ground, curl your body into a ball, cover your head, and play dead. If the animal no longer perceives you as a threat, it will probably leave.

When camping in the backcountry, it is important that you don't let bears come into contact with your food, so as to maintain their wild instinct to avoid humans. Select a campsite with two separate areas at least 100 feet apart—one area is for sleeping and the other is for food storage, preparation, and consumption. Whenever you are not eating, hang food, garbage, stoves, eating utensils, and all gear that has any kind of odor. Hang these items at least 10 feet above the ground and 4 feet away from the trunk of the tree. Never store food in your tent or leave food unattended even for a moment. Be sure to notify a ranger if a bear does access your food, so that those hiking behind you have a safe experience.

Mountain lions: Conflicts with cougars are also extremely rare, but in the event of an attack, fight back.

Moose and other large ungulates: A cow moose with young is perhaps the most dangerous animal in Montana, especially when surprised at a short distance. Do not approach any large ungulate, especially females with offspring or males during the fall rut.

Rattlesnakes: Rattlesnakes inhabit very few of the hiking areas in this book. However, if you are hiking in dry, rocky environments at lower elevations, carry a snakebite kit and be alert for snakes resting on the trail.

Ticks: To prevent contracting an illness such as Lyme disease or Rocky Mountain fever, check yourself and your children and pets for ticks during and after each hike, especially during the late winter and spring. Ticks seek moist, warm places and will often hide in your clothes until they get an opportunity to move onto your body. Some insect repellents are effective in deterring them. It takes several hours for a tick to latch onto your skin, so you can locate and remove them before they are able to bite. If you do find a tick attached to your body, use fine tweezers to grip the tick as close to the skin as possible and pull backward gently but firmly until it is removed. Wash the area with soap and water and keep the tick in a small bag in case later identification is necessary.

Driving on rough back roads: Many trailheads in this book require driving on dirt and gravel back roads. When traveling on these narrow, winding byways, maintain a safe speed to avoid encountering oncoming traffic on sudden curves and to prevent tire damage. Turn back when roads are icy, slushy, or muddy, so as to not end up in a ditch or at the bottom of a ravine.

Other hazards: Be cautious and use common sense to avoid other potential dangers such as flash floods, forest fires, falling rocks and trees, sunburn, heatstroke, altitude sickness, and getting lost.

Zero Impact

To preserve the natural beauty of the backcountry for those who will hike the trail after you, it is essential to uphold zero-impact principles on every trip. These practices are easy and can quickly become effortless habits. The following guidelines will help you leave no trace and keep the wildlands wild for many generations to come:

- Pack out all trash and food waste, and pick up any garbage others leave behind.
- Keep streams clean by never putting anything in the water.
- Stay on the trail at switchbacks. Cutting causes serious erosion.
- Avoid walking on vegetation along the side of the trail.
- Be gentle when exploring waterfalls off-trail. Walk only on hard surfaces such as rock and dirt and avoid stepping on sensitive plants like moss, lichens, and wildflowers.
- Keep your noise level to a minimum, except when alerting bears of your presence in areas of low visibility.
- Carry a trowel to bury human waste at least 6 inches below the ground and at least 200 feet from any water source or trail.
- Use only existing fire rings and consider not having a campfire at all, especially in areas where wood is scarce. Use stoves to cook and a flashlight or headlamp for light.
- Use only existing campsites and camp on hard surfaces so as not to damage delicate plant life.

- Keep food out of reach of animals by keeping it inside your pack while hiking or strung high on a tree while camping.
- Visit the backcountry in small groups of ten or fewer hikers.
- Be informed and ready to follow conservation regulations that are specific to the areas you visit.

Packing for the Hike

Be prepared for a successful day-hike or backpacking trip by packing all the essential gear. Here is a list of the most important items to take along:

Day-Hikes
- Daypack
- Hiking boots or shoes
- Comfortable, layered clothing
- Bottle of water, at least 1 liter
- High-energy food
- Rain jacket
- Bear spray, quickly accessible while hiking
- First aid kit
- Survival kit
- Trail map and compass
- Headlamp or flashlight
- Sun protection
- Insect repellent
- Lightweight sandals or other extra footwear for crossing streams

Extra Gear for Overnight Backpacking Trips
- Backpack
- Tent
- Sleeping bag
- Sleeping pad
- High-energy rations
- Camp stove and fuel
- Cooking pot and eating utensils
- Rope for hanging food
- Water filter
- Knife
- Waterproof lighters or matches
- Extra changes of warm clothes

Montana Wildlife

The diversity and observability of Rocky Mountain fauna is something truly exceptional. On a given day, a wildlife watcher in Montana can spot an array of large game animals, and many wildlife species can be seen from the trails featured in this book.

While it is our privilege to enjoy encounters with wildlife, it is also our responsibility to protect vulnerable species and the ecosystems in which these creatures thrive. Remember to keep a distance from all wildlife, especially from predators and animals with young, and be respectful of the natural resources that these species depend on for survival.

Many of the hike profiles in this book mention wildlife you are likely to find in each area. Large mammals that are most commonly seen on hikes in Montana are white-tailed deer, mule deer, elk, moose, black bear, mountain goat, bighorn sheep, pronghorn, coyote, beaver, and fox. Other species that are often present but less often observed include grizzly bear, bison, wolf, mountain lion, wolverine, bobcat, marten, and lynx.

Montana is also an excellent place for bird watchers. From raptors to waterfowl to songbirds, you may encounter dozens of different bird species while out on a hike.

A herd of young bighorn sheep crossing a stream.

Trail Finder

#	Hike Name	Best Hikes to Tall Waterfalls	Best Hikes to Secluded Waterfalls	Best Waterfall Hikes for Swimming	Best Waterfall Hikes for Children	Best Waterfall Hikes for Wildlife Watchers	Best Waterfall Hikes for Mountain Views	Best Waterfall Hikes for Backpackers	Waterfall Hikes with Challenging Final Approaches	Waterfall Hikes a Short Distance from the Road	Best Waterfall Hikes with Lake Views
1.	West Fork Yaak Falls			*					*	*	
2.	Turner Falls		*			*	*	*			*
3.	Little North Fork Falls				*					*	
4.	Leigh Creek Falls		*		*	*	*		*		*
5.	Granite Creek Falls		*	*	*	*		*			
6.	Rock Creek Falls		*		*	*	*	*			*
7.	Baree Creek Falls		*			*			*		
8.	South Fork Ross Creek Falls		*		*				*		
9.	Kootenai Falls			*	*	*				*	
10.	Pinkham Falls			*					*	*	

#	Hike Name	Best Hikes to Tall Waterfalls	Best Hikes to Secluded Waterfalls	Best Waterfall Hikes for Swimming	Best Waterfall Hikes for Children	Best Waterfall Hikes for Wildlife Watchers	Best Waterfall Hikes for Mountain Views	Best Waterfall Hikes for Backpackers	Waterfall Hikes with Challenging Final Approaches	Waterfall Hikes a Short Distance from the Road	Best Waterfall Hikes with Lake Views
11.	Sunday Falls			*	*					*	
12.	Martin Falls		*		*					*	
13.	Beaver Chief Falls	*	*	*		*	*	*			*
14.	Beaver Medicine Falls	*	*			*	*	*			*
15.	McDonald Falls and Sacred Dancing Cascade				*	*	*			*	*
16.	Monument Falls and Avalanche Gorge	*		*		*	*				*
17.	Florence Falls and Deadwood Falls	*	*	*		*	*	*			
18.	Baring Falls				*	*	*				*
19.	St. Mary and Virginia Falls	*			*	*	*				*

#	Hike Name	Best Hikes to Tall Waterfalls	Best Hikes to Secluded Waterfalls	Best Waterfall Hikes for Swimming	Best Waterfall Hikes for Children	Best Waterfall Hikes for Wildlife Watchers	Best Waterfall Hikes for Mountain Views	Best Waterfall Hikes for Backpackers	Waterfall Hikes with Challenging Final Approaches	Waterfall Hikes a Short Distance from the Road	Best Waterfall Hikes with Lake Views
20.	Rose Creek Falls					*	*	*			*
21.	Pyramid Falls	*	*	*		*	*	*			*
22.	Raven Quiver Falls	*	*	*		*	*	*			*
23.	Dawn Mist Falls		*			*	*	*			
24.	Apikuni Falls	*			*	*	*		*		*
25.	Morning Eagle Falls	*				*	*				*
26.	Ptarmigan Falls				*	*	*				
27.	Redrock Falls			*	*	*	*				*
28.	Atlantic Falls					*	*	*			
29.	Running Eagle Falls				*		*			*	
30.	Appistoki Falls				*	*	*			*	
31.	Twin Falls			*	*	*	*				*
32.	Aster Falls and Rockwell Falls			*	*	*	*				

#	Hike Name	Best Hikes to Tall Waterfalls	Best Hikes to Secluded Waterfalls	Best Waterfall Hikes for Swimming	Best Waterfall Hikes for Children	Best Waterfall Hikes for Wildlife Watchers	Best Waterfall Hikes for Mountain Views	Best Waterfall Hikes for Backpackers	Waterfall Hikes with Challenging Final Approaches	Waterfall Hikes a Short Distance from the Road	Best Waterfall Hikes with Lake Views
33.	Dean Falls		*	*		*	*	*	*		
34.	Spotted Bear Falls			*	*	*			*	*	
35.	Graves Creek Falls			*	*					*	
36.	Bond Creek Falls				*	*	*	*			
37.	Arnica Falls		*				*		*		
38.	Rumble Creek Falls	*	*			*	*	*			*
39.	Holland Falls				*	*	*				*
40.	Big Salmon Falls and Upper Holland Falls		*	*		*	*	*			*
41.	Morrell Falls	*			*	*					*
42.	Monture Falls		*			*	*	*	*		
43.	Lodgepole Falls	*	*						*		

#	Hike Name	Best Hikes to Tall Waterfalls	Best Hikes to Secluded Waterfalls	Best Waterfall Hikes for Swimming	Best Waterfall Hikes for Children	Best Waterfall Hikes for Wildlife Watchers	Best Waterfall Hikes for Mountain Views	Best Waterfall Hikes for Backpackers	Waterfall Hikes with Challenging Final Approaches	Waterfall Hikes a Short Distance from the Road	Best Waterfall Hikes with Lake Views
44.	North Fork Falls		*				*	*	*		
45.	North Crow Creek Falls			*	*		*				
46.	Mission Falls	*				*	*		*		
47.	Glacier Creek Falls	*	*	*	*	*	*				*
48.	Cascade Falls				*	*	*		*		
49.	Dipper Falls		*		*	*	*	*			*
50.	Lost Creek Falls		*		*	*					*
51.	Emerald Sun Falls and Trout Creek Cascades		*	*			*		*		
52.	Stepladder Falls		*			*	*	*			
53.	Abha Falls		*						*		
54.	Sweathouse Falls						*	*			

#	Hike Name	Best Hikes to Tall Waterfalls	Best Hikes to Secluded Waterfalls	Best Waterfall Hikes for Swimming	Best Waterfall Hikes for Children	Best Waterfall Hikes for Wildlife Watchers	Best Waterfall Hikes for Mountain Views	Best Waterfall Hikes for Backpackers	Waterfall Hikes with Challenging Final Approaches	Waterfall Hikes a Short Distance from the Road	Best Waterfall Hikes with Lake Views
55.	Brave Bear Falls			*	*		*				
56.	Mill Canyon Falls			*		*	*	*			
57.	Blodgett Falls			*	*	*	*	*			*
58.	Canyon Falls	*					*	*	*		
59.	Rock Creek Falls				*	*	*	*			*
60.	Little Rock Creek Falls		*			*	*	*	*		*
61.	Trapper Creek Falls		*	*			*				
62.	Boulder Falls		*	*			*		*		
63.	Overwhich Falls	*	*			*	*	*	*		
64.	Star Falls			*		*		*			
65.	Pintler Falls		*	*	*	*				*	
66.	Lost Creek Falls				*		*			*	*

#	Hike Name	Best Hikes to Tall Waterfalls	Best Hikes to Secluded Waterfalls	Best Waterfall Hikes for Swimming	Best Waterfall Hikes for Children	Best Waterfall Hikes for Wildlife Watchers	Best Waterfall Hikes for Mountain Views	Best Waterfall Hikes for Backpackers	Waterfall Hikes with Challenging Final Approaches	Waterfall Hikes a Short Distance from the Road	Best Waterfall Hikes with Lake Views
67.	Rock Creek Falls	*			*			*	*		*
68.	Crow Creek Falls					*		*			
69.	Dearborn River Cascades					*	*	*			
70.	Cataract Falls	*			*					*	
71.	Double Falls				*					*	
72.	Willow Creek Falls		*	*		*	*				
73.	Mill Falls				*	*				*	
74.	Our Lake Falls	*			*	*	*	*			*
75.	Muddy Creek Falls		*			*	*				
76.	Rainbow Falls and Crooked Falls				*	*					
77.	Big Falls				*	*				*	
78.	Memorial Falls				*					*	

#	Hike Name	Best Hikes to Tall Waterfalls	Best Hikes to Secluded Waterfalls	Best Waterfall Hikes for Swimming	Best Waterfall Hikes for Children	Best Waterfall Hikes for Wildlife Watchers	Best Waterfall Hikes for Mountain Views	Best Waterfall Hikes for Backpackers	Waterfall Hikes with Challenging Final Approaches	Waterfall Hikes a Short Distance from the Road	Best Waterfall Hikes with Lake Views
79.	Crystal Cascades		*						*		
80.	Pioneer Falls		*		*	*	*				
81.	Ousel Falls				*	*					
82.	Cedar Falls	*	*	*		*	*	*	*		*
83.	Waterfalls of Hyalite Creek				*	*	*	*			*
84.	Palisade Falls	*			*					*	
85.	Horsetail Falls		*				*		*		
86.	Pine Creek Falls	*		*	*	*	*	*			*
87.	Passage Falls		*		*		*				
88.	Knowles Falls		*	*		*	*	*			
89.	Natural Bridge Falls				*	*	*			*	
90.	Great Falls Creek Falls		*				*		*		
91.	Bridal Falls		*		*		*			*	

#	Hike Name	Best Hikes to Tall Waterfalls	Best Hikes to Secluded Waterfalls	Best Waterfall Hikes for Swimming	Best Waterfall Hikes for Children	Best Waterfall Hikes for Wildlife Watchers	Best Waterfall Hikes for Mountain Views	Best Waterfall Hikes for Backpackers	Waterfall Hikes with Challenging Final Approaches	Waterfall Hikes a Short Distance from the Road	Best Waterfall Hikes with Lake Views
92.	Silver Falls	*	*		*	*	*				
93.	Sheep Creek Falls	*	*	*			*		*		
94.	Woody Falls	*	*		*		*				
95.	Upper Big Timber Falls				*	*	*	*			
96.	Woodbine Falls	*			*	*	*				
97.	Stillwater River Cascades			*	*			*		*	
98.	Impasse Falls	*	*	*		*	*	*	*		*
99.	Sentinel Falls and Calamity Falls			*	*		*	*			
100.	Silver Falls		*			*	*	*	*		*

Map Legend

Municipal

≡⟨90⟩≡   Interstate Highway

⟨287⟩   US Highway

⟨141⟩   State Road

⟨510⟩   County/Forest Road

-------   State Boundary

-------   International Boundary

Trails

-------   Featured Trail

-------   Trail

Water Features

⬭   Lake/Reservoir

〜   River/Creek

⁀⁀   Intermittent Stream

≋   Waterfall

∥   Rapid

⌀⟋   Spring

Symbols

▲   Backcountry campsite

≋   Boat Ramp

⏑   Bridge

▲   Campground

✪   Capital

🅿   Parking

⏓   Pass

🛱   Picnic Area

■   Point of Interest/Structure

🛉   Ranger Station

○   Town

①   Trailhead

🖾   Viewpoint/Overlook

❷   Visitor/Information Center

Land Management

▭   National Park/Forest/Recreation Area

▭   National Wilderness

Purcell Mountains

Most of the Purcell Mountains are located in British Columbia, but a small portion extends into northwest Montana. Both Rocky Mountain and Pacific Coast tree species are present in this heavily forested region. The Yaak River flows south through the range and Lake Koocanusa forms the mountains' eastern boundary.

Spiraea douglasii *in the Purcell Mountains.*

1 West Fork Yaak Falls

There are two waterfalls on the West Fork Yaak River that are both excellent places to get in the water on a hot day. Lower West Fork Yaak Falls is a scenic destination for a short, family hike. Stroll peacefully through a diverse array of old-growth trees to a viewing platform over the creek. The waterfall plummets through columns of sedimentary rock and into a deep and inviting pool. There is a rugged path to the bottom for swimmers' access as well as places for children to wade in the creek near the trailhead.

Upper West Fork Yaak Falls is accessed by a short but steep path that descends to the river. A large column stands in the middle of the gorge and water spills around it. The falls create a large pool that is perfect for cooling off. For the most impressive display, come during spring runoff when the water level is at its maximum.

Stream: West Fork Yaak River
Height: Lower Falls, 25 feet; Upper Falls, 20 feet
Distance: Lower Falls, 0.4 mile out and back; Upper Falls, 0.2 mile out and back
Elevation loss: Lower Falls, 30 feet; Upper Falls, 25 feet
Difficulty: Lower Falls, easy; Upper Falls, challenging terrain
Trail surface: Lower Falls, dirt; Upper Falls, loose dirt, rock, shale, river
Hiking time: Lower Falls, 5–10 minutes; Upper Falls, 10–20 minutes

Canine compatibility: Dogs are allowed
Seasons: Mar to Dec
County: Lincoln
Land status: National forest
Fees and permits: No fees required
Trail contact: Kootenai National Forest, 31374 US 2, Libby, MT 59923-3022; (406) 293-6211; fs.usda.gov/kootenai
Maps: *DeLorme Atlas and Gazetteer Montana* Page 20, A4; *USGS Quad* Bonnet Top
Camping: Caribou Campground is a tent-only campground located at mile 52 of MT 508, and has three no-fee sites.

Finding the Trailhead:

Lower Falls: From Yaak, drive north on Yaak River Road, MT 508, for 9.0 miles. Turn left into the West Fork Yaak Falls parking area.

Upper Falls: Turn left from West Fork Yaak Falls parking area and continue north on Yaak River Road for 0.1 mile. Turn left on West Fork Yaak Road #276 and drive west on this narrow gravel road for 2.1 miles. There is an unmarked pullout on the left. The trail begins on the south side of the road.

GPS: Lower Falls, 48.9341, -115.6741 Elevation: 3,100 feet
GPS: Upper Falls, 48.9319, -115.7173 Elevation: 3,380 feet

The Hike

Lower Falls: The path on the left leads to a small sandy beach on the river for wading and picnicking. Take the wider path on the right to the falls. You pass a magnificent

Lower West Fork Yaak Falls.

stand of old-growth western white pine that soar high in the canopy of the forest. You begin to hear the rumble of the falls and suddenly reach a wooden platform with a spectacular view. Lower West Fork Falls drops through a box-shaped opening in the bedrock and then makes a final pour into an enormous green pool. If the glistening

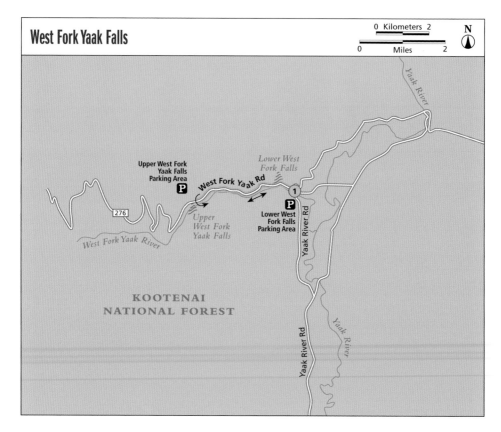

0 Kilometers 2

0   Miles   2

N

Upper West Fork
Yaak Falls
Parking Area

Lower West
Fork Falls

West Fork Yaak Rd

276

Upper
West Fork
Yaak Falls

West Fork Yaak River

Lower West
Fork Falls
Parking Area

Yaak River Rd

Yaak River Rd

Yaak River

Yaak River

KOOTENAI
NATIONAL FOREST

waters entice you for a cool dip, take the steep path down to paradise. A second path follows the rim of the canyon to a precarious view from the brink of the falls.

Upper Falls: Start descending carefully down a steep, worn path of loose dirt and shale. Some hikers will find this terrain too difficult. Be very careful as you come to the rim of the gorge. After spring runoff, the waterfall is concealed from this lookout but more visible if you hike to the other side of the river. Take the path downstream and drop steeply to the crystal-clear water of the West Fork Yaak River. At normal water level, you can ford the thigh-high stream to the rocks on the other side. Walk to the far wall and peer up the gorge into a dark cave. A small 20-foot waterfall drops almost vertically into a deep pool. Watch for toads and trout in this cool aquatic environment. While you're down at the river, take a swim or maybe jump into the water from one of the nearby boulders.

Miles and Directions

Lower Falls:

0.0 Lower West Fork Yaak Falls parking area

0.2 Viewing platform

0.2 Base of Lower West Fork Yaak Falls
GPS: 48.9342, -115.6774 Elevation: 3,070 feet

0.4 Arrive back at the trailhead.

Upper Falls:

0.0 Upper West Fork Yaak Falls parking area

0.1 Base of Upper West Fork Yaak Falls
GPS: 48.9313, -115.7173 Elevation: 3,355 feet

0.2 Arrive back at the trailhead.

2 Turner Falls

Vinal Creek Trail takes you to a spectacular waterfall and a chain of turquoise lakes in the Purcell Mountains north of Libby. This rugged route was designated a Pacific Northwest National Recreation Trail for its sheer beauty and popularity with day-hikers and backpackers. The trail follows Vinal Creek through an old-growth temperate rainforest to a rocky canyon where Turner Falls plunges for over 75 feet. Shortly beyond the falls, you visit the Fish Lakes, a series of small lakes with decent fishing and camping. There is a good chance of encountering wildlife and edible berries along the way.

Stream: Turner Creek
Height: 75 feet
Distance: 6.8 miles out and back
Elevation gain: 465 feet
Difficulty: Moderate
Trail surface: Dirt and rock
Hiking time: 6–7 hours
Canine compatibility: Dogs are allowed
Seasons: May to Nov
County: Lincoln
Land status: National forest

Fees and permits: No fees required
Trail contact: Kootenai National Forest, 31374 US 2, Libby, MT 59923-3022; (406) 293-6211; fs.usda.gov/kootenai
Maps: *DeLorme Atlas and Gazetteer Montana* Page 20, A5; *USGS Quad* Lost Horse Mountain
Camping: There are primitive campsites for backpackers at Turner Falls and at the second lake. Caribou Campground is a tent-only campground located at mile 52 of MT 508, and has three no-fee sites.

Finding the Trailhead: From Yaak take South Fork Road, County Highway 567, southeast for 4.2 miles. Turn left on gravel Vinal Lake Road #746 and travel 6.0 miles. After crossing a bridge over Vinal Creek, turn into the trailhead parking area on the right.

From Libby, travel north for 31.8 miles on Pipe Creek Road, County Highway 567, which becomes South Fork Road after crossing Flat Iron Summit. Turn right on Vinal Lake Road #746 and travel 6.0 miles to the trailhead parking area on the right.

GPS: 48.8610, -115.6438 Elevation: 3,110 feet

The Hike

Start climbing gently up the hillside north of the creek. Watch your footing as you walk—Vinal Creek Trail has frequent rough patches where you have to clamber over rocks, roots, and other obstacles. While ambling pleasantly under monstrous cedars, hemlocks, and larch, listen to the chorus of songbirds and the soft murmur of the stream. After more than a mile, you reach a large talus slope beneath giant gray boulders.

Pika, a small rock-loving member of the rabbit family, can be easily spotted in this area. You enter an area of rock formations and open terrain on both sides of the

Turner Falls.

canyon. The added sunlight gives way to new tree species such as juniper, aspen, and birch.

Over the course of the next mile, you proceed to cross Vinal Creek five times on well-maintained footbridges. After the first bridge, a wooden walkway takes you over a marshy area in the forest. Wild rose, fireweed, and delphinium add color to the scene.

A second wooden footbridge takes you back to the north side of Vinal Creek and into an old cedar grove. As you advance through more rocky terrain, keep an eye out for delicious raspberries in July. You cross the next two footbridges and then the trail

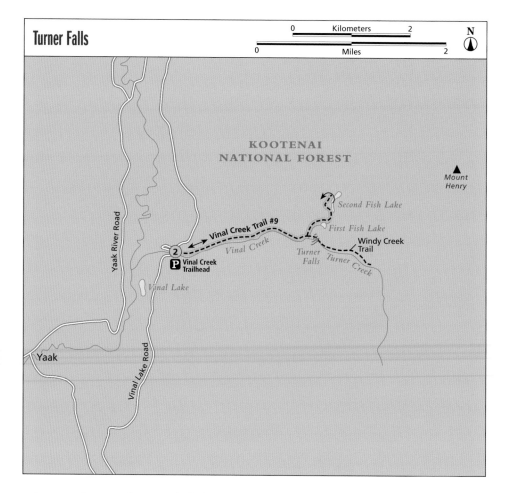

increases in ruggedness, with shale and tree roots creating more tripping hazards. The scenery is lush and beautiful, but keep your eyes on the path during rough sections.

The last bridge crosses Vinal Creek's largest tributary, Turner Creek, and you arrive at a campsite and a path to Turner Falls. Turn right and walk a few hundred feet to an impressive view of the waterfall from the bottom of a 100-foot cliff. After a vertical drop, the creek feathers out and cascades into a round pool between mossy boulders. The pool empties into a tight logjam and then falls a final 5 feet into a lower pool. Find a seat near the top pool and feel the cool breeze and mist produced by 75 feet of falling water.

To continue to Fish Lakes, return to the main trail and turn right. Keep left on Windy Creek Trail at the Y-junction and hike a quarter mile to the first lake. Watch for bald eagles, waterfowl, and moose at this small body of water surrounded by talus slopes and healthy stands of western larch. Continue up the trail to more picturesque lakes nestled throughout the canyon. There are several well-developed campsites for backpackers. The second lake is much larger and more scenic but can be crowded on summer weekends.

Miles and Directions

0.0 Vinal Creek Trailhead #9

1.3 First bridge over Vinal Creek

1.6 Second bridge over Vinal Creek

2.0 Third and fourth bridges over Vinal Creek

2.3 Fifth bridge over Vinal Creek

2.5 Bridge over Turner Creek

2.6 Turn right on side trail to Turner Falls.
GPS: 48.8655, -115.5847 Elevation: 3,440 feet

2.6 Base of Turner Falls
GPS: 48.8654, -115.5843 Elevation: 3,525 feet

2.6 Return to main trail. Turn right to Fish Lakes.

2.7 Turn left on Windy Creek Trail #397 at Y-junction.

3.0 First of the Fish Lakes

3.4 Second of the Fish Lakes
GPS: 48.8719, -115.5739 Elevation: 3,575 feet

6.8 Arrive back at the trailhead.

3 Little North Fork Falls

Located in the eastern Purcell Mountains just west of Lake Koocanusa, Little North Fork Falls pours over tall ledges into a narrow ravine. Along the National Recreational Trail, interpretive signs educate you about the flora, fauna, and geology of the place. The short walk up the well-maintained trail is suitable for all hikers, and the shady forest is a pleasant escape from summer heat. Stay a night at a nice camping area near the banks of trout-laden Big Creek by the trailhead.

Stream: Little North Fork Creek
Height: 50 feet
Distance: 0.3 mile out and back
Elevation gain: 85 feet
Difficulty: Easy
Trail surface: Dirt
Hiking time: 5–10 minutes
Canine compatibility: Dogs are allowed
Seasons: May to Nov
County: Lincoln

Land status: National forest
Fees and permits: No fees required
Trail contact: Kootenai National Forest, 31374 US 2, Libby, MT 59923-3022; (406) 293-6211; fs.usda.gov/kootenai
Maps: *DeLorme Atlas and Gazetteer Montana* Page 21, B6; *USGS Quad* Boulder Lakes and Webb Mountain
Camping: There is a campsite at the banks of Big Creek near the trailhead parking area.

Finding the Trailhead: From Rexford, drive southeast on MT 37 for 7.5 miles along the east side of Lake Koocanusa. Turn right and cross Lake Koocanusa Bridge for 0.5 mile. After the bridge, take a left on paved FR 228 and travel for 8.5 miles. Turn right on gravel Big Creek Road #336 and drive for 1.6 miles to the bridge over Little North Fork Creek.
GPS: 48.7519, -115.3719 Elevation: 2,665 feet

The Hike

Find the small path east of Little North Fork Creek and climb gradually through diverse forest. Tall trees like cottonwood, larch, cedar, and pine dominate the canopy while dogwood, alder, birch, and maple inhabit the understory. Continue up the shady, fern-lined path past mossy cliff overhangs dripping with water.

Although not the tastiest of edible berries, there are thimbleberries galore along the sides of the trail. The deeper you go into the lush woods, the more you notice the moisture of the temperate rainforest. There is a halfway bench to rest on after a steady uphill climb as well as a metal bridge where you can watch the creek's endless cascading and pooling motion.

A few steps later, you arrive at the end of the trail, with a perfect view from the base of Little North Fork Falls. The 50-foot waterfall makes three drops through a narrow gorge of mossy sedimentary rock. If you're looking for a greater challenge, clamber up a path on the left to the top of the falls. Just be extremely careful on the loose dirt near the edges of the cliff.

Little North Fork Falls.

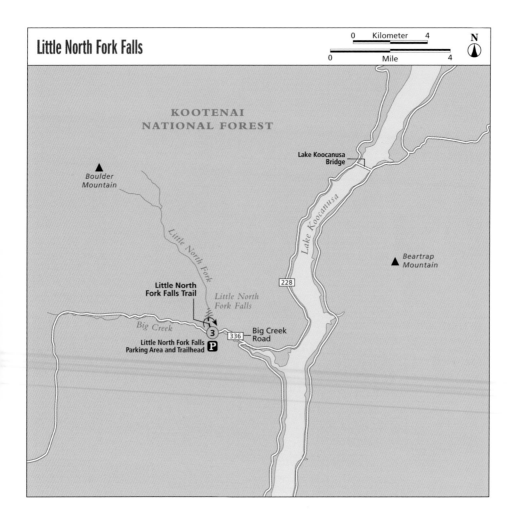

Little North Fork Falls

Miles and Directions

0.0 Little North Fork Falls Trailhead

0.1 Bridge over Little North Fork Creek

0.15 Base of Little North Fork Falls

GPS: 48.7536, -115.3732 Elevation: 2,750 feet

0.3 Arrive back at the trailhead.

Cabinet Mountains

The Cabinet Mountains are situated between the Idaho border and the Kootenai and Clark Fork Rivers south of the Purcell Mountains. An excellent trail system leads into the subalpine terrain and high peaks of the Cabinet Mountain Wilderness. The range's highest peak, Snowshoe Peak, stands at 8,700 feet and has the highest elevation of any mountain between Glacier Park and the Cascades. The north end of the range slopes down to the lowest point in Montana at 1,820 feet.

Mountain goats at Leigh Lake.

4 Leigh Creek Falls

The hike to Leigh Creek Falls and beyond is steep and strenuous but the payoff is enormous. You get to see not only a spectacular waterfall but also Leigh Lake, the largest lake in the Cabinet Mountains Wilderness, and Snowshoe Peak, the tallest point in the range. On the way, you stand a good chance of seeing mountain goats in the rocky subalpine environment. There is no camping within 300 yards of the lake, which makes the trek most suitable as a day-hike. The mountain grandeur you find on this hike is hard to beat anywhere.

Stream: Leigh Creek
Height: 80 feet
Distance: 2.5 miles out and back
Elevation gain: 1,180 feet
Difficulty: Strenuous
Trail surface: Dirt and rock
Hiking time: 2–3 hours
Canine compatibility: Dogs are allowed
Seasons: July to Oct
County: Lincoln

Land status: Wilderness area, national forest
Fees and permits: No fees required
Trail contact: Kootenai National Forest, 31374 US 2, Libby, MT 59923-3022; (406) 293-6211; fs.usda.gov/kootenai
Maps: *DeLorme Atlas and Gazetteer Montana* Page 20, F5; *USGS Quad* Snowshoe Peak
Camping: Pleasant Valley Campground is located 32 miles southwest of Libby on US 2 and has seven no-fee sites.

Finding the Trailhead: From Libby, drive south on US 2 for 8.0 miles to the turnoff for Bear Creek Road #278. Turn right on this rough, paved road and drive for 3.0 miles to Cherry Creek Road #837. Turn right onto this bumpy, gravel road and drive for 4.4 miles to FR 4786 with a sign for Leigh Lake Trail. Drive a final 1.8 miles to the trailhead at the end of the road. A high-clearance vehicle is recommended on this last road. Take it slow to avoid a flat tire.
GPS: 48.2245, -115.6413 Elevation: 3,940 feet

The Hike

The rugged trail starts climbing the steep mountainside right off the bat. You come to an overlook at the edge of the timber where you hear cascading water and view the brushy open slopes around Leigh Creek. Continue your grueling ascent past a sign marking the entrance into the Cabinet Mountain Wilderness. Peeks at cascading whitewater through the trees motivate you to keep hiking the steep switchbacks up the mountain.

After climbing nearly 1,000 feet, you finally reach a rise where you catch your first glimpse of Leigh Creek Falls with the majestic 8,740-foot Snowshoe Peak rising behind it. Walk past an avalanche-formed rocky ravine to a pool at the base of the waterfall. It's hard to determine the total stature of Leigh Creek Falls. It possesses multiple drops and cascades that plummet forcefully down the rocky slope. The view

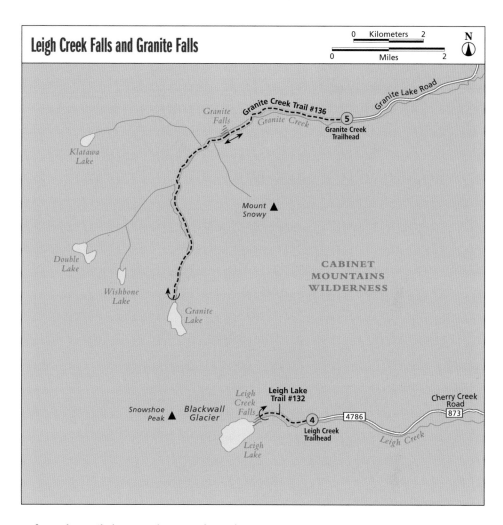

0 Kilometers 2

N

0 Miles 2

Granite Creek Trail #136

Granite Lake Road

Granite Falls

Granite Creek

5

Granite Creek Trailhead

Klatawa Lake

Mount Snowy ▲

CABINET MOUNTAINS WILDERNESS

Double Lake

Wishbone Lake

Granite Lake

Leigh Creek Falls

Leigh Lake Trail #132

Cherry Creek Road

Snowshoe Peak ▲

Blackwall Glacier

4

4786

873

Leigh Creek Trailhead

Leigh Creek

Leigh Lake

from the trail shows at least 80 feet of continuous terraces and falls. If you need to cool off, the welcoming pool is large enough for an ice-cold dip.

Climb another 300 feet up the trail with continued views of Leigh Creek Falls tumbling down slabs of rock. You slowly enter the subalpine landscape and reach a wonderful view of Leigh Lake sitting in a glacial cirque. Make noise to alert bears of your presence as you drop to the lakeshore through thick brush. Scan the alpine tundra around the edge of the lake for mountain goats and other wildlife. Large chunks of ice drift about the clear waters of the lake until as late as July.

Miles and Directions

0.0 Leigh Lake Trailhead #132

0.3 Sign marking entrance to Cabinet Mountains Wilderness

0.5 First view of Leigh Creek Falls

Leigh Creek Falls.

- **0.9** Base of Leigh Creek Falls
  GPS: 48.2258, -115.6552 Elevation: 4,900 feet
- **1.1** First view of Leigh Lake
- **1.2** Shore of Leigh Lake
  GPS: 48.2246, -115.6607 Elevation: 5,120 feet
- **2.5** Arrive back at the trailhead.

5 Granite Creek Falls

Granite Creek Falls is a small, graceful waterfall nestled in a cool and pristine old-growth cedar-hemlock forest. Other than a few steep climbs and log crossings, it's an easy trail. Bring your family or friends to spend a few hours in the woods and maybe do some swimming or fishing below the falls. Day-hikers and backpackers can extend the hike to Granite Lake.

See map on p. 35.
Stream: Granite Creek
Height: 15 feet
Distance: 4.0 miles out and back
Elevation gain: 430 feet
Difficulty: Easy to moderate
Trail surface: Dirt and rock
Hiking time: 2-3 hours
Canine compatibility: Dogs are allowed
Seasons: June to Nov
County: Lincoln
Land status: Wilderness area, national forest

Fees and permits: No fees required
Trail contact: Kootenai National Forest, 31374, US 2, Libby, MT 59923-3022; (406) 293-6211; fs.usda.gov/kootenai
Maps: *DeLorme Atlas and Gazetteer Montana* Page 20, F4 and F5; *USGS Quad* Treasure Mountain
Camping: There is a backcountry campsite at the falls as well as a primitive campsite at the trailhead. Fireman Memorial Campground in Libby has shaded campsites for a fee.

Finding the Trailhead: From Libby, drive south on US 2 for 1.1 miles until you reach the turnoff for Shaugnessy Road on the right. Drive for 0.7 mile and make a left on Snowshoe Road. Travel for 0.5 mile and turn right on Granite Lake Road. Drive for 7.6 miles to the trailhead at the end of the gravel road.
GPS: 48.2953, -115.6259 Elevation: 3,035 feet

The Hike

An old mining road takes you along the creek through an impressive grove of western red cedar. The path narrows and climbs over a hill and back to the creek bottom.

Make a sharp turn at a switchback and climb through an open forest of Douglas fir and grand fir. From your vantage point along the slope, take a moment to contemplate the avalanche-cut path between the forests on the south side of the drainage.

Hundreds of giant logs are strewn about like toothpicks.

Enter the forest again and drop to some large boulders with views of the cascading stream. Resume climbing along the north hillside until you begin to glimpse the peaks to the west in the vicinity of Gus Brink Mountain. Then cross a small tributary stream in a bushy open slope and pass a lovely grove of quaking aspen. Drop through dense fir back to the banks of Granite Creek for a pleasant stroll along a level trail.

A large fallen hemlock forms a natural bridge to the south side of the stream where the trail continues through the temperate rainforest. A sign welcomes you into

A hiker contemplates Granite Creek Falls from a ledge.

the Cabinet Mountains Wilderness minutes before you reach a large campsite near the falls. Hike to the rocky banks of Granite Creek for a perfect view.

Situated at a wall of exposed rock in shady forest, Granite Creek Falls has an impressive, 8-foot width. After dropping vertically for 15 feet, whitewater slips into a deep, jade-green pool. This is the ultimate place to cool off on a hot day, and the pristine scene is worth pondering for a while. To extend the hike, continue about five more miles up to Granite Lake. The large lake is fed by meltwater from Blackwell Glacier, the Cabinet Mountains' only glacier.

Miles and Directions

0.0 Granite Creek Trailhead #136

1.2 Cross tributary stream.

1.6 Cross large log over Granite Creek.

1.7 Enter Cabinet Mountains Wilderness.

2.0 Base of Granite Creek Falls
GPS: 48.2920, -115.6706 Elevation: 3,465 feet

4.0 Arrive back at the trailhead.

6 Rock Creek Falls

Rock Creek Falls is located next to the abandoned Heidelberg Mine in a wooded canyon in the southern Cabinet Mountains. The lightly used trail passes through a variety of terrain before terminating at subalpine Rock Lake. Lush forests lead to Rock Creek Meadows and a couple of sky-reflecting ponds. You have a good chance of seeing waterfowl, whitetail deer, mountain goats, and other wildlife as you trek through the diverse and changing habitats. The hike to the lake is suitable as a day-hike or as an overnighter, and there are several backcountry campsites to choose from along the route.

Stream: Rock Creek
Height: 30 feet
Distance: 5.5 miles out and back to falls, 7.4 miles out and back to lake
Elevation gain: 925 feet to falls, 1,765 feet to lake
Difficulty: Easy
Trail surface: Dirt and rock
Hiking time: 3–5 hours to falls, 4–6 hours to lake
Canine compatibility: Dogs are allowed
Seasons: May to Oct

County: Sanders
Land status: National forest
Fees and permits: No fees required
Trail contact: Kaniksu National Forest/Kootenai National Forest, 31374 US 2, Libby, MT 59923-3022; (406) 293-6211; fs.usda.gov/kootenai
Maps: *DeLorme Atlas and Gazetteer Montana* Page 36, B5; *USGS Quad* Elephant Peak
Camping: In addition to backcountry camping, there are primitive campsites along Rock Creek Road and at the trailhead.

Finding the Trailhead: From Trout Creek, drive northwest on US 200 for 12.4 miles. Turn right on Government Mountain Road and travel this gravel road for 0.2 mile until it intersects with Rock Creek Road #150. Turn right and drive for 5.3 miles on this bumpy, potholed gravel road. Take a right onto FR 150A at a sign for Rock Creek Lake Trail. Drive for 1.2 miles to the end of this steep and narrow road. High clearance is recommended but not required.
GPS: 48.0401, -115.68 Elevation: 3,125 feet

The Hike

The route to the falls begins on an old, abandoned mining road. The drainage is heavily wooded with a great diversity of trees. Cedar, hemlock, and white pine dominate the lowlands and western larch and grand fir abound on the mountainsides. Deciduous trees like birch, maple, and aspen also mingle among the conifers and speckle the landscape with shades of orange and yellow in September.

After some up-and-down climbing along the north slope, you reach Rock Creek, a medium-sized creek that flows along a bed of dark rocks and boulders. You come to a bridge with views of cliffy open slopes to the north that are especially beautiful with fall color. Continue the roller-coaster climbing to a bridge over a tributary

Rock Creek Falls. Photo by Martha Gunsalam.

and then to another bridge back to the north side of Rock Creek. Look for white pines along the trail and scan for mountain goats on the rocky outcroppings to the north. Follow the flat and wide roadbed to an old mining cabin and still-operational outhouse. Just before the meadows, there is a spacious campsite in a shady grove of cedars. As you emerge from the woods, look southeast toward Flat Top Mountain, the

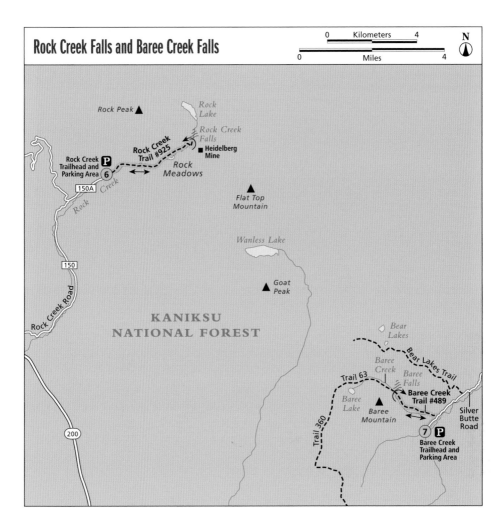

Rock Creek Falls and Baree Creek Falls

Kilometers 0 — 4

Miles 0 — 4

N

Rock Peak ▲

Rock Lake

Rock Creek Falls

Rock Creek Trail #925

Heidelberg Mine

Rock Creek Trailhead and Parking Area ⑥

P

150A

Rock Creek

Rock Meadows

Flat Top Mountain ▲

Wanless Lake

Goat Peak ▲

150

Rock Creek Road

KANIKSU NATIONAL FOREST

Bear Lakes

Baree Creek

Bear Lakes Trail

Trail 63

Baree Falls

Baree Creek Trail #489

Baree Lake

Baree Mountain ▲

Silver Butte Road

Trail 360

200

⑦ P Baree Creek Trailhead and Parking Area

tallest mountain in sight, and observe a waterfall dropping over its steep ledges. Watch closely for wildlife as you pass a couple of ponds in the brushy Rock Creek Meadows. Ducks and songbirds are common, and you may also spot a hoofed mammal coming in for a drink.

After entering thick woods again, you pass another campsite, then a second miner's cabin. A third bridge takes you across the creek and then finally to the remnants of Heidelberg Mine a quarter mile later. Walk to the left and scramble down to the creek for the best view of Rock Creek Falls. Water splashes down a crack in the face of a large, exposed boulder and then spews into a small pool. Early-season viewing is recommended as only a thin horsetail of water remains in the late season.

To make the final 800-foot climb to Rock Lake, find the small single-track trail that leaves the main trail just before arriving at the mine area. After climbing to the end of a quarter-mile-long switchback, continue along the trail as it curves sharply to

Rock Lake.

the north. The higher you get the more you can appreciate the gorgeous landscape to the west. Just before the lake, you pass a sign marking entrance to the Cabinet Mountains Wilderness. Views open up of beautiful subalpine scenery as you approach the Rock Lake basin. The lake is surrounded by steep talus slopes and hillsides of alpine grasses and shrubs. Look for mountain goats along the lakeshore and up into the rocky ridges below Rock Peak. There are a couple of campsites in the spruce near the end of the trail.

Miles and Directions

0.0 Rock Creek Lake Trailhead #935

2.4 Large pond at Rock Creek Meadows. View of seasonal waterfall on cliffs to the southeast.

3.1 Base of Rock Creek Falls at remnants of Heidelberg Mine
GPS: 48.0528, -115.6302 Elevation: 4,050 feet

6.2 Arrive back at the trailhead.

Extended Hike to Rock Lake:

4.1 Enter Cabinet Mountains Wilderness.

4.3 Rock Lake
GPS: 48.0593, -115.6282 Elevation: 4,890 feet

8.6 Arrive back at the trailhead.

7 Baree Creek Falls

Baree Creek Falls gives you, on a much larger scale, the style of picturesque waterfall that landscapers try to imitate at the entrances of modern-day subdivisions. In nature, it's much more convincing. Gentle stair-stepping cascades of whitewater fall over colorful slabs of stone. This short walk in the Cabinet Mountains is ideal for families and beginner hikers. Options exist to extend the trip to Baree Lake and beyond. This is one of the few waterfalls in Montana that you can potentially access in winter on cross country skis or snowshoes.

See map on p. 41.
Stream: Baree Creek
Height: 75 feet
Distance: 2.4 miles out and back
Elevation gain: 865 feet
Difficulty: Easy
Trail surface: Dirt and rock
Hiking time: 1-2 hours
Canine compatibility: Dogs are allowed
Seasons: June to Nov. Winter access is possible by ski or snowshoe depending on road access.
County: Lincoln

Land status: Wilderness area, national forest
Fees and permits: No fees required
Trail contact: Kootenai National Forest, 31374 US 2, Libby, MT 59923-3022; (406) 293-6211; fs.usda.gov/kootenai
Maps: *DeLorme Atlas and Gazetteer Montana* Page 36, B5, and Page 37, B6; *USGS Quad* Goat Peak
Camping: Primitive camping is allowed at the trailhead. Pleasant Valley Campground is located 32 miles southwest of Libby on US 2 and has seven no-fee campsites.

Finding the Trailhead: From Libby drive south on US 2 for 28.2 miles to Silver Butte Road. Turn right and drive southwest on this gravel road for 10.0 miles. Turn right when you come to a sign for Baree Creek Trail #489 and drive for 0.2 mile to the trailhead.
GPS: 47.952, -115.4949 Elevation: 3,745 feet

The Hike

An interesting blend of lichen-covered hemlocks, lodgepole pines, and western white pines welcomes you at the beginning of the hike. In July and August, there are large amounts of huckleberries along the sides of the trail for you to snack on as you gently climb.

After crossing a couple of tributaries and a wet area of the trail, you begin to hear Baree Creek down in the drainage below. You finally reach the white rapids of the stream and begin to follow its soft cascades along the north side. A tenth of a mile later, you arrive at a faint view of Baree Creek Falls through the trees. There is no side trail leading closer, but you can carefully bushwhack to the base area for a better view.

Baree Creek Falls is a multiterraced waterfall on a small stream lined with thick bushes and trees. Water cascades for 75 feet in a braided manner over many shelves of

Baree Creek Falls.

sedimentary rock. Lacking the powerful roar of some waterfalls, this waterfall offers you a more relaxed and peaceful experience. During spring runoff, the falls rage with more intensity. If you decide to scramble around the falls area, be careful not to disturb the delicate moss or slip on wet rock. Baree Lake is located a few more miles up the trail if you wish to extend the hike.

A popular 11-mile loop option for a long day-hike or an overnighter involves hiking up Baree Creek Trail #489, taking crossover trails #360 and #63 to the north, and descending Bear Lakes Trail #178.

Miles and Directions

0.0   Baree Creek Trailhead #489

0.3   Cross small tributary stream.

1.1   Faint view of Baree Falls from trail

1.2   Base of Baree Falls
   GPS: 47.9598, -115.5161 Elevation: 4,610 feet

2.4   Arrive back at the trailhead.

8 South Fork Ross Creek Falls

Ross Creek is located near Bull Lake in the Cabinet Mountains south of Troy. The hike to South Fork Ross Creek Falls is a spectacular, yet challenging adventure for waterfall enthusiasts who don't mind getting their feet wet and scrambling off-trail on difficult terrain. First, you amble along a beautiful stream through ancient groves of cedar and hemlock and then come to a series of stream crossings. Bring extra footwear, and don't attempt the fords at high water. After ascending a steep mountainside to the falls area, bushwhack into a steep gorge where water tumbles violently over the rocks. The difficulty of the hike makes this waterfall a seldom-visited treasure.

Stream: South Fork Ross Creek
Height: 50 feet
Distance: 5.8 miles out and back
Elevation gain: 1,260 feet
Difficulty: Difficult due to multiple fords, a steep ascent during the last mile, and a tricky final scramble to views of the waterfall
Trail surface: Dirt, rock, creek
Hiking time: 5–7 hours
Canine compatibility: Dogs are allowed
Seasons: June to Nov

County: Lincoln
Land status: National forest
Fees and permits: No fees required
Trail contact: Kootenai National Forest, 31374 US 2, Libby, MT 59923-3022; (406) 293-6211; fs.usda.gov/kootenai
Maps: *DeLorme Atlas and Gazetteer Montana* Page 20, F3; *USGS Quad* Sawtooth Mountain
Camping: Bad Medicine Campground is located on West Bull Lake Road and has eighteen sites for a fee.

Finding the Trailhead: From Trout Creek, drive northwest on US 200 for 15.5 miles to a junction with MT 56, Bull River Road. Turn right and drive along the Bull River for 16 miles until you reach a sign for Ross Creek Cedars and Bad Medicine Campground. Turn left and drive west on FR 398 for a mile. Make another left to continue on FR 398 at a sign for Ross Creek Cedars. Drive 3.2 miles to the trailhead at the end of the paved road.
GPS: 48.2085, -115.9152 Elevation: 2,840 feet

The Hike

The trail begins at a scenic picnic area where Ross Creek meanders through the dense forest along a braided, rocky streambed. The first stretch of the hike is part of an interpretive loop nature trail, and you can complete the other side of the loop on the way back. The path enters a magical grove of western red cedar that has certainly stood the test of time. Some specimens are as old as 500 to 1,000 years. In the early season, look for delicate white trillium flowers blooming all over the shady forest floor.

When Trail #142 diverges from the loop, take a right and start hiking away from the stream. You cross a small tributary flowing down from the north, and shortly after, you reunite with Ross Creek. The trail follows the stream closely for a while and then

South Fork Ross Creek Falls.

crosses North Fork Ross Creek. There is no bridge so you should change into extra footwear for this easy ford. After crossing, the forest opens up a bit at a lookout of rugged Ross Point looming over the drainage to the south.

Continue over a few forested hills until you reach a difficult ford of Ross Creek at the location where South Fork Ross Creek joins its parent stream. The safest way to make the crossing is to find the widest spot in the creek and ford with sandals or river shoes and a strong stick. Because this ford is potentially dangerous, do not attempt to reach the waterfall during high-water season. A short distance after crossing Ross Creek, carefully use fallen logs to make a dry crossing over South Fork Ross Creek.

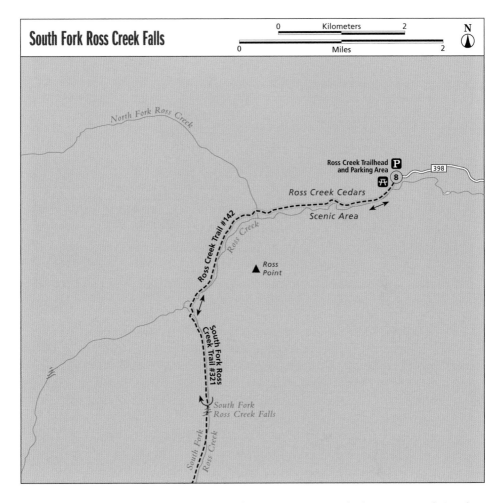

South Fork Ross Creek Falls

0   Kilometers   2

0   Miles   2

N

North Fork Ross Creek

Ross Creek Trailhead and Parking Area

398

Ross Creek Cedars

Scenic Area

8

Ross Creek Trail #142

Ross Creek

Ross Point

South Fork Ross Creek Trail #321

South Fork Ross Creek Falls

South Fork Ross Creek

A less-worn path continues beyond the crossings to a marked junction with South Fork Ross Creek Trail #321. Turn left and begin scaling the mountainside along the west side of South Fork Ross Creek. After almost a mile of strenuous climbing, you reach a glimpse of whitewater through the trees. Leave the trail and descend toward the sound of the falls, being careful to avoid stepping on the moss, loose soil, and slippery rocks. This is a difficult scramble, so exercise extreme caution. Grab on to the young cedars to help you lower yourself safely down to the base of the falls. The 50-foot waterfall splits into two sections, dropping around a group of trees growing at the brink. The rising mist creates a perfect climate for the vibrant, green moss that carpets the rock surfaces. Below South Fork Ross Creek Falls, the stream flows into a deep, rocky gorge with vertical walls. Return to the trail and continue climbing a short distance to a smaller, yet very pretty cascade. This flat and easily accessible spot is a good location to relax after the many challenges you faced on the hike.

Hidden waterfall in dense forest at a tributary of Ross Creek.

If you're interested in continuing your hike and overcoming more obstacles, return to Trail #142 and follow the scant path southwest along Ross Creek. After about a mile, search the tributaries flowing in from the northwest for some nice cascades with drops of up to 30 feet. This extension to your hike is considered very difficult. Prepare yourself for two more difficult fords over Ross Creek and some rough bushwhacking to locate the waterfalls hidden in the dense forest.

Miles and Directions

0.0 Ross Creek Cedars Trailhead #142

0.7 Cross first small tributary.

1.0 Moderate ford over North Fork Ross Creek.

1.2 View of creek and Ross Point to the south

1.9 Difficult ford over Ross Creek followed immediately by dry crossing over South Fork Ross Creek.

2.0 Make a left onto South Fork Ross Creek Trail #321 at junction.
GPS: 48.1919, -115.9558 Elevation: 3,185 feet

2.8 Obstructed view of South Fork Ross Creek Falls from the trail. Carefully bushwhack down the hill to the creek.

2.8 Base of South Fork Ross Creek Falls
GPS: 48.1798, -115.9511 Elevation: 4,095 feet

2.9 Upper South Fork Ross Creek Falls

5.8 Arrive back at the trailhead.

9 Kootenai Falls

Kootenai Falls has the lowest elevation of any major waterfall in Montana. Being one of the most awesome natural features in the state, it's a very popular area for hikers of all ages and ability levels. A large volume of water cascades and falls in several places over interesting rock formations in the Kootenai River. Considered a sacred site for the Kootenai tribe, many have worked hard to ensure the waterfall remains in its undammed, natural state. If you come during the right season, you may be able to swim in crystalline pools or spot bighorn sheep on the cliffs around the falls. You can also access views of the spectacle from above if you wish to extend the hike.

Stream: Kootenai River
Height: 55 feet
Distance: 1 mile out and back to falls, 2.3 miles out and back to overlook
Elevation change: 175 feet loss to falls, 270 feet gain to overlook
Difficulty: Easy to falls; moderate to overlook
Trail surface: Dirt and rock, some asphalt
Hiking time: 1 hour to falls, 2–3 hours to overlook
Canine compatibility: Dogs are allowed
Seasons: Apr to Nov

County: Lincoln
Land status: National forest
Fees and permits: No fees required
Trail contact: Kootenai National Forest, 31374 US 2, Libby, MT 59923-3022; (406) 293-6211; fs.usda.gov/kootenai
Maps: *DeLorme Atlas and Gazetteer Montana* Page 20, E4; *USGS Quad* Kootenai Falls
Camping: Yaak River Campground is located 7 miles northwest of Troy on US 2 and has forty-four campsites for a fee.

Finding the Trailhead: Drive 5 miles east from Troy or 11 miles west from Libby along US 2. Turn into a parking pullout on the north side of the road.
GPS: 48.4527, -115.7688 Elevation: 2,085 feet

The Hike

The first tenth of a mile is flat and paved and takes you through a shady cedar forest. After you pass an overlook of the falls at a distance, the asphalt ends and the trail begins to drop steeply down a couple of switchbacks. Next, you cross a steel footbridge over Burlington Northern train tracks and reenter the forest.

At a T-junction, turn right and walk another tenth of a mile to the falls. The gorge exposes layers of sandstone and shale from the Belt Supergroup. The stair-stepping features are a result of ledges sliding over others in what is known as thrust faulting. As you scramble along the rocky outcroppings in search of your favorite views, stay clear of wet, slippery rocks and be especially careful if the water level is high. Signs warn hikers of accidents in the area that have claimed lives. Hike upriver along small paths that eventually peter out at a long cascade that spans the width of the river. Explore downriver as well to some swimming holes beneath white curtains of falling water.

Kootenai Falls.

After enjoying Kootenai Falls at the river's edge, consider extending your hike to the ridge across the canyon. Adding only 1.5 miles to your total hike, the vantage point from above lets you appreciate the entirety of the gorge. Retrace your steps back to the T-junction, and follow the trail to the right toward the swinging bridge.

The path takes you along the edge of the canyon, with views of water tumbling down shelves of rock. Here, the rugged riverbanks are populated by two tree cousins, Rocky Mountain juniper and western red cedar.

While up on the swinging bridge at midcanyon, you'll notice a sudden increase in wind—make sure you secure your children and belongings as you cross. Up ahead

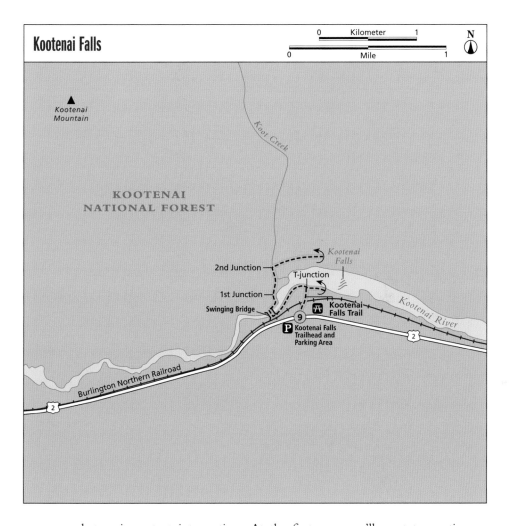

Kootenai Falls

KOOTENAI NATIONAL FOREST

you reach two important intersections. At the first one, you'll want to continue straight. The second is at a creek crossing and you'll want to turn right. Scramble up the very steep trail for a final push to an overlook view of the gorge. If skies are clear, you'll also be treated with a backdrop of Scenery Mountain high up in the Cabinet Mountains Wilderness.

Miles and Directions

0.0 Kootenai Falls Trailhead

0.1 First view of falls at end of paved trail

0.15 Cross railroad tracks using overpass.

0.2 Turn right at the T-junction.

GPS: 48.4545, -115.7681 Elevation: 1,905 feet

0.3   Kootenai Falls viewed from riverside
GPS: 48.4547, -115.7652 Elevation: 1,910 feet

0.4   Continue upstream to end of trail at pools and falls.

0.8   Arrive back at the trailhead.

Extended Hike to Overlook:

0.6   Return to T-Junction and turn right.

0.8   Cross swinging bridge.

0.9   Go straight at the first junction.
GPS: 48.4549, -115.7723 Elevation: 1,970 feet

1.0   Cross creek at the second junction and turn right up steep trail.
GPS: 48.4564, -115.7719 Elevation: 1,980 feet

1.3   Overlook view of canyon and falls
GPS: 48.4574, -115.7664 Elevation: 2,170 feet

2.3   Arrive back at the trailhead.

Salish Mountains

The Salish Mountains extend from the west shore of Flathead Lake to the east shore of Lake Koocanusa and north into Canada. They are composed of rolling forested hills and low mountains with no peaks over 7,000 feet. Several large lakes in the northern Salish are a dominant feature.

Rocky Mountain clematis in the Salish Mountains.

10 Pinkham Falls

Pinkham Falls is a favorite of Eureka locals, but overuse has resulted in braids of eroded dirt roads and paths that weave their way down to the falls. While most of the route is easy to follow, the short trek is best for skilled hikers. The combination of a steep grade and loose gravel makes it easy to slip on the way down. The two small waterfalls at both ends of the gorge are very scenic, but the dangerous rim of the canyon should be approached carefully.

Stream: Pinkham Creek
Height: Upper Pinkham Falls, 20 feet and Lower Pinkham Falls, 15 feet
Distance: 0.8 mile out and back
Elevation loss: 245 feet
Difficulty: Difficult
Trail surface: Dirt, rock, loose gravel
Hiking time: 30-60 minutes
Canine compatibility: Dogs are allowed
Seasons: May to Nov
County: Lincoln

Land status: National forest
Fees and permits: No fees required
Trail contact: Kootenai National Forest, 31374 US 2, Libby, MT 59923-3022; (406) 293-6211; fs.usda.gov/kootenai
Maps: *DeLorme Atlas and Gazetteer Montana* Page 21, B7; *USGS Quad* Beartrap Mountain
Camping: Camp 32 is located on FR 7182 off MT Hwy. 37, 12 miles southwest of Eureka. It has eight no-fee campsites.

Finding the Trailhead: From Eureka, turn off US 93 at the south edge of town and onto paved Tobacco Road. Drive west for 0.6 mile and then turn right onto paved Othorp Lake Road #854. Drive west for 5.1 miles, and when the road splits, keep left on FR 856, Pinkham Creek Road. Drive for 0.8 mile to a small dirt road on the right. Park off the side of the dirt road where it begins. Don't attempt to drive farther on this road since it's already severely eroded. This is an unofficial trailhead with no sign. The area is bordered by private land, so stay on the road and trails.
GPS: 48.8403, -115.1412 Elevation: 3,245 feet

The Hike

Walk along the rutted dirt road through heavily logged forest of Douglas fir and ponderosa pine. The road splits and rejoins several times, and as the path curves to the right, it steepens and drops down a big switchback. Be careful not to slip on the loose dirt as you descend to a few scattered campsites at the creek. A path heads a short distance downstream to the 20-foot-tall Upper Pinkham Falls. Water spills sideways into a deep box canyon and then cascades through a chasm and over flat shelves of rock.

To reach the lower falls, cross the stream over rocks and logs upstream from the upper falls. Find a small path and hike carefully along the rim of the gorge. Lower Pinkham Falls plummets for 15 feet into a very deep pool at the end of the gorge.

Swimmers have tied a rope to a nearby tree to use to climb out of the pool after jumping in from the ledges.

Lower Pinkham Falls.

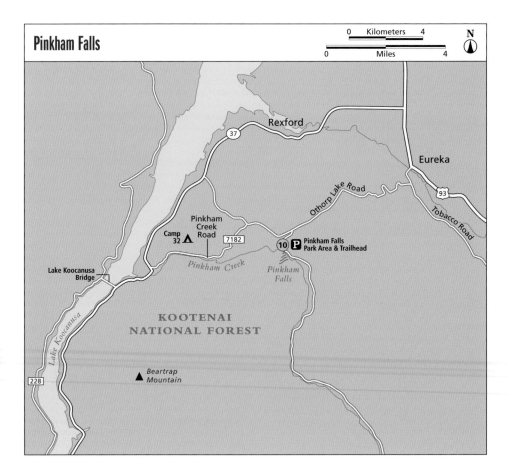

Miles and Directions

0.0 Pinkham Falls parking area

0.3 Upper Pinkham Falls
GPS: 48.8375, -115.1424 Elevation: 3,140 feet

0.4 Lower Pinkham Falls
GPS: 48.8385, -115.1429 Elevation: 3,000 feet

0.8 Arrive back at the trailhead.

11 Sunday Falls

Located in the tall temperate rainforest of the Salish Mountains, Sunday Falls is an exhilarating sight that you won't want to miss if you're driving between Eureka and Whitefish. The hike to the 30-foot waterfall is an easy stroll for all ability levels. Bring your family or friends to picnic, wade, and spend time together in the outdoors. It is popular with the locals, but you won't find crowds here on weekdays.

Stream: Sunday Creek
Height: 30 feet
Distance: 0.3 mile out and back
Elevation loss: 30 feet
Difficulty: Very easy
Trail surface: Dirt
Hiking time: 5–10 minutes
Canine compatibility: Dogs are allowed
Seasons: May to Nov
County: Flathead

Land status: National forest
Fees and permits: No fees required
Trail contact: Flathead National Forest, 650 Wolfpack Way, Kalispell, MT 59901; (406) 758-5208; fs.usda.gov/flathead/
Maps: *DeLorme Atlas and Gazetteer Montana* Page 21, C10; *USGS Quad* Sunday Mountain
Camping: One no-fee campsite is located near the trailhead.

Finding the Trailhead: From Whitefish, drive 31 miles north on US 93 to the town of Stryker. Turn left on gravel Sunday Creek Road #315. Travel for 3.8 miles, passing scenic Sunday Lake on the left. Turn left on FR 3734, which is marked for Sunday Falls, and follow it for 0.2 mile to the trailhead at a bridge.
GPS: 48.6277, -114.7499 Elevation: 3,480 feet

The Hike

Find the path entering the forest on the south side of the bridge. The well-maintained trail can even be traversed with a wheelchair if the surface isn't muddy. As you advance toward the falls, you follow the clear waters of Sunday Creek through majestic forest of cedar, larch, and hemlock. The presence of Rocky Mountain maple adds bright shades of red, orange, and yellow to the forest in the fall. After passing a small cascade, you come to the base of Sunday Falls at the end of the trail. Water cascades over a tan-colored rock protrusion and then makes a vertical plunge into a deep pool. There is a bench to sit, relax, and take in the peaceful atmosphere created by the falls.

Sunday Falls.

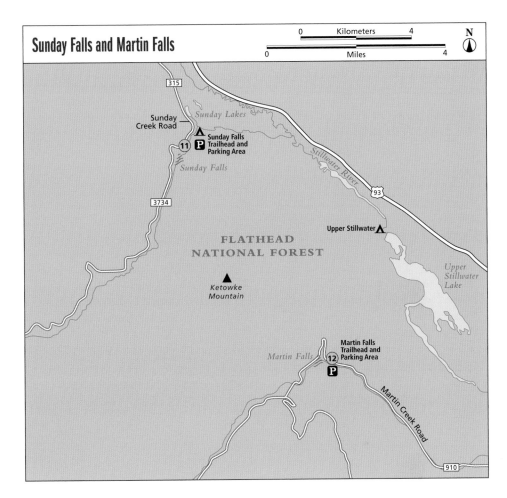

Miles and Directions

0.0 Sunday Falls Trailhead

0.15 Base of Sunday Falls

GPS: 48.6260, -114.7519 Elevation: 3,450 feet

0.3 Arrive back at the trailhead.

12 Martin Falls

Located in the foothills of the Salish Mountains, this short nature trail is a perfect hike for families and hikers of all ages. Tall, old-growth trees encircle the gorgeous cascade. It's a great spot to relax for a while and enjoy the beauty of nature. Despite its closeness to Whitefish and Kalispell, it doesn't receive too many visitors.

See map on p. 59.
Stream: Martin Creek
Height: 50 feet
Distance: 0.1 mile out and back
Elevation gain: 95 feet
Difficulty: Very easy
Trail surface: Dirt
Hiking time: 5–10 minutes
Canine compatibility: Dogs are allowed
Seasons: May to Nov
County: Flathead

Land status: National forest
Fees and permits: No fees required
Trail contact: Flathead National Forest, 650 Wolfpack Way, Kalispell, MT 59901; (406) 758-5208; fs.usda.gov/flathead/
Maps: *DeLorme Atlas and Gazetteer Montana* Page 21, D10; *USGS Quad* Radnor
Camping: Upper Stillwater Lake Campground is located 6 miles north of Good Creek Road on US 93 and has five heavily used sites.

Finding the Trailhead: From Whitefish, drive north on US 93 for 15.7 miles. Turn left on paved Good Creek Road and drive for 3.4 miles. Turn right on gravel Martin Creek Road #910 and drive for 4.7 miles to the pullouts on the side of the road.
GPS: 48.5670, -114.6848 Elevation: 3,700 feet

The Hike

The Martin Falls Nature Trail winds through mature forests of larch, cedar, fir, and hemlock. The dry temperate rainforest hosts a variety of plants and animals in its diverse layers of canopy. After only a few hundred feet of walking up a gentle trail, you reach the base of Martin Falls with a perfect head-on view. Exposed rock appears out of nowhere in the dense woods, and the small creek descends a tall whitewater staircase.

Fallen logs are tossed like toothpicks around the opening in the forest. With an upper and lower cascade, the waterfall stands about 50 feet tall. There are comfortable places to sit and listen to the birds, feel the breeze, and enjoy the sight. Ambitious hikers can make a steep climb up a rough path on the right side to explore the top of the falls.

Martin Falls.

Miles and Directions

0.0 Martin Falls Trailhead

0.05 Base of Martin Falls

GPS: 48.5669, -114.6859 Elevation: 3,795 feet

0.1 Arrive back at the trailhead.

Lewis Range

The area of Glacier National Park extends principally over two mountain ranges, and the Lewis Range covers the eastern region. These mountains have the greatest relief of any range in the state and rival the Beartooths in fame. Many trails lead into the backcountry and allow you to discover the great diversity of flora and fauna and contemplate the area's fascinating glacial history.

Mount Jackson, one of four peaks over 10,000 feet, is visible along the trail to Beaver Chief Falls.

The 960-foot Bird Woman Falls from Going-to-the-Sun Park Road in the Lewis Range.

13 Beaver Chief Falls

Lincoln Lake Trail takes you from the shores of Lake McDonald to a glacier-carved amphitheater where Beaver Chief Falls, the tallest trail-accessible waterfall in Montana, makes its awe-inspiring descent behind the crystalline waters of Lincoln Lake. The long day-hike or overnight backpacking trip is a challenging but extremely rewarding trek that sees few hikers due to elevation change and a sometimes muddy, overgrown trail. Much of the forest was burned in the Sprague Fire of 2017, which devastated almost 17,000 acres of forest in Glacier National Park. Due to limited shade, try taking this hike on a cooler day.

Stream: Lincoln Creek
Height: 1,290 feet
Distance: 15 miles out and back
Elevation gain: 2,200 feet to the lake, 800 feet back to trailhead
Difficulty: Difficult
Trail surface: Dirt, rock, mud
Hiking time: 10-14 hours as a long day-hike or overnight backpack
Canine compatibility: Dogs are not allowed
Seasons: June to Oct
County: Flathead
Land status: National park

Fees and permits: Backcountry camping permit must be obtained in Apgar. National Park Pass is required to enter Glacier National Park, nps.gov/glac/planyourvisit/fees.htm
Trail contact: Glacier National Park, Park Headquarters, PO Box 128, West Glacier, MT 59936; (406) 888-7800; nps.gov/glac/
Maps: *DeLorme Atlas and Gazetteer Montana* Page 23, D6; *USGS Quad* Lake McDonald East
Camping: Sprague Creek Campground is located along Lake McDonald and has twenty-five sites for a fee. Avalanche Creek Campground is located near the trailhead and has eighty-seven sites for a fee.

Finding the Trailhead: From the park entrance at West Glacier, drive east for 9.7 miles on Going-to-the-Sun Road to the Lincoln Lake Trailhead on the south side of the road. You can also use the shuttle bus to avoid driving and parking issues.
GPS: 48.5994, -113.8877 Elevation: 3,280 feet

The Hike

The hike begins near the south shore of Lake McDonald, where you begin to climb back and forth up the mountainside in a steep first mile. Old groves of cedar and hemlock completely shade the forest floor, creating a cool, mossy environment. As you gain your first 1,000 feet, the forest slowly changes into the burned zone that was scorched by wildfire in 2017. The opened forest gives life to a sea of fireweed, huckleberries, and bear grass.

After crossing a small creek, you come to a junction with Snyder Ridge Fire Trail that leads to Fish Lake. Keep walking straight to stay on Lincoln Lake Trail.

Beaver Chief Falls behind Lincoln Lake.

While climbing through the burned landscape, look for colorful birds like the pileated woodpecker or Stellar's jay. Notice the small trees emerging to regenerate the forest.

After about 3 miles of climbing, the trail starts descending into the Lincoln Creek drainage and offers occasional views of snow-capped peaks of the Flathead Range to the south. Turn left when you reach the merging Lincoln Creek Trail from the south and begin following the sound of the stream. You first meet Lincoln Creek at a meadow where the stream meanders calmly between banks of tall grass and splashes over scattered beaver dams. The marsh habitat supports a variety of wildlife including

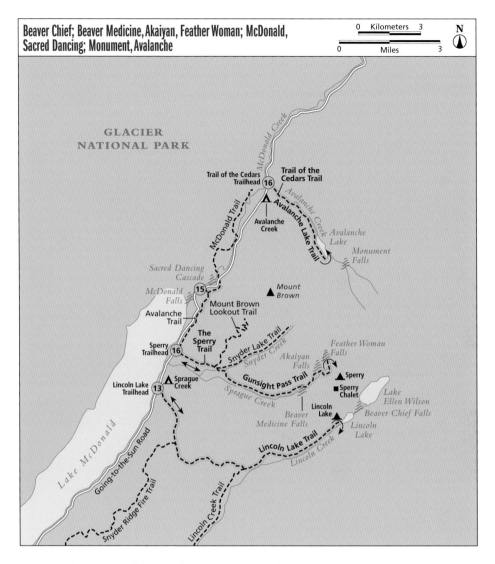

GLACIER
NATIONAL PARK

McDonald Creek

Trail of the Cedars Trailhead 16

Trail of the Cedars Trail

Avalanche Creek

Avalanche Creek

McDonald Trail

Avalanche Lake Trail

Avalanche Lake

Monument Falls

Sacred Dancing Cascade

McDonald Falls 15

Avalanche Trail

Mount Brown

Mount Brown Lookout Trail

The Sperry Trail

Sperry Trailhead 16

Snyder Lake Trail

Snyder Creek

Feather Woman Falls

Akaiyan Falls

Sperry

Lincoln Lake Trailhead 13

Sprague Creek

Gunsight Pass Trail

Sperry Chalet

Lake Ellen Wilson

Sprague Creek

Lincoln Lake

Beaver Chief Falls

Beaver Medicine Falls

Lincoln Lake

Lake McDonald

Going-to-the-Sun Road

Lincoln Lake Trail

Lincoln Creek

Snyder Ridge Fire Trail

Lincoln Creek Trail

moose, bear, spotted frog, and trout. As you circle the meadow, enjoy majestic views of Mount Jackson, which rises proudly to the east. Find a place to sit and rest and take in the scenery for a while.

The final portion of the trail can be a wet and muddy slog with the path often completely overgrown and hard to see. The underbrush on the sides of the trail can soak you even in sunny weather. While sloshing through, look for ripe huckleberries, wild strawberries, and thimbleberries to power you along. The trail passes a few steep avalanche slopes on the right with tall strings of falling snowmelt. As you follow the creek between glacially sculpted headwalls, you begin to faintly glimpse the upper portions of the falls through the trees.

The trail finally reaches the campground at the foot of Lincoln Lake, with a magnificent vista of Beaver Chief Falls descending gracefully behind the lake. The massive cataract zigzags down a cliff face in several drops, fans and feathers out into different channels, and finally reunites its volume to make a brisk final drop. Standing over 1,290 feet high, this is the tallest waterfall featured in this guide. The cascade is fed by Lake Ellen Wilson, a much larger body of water that sits in the glacial valley high above Lincoln Lake.

Rugged mountains, including Lincoln Peak to the north and Mount Jackson to the east, surround the lake. The subalpine, rocky slopes provide good habitat for mountain goats. Because of the challenge of the hike and the fact that it's not a through-trail, you're likely to have this amazing place to yourself, or see only a few people. There are several campsites at the lake to extend your time at one of the greatest gems of the Treasure State. Be sure to get your backcountry camping permit in advance in Apgar Village.

Miles and Directions

0.0   Lincoln Lake Trailhead

1.4   Continue forward at junction with Snyder Ridge Fire Trail.
GPS: 48.5807, -113.8763 Elevation: 4,425 feet

4.1   Turn left at junction with Lincoln Creek Trail.
GPS: 48.5704, -113.8330 Elevation: 4,185 feet

4.7   Meadows at Lincoln Creek with views of Mount Jackson

7.5   Foot of Lincoln Lake with views of Beaver Chief Falls
GPS: 48.5886, -113.7751 Elevation: 4,565 feet

15.0   Arrive back at the trailhead.

14 Beaver Medicine Falls, Akaiyan Falls, and Feather Woman Falls

This is one of Montana's most difficult yet rewarding waterfall day-hikes. Gunsight Pass Trail gains about 3,800 feet in 6 miles, taking you from the shores of Lake McDonald to the alpine splendor of Edwards Mountain, Gunsight Mountain, and Glacier Basin. You follow crystalline streams to three large, dynamic waterfalls. Except for the first mile of dense cedar hemlock forest, the trail mostly passes through forests burned by the Sprague Fire of 2017. Extend your visit to some high-mountain lakes and to an observation point of Sperry Glacier. There is a good chance of seeing wildlife along the way—deer and black bear inhabit the lower-elevation terrain and mountain goats and grizzlies prefer the higher areas. Stay at the recently rebuilt Sperry Chalet or at Sperry Backcountry Campground if you want to spend more time in the area.

See map on p. 65.
Stream: Sprague Creek
Height: Beaver Medicine Falls, 120 feet; Feather Woman Falls, 350 feet; Akaiyan Falls, 280 feet
Distance: 12.2 miles out and back as a long day-hike or overnight backpack
Elevation gain: 3,765 feet
Difficulty: Difficult
Trail surface: Dirt and rock
Hiking time: 10–12 hours
Canine compatibility: Dogs are not allowed
Seasons: July to Oct
County: Flathead

Land status: National park
Fees and permits: National Park Pass is required to enter Glacier National Park, nps.gov/glac/planyourvisit/fees.htm
Trail contact: Glacier National Park, Park Headquarters, PO Box 128, West Glacier, MT 59936; (406) 888-7800; nps.gov/glac/
Maps: *DeLorme Atlas and Gazetteer Montana* Page 23, C6; *USGS Quad* Lake McDonald East
Camping: Sprague Creek Campground is located along McDonald Lake and has twenty-five sites for a fee. Avalanche Creek Campground is located near the trailhead and has eighty-seven sites for a fee.

Finding the Trailhead: From the park entrance at West Glacier, drive east for 10.0 miles on Going-to-the-Sun Road to the Sperry Trailhead. There is parking on the north side of the road near Lake McDonald Lodge. You can also use the shuttle bus to avoid driving and parking issues. The trail begins on the south side of the road.
GPS: 48.6167, -113.8757 Elevation: 3,195 feet

The Hike

Sperry Trail immediately begins to climb the lower slope of Mount Brown to the east of Snyder Creek. Keep going straight on what becomes Gunsight Pass Trail when you reach a junction with Avalanche Trail. Hike through majestic forest of western red cedar, western hemlock, and western larch. Western white pines increase in frequency as you climb the switchbacks of the ridge above Snyder Creek. A couple of short side trails lead to lookouts of the stream and of indigo-colored Lake McDonald. After less than a mile of climbing you leave the shade of the temperate rainforest and enter a burned landscape. You come to a junction where Mount Brown Lookout Trail exits on the left. Keep going straight to a Y-junction with Snyder Lake Trail. Stay to the right and drop down to a pack bridge over the creek at a pretty location called Crystal Ford. The green forest along the creek makes this a shady break spot. The trail splits again after the bridge, and this time you take a left to continue on Gunsight Pass Trail. Climb a shady, wooded slope past a small but loud cascade on Snyder Creek.

For the next two miles, the path traverses the slope to the Sprague Creek drainage. You ascend steep switchbacks and arrive at a view of Sperry Chalet sitting atop a hill next to Glacier Basin. Glimpses of wondrous Beaver Medicine Falls begin to appear ahead of you as you climb the yarrow- and fireweed-lined trail. Beneath a rock wall, you come to a wide-open view of the 120-foot waterfall that splashes down the rocky terrain of Sprague Creek. Lincoln Peak and the ridges around Lincoln Pass provide a splendid backdrop.

As you hike past the roaring falls, you enter a subalpine landscape with breathtaking alpine views. Make lots of noise when passing areas of running water so as not to surprise a bear. Almost a mile later, you gain your first view of Feather Woman Falls straight ahead on the far end of Glacier Basin. The trail flattens as you climb onto the glacial cirque toward the 350-foot cascade.

Suddenly, you approach a footbridge over the creek and the majestic Akaiyan Falls comes into view on the left. Water cascades down a treeless, cliffy slope, making both vertical drops and terraced cascades for a total of 280 feet.

Here, you reach a junction with Gunsight Pass Trail and Sperry Glacier Trail. Take a right to access the Sperry Backcountry Campground and Sperry Chalet. Make sure you get a permit in advance if you plan on camping. The two stone structures of the chalet were built in 1913. The dormitory building was burned in the Sprague Fire on August 2017. It has since been rebuilt and the Sperry Chalet still provides food and lodging to guests.

To complete the waterfalls hike, take a left on Sperry Glacier Trail and enjoy clear views of both cataracts as you hike north. Feather Woman Falls on the right distinguishes itself by dividing into several vertically plunging channels. Akaiyan Falls on the left crashes with force as a large amount of water descends the slopes of Edwards Mountain in multiple cascades and drops.

The trail crosses parks and talus fields to a creek crossing at the base of the elegant, lacy Feather Woman Falls. Continue on a gentle curve along the slope below vertical walls of granite. You finally round a bend in the cliff and arrive at the base of a spectacular section of Akaiyan Falls. Whitewater plunges down the boulders and between the crevices of the rock face. Sit down on some flat rock ledges and look southwest at the gorgeous alpine landscape of Glacier Basin, Gunsight Mountain, and Lincoln Peak. Mountain goats, grizzly bears, marmots, and pikas are common in this

Beaver Medicine Falls.

high-altitude environment. To extend the hike, continue a couple more miles to a higher basin with vistas of more waterfalls emptying into Akaiyan Lake and Feather Woman Lake. There is an observation point of Sperry Glacier at the end of the trail.

Miles and Directions

1.0 Sperry Trailhead

0.1 Continue forward on Gunsight Pass Trail at a junction with Avalanche Trail.

0.5 First lookout of Snyder Creek and Lake McDonald

0.8 Second lookout of Snyder Creek and Lake McDonald

1.3   Continue forward on Gunsight Pass Trail at junction with Mount Brown Lookout Trail.

1.4   Keep right on Gunsight Pass Trail at Y-junction with Snyder Lake Trail.

1.5   Take a left on Gunsight Pass Trail after crossing the pack bridge over Snyder Creek.

4.0   View of Beaver Medicine Falls from the west
       GPS: 48.6027, -113.7994 Elevation: 5,355 feet

4.8   First view of Feather Woman Falls

5.1   Footbridge and first view of Akaiyan Falls

5.3   Take a left on Sperry Glacier Trail at Y-junction. Use Gunsight Pass Trail on the right to access Sperry Chalet and Sperry Chalet Campground, if desired.

5.8   Trail crosses stream below Feather Woman Falls.
       GPS: 48.6117, -113.7818 Elevation: 6,460 feet

6.1   Trail reaches vista point below Akaiyan Falls.
       GPS: 48.6135, -113.7860 Elevation: 6,960 feet

12.2   Arrive back at the trailhead.

15 McDonald Falls and Sacred Dancing Cascade

Thousands of Glacier Park visitors see McDonald Falls and Sacred Dancing Cascade from the roadside overlooks, but the experience is much better if you visit them along the footpath on the opposite side of the stream. The hike takes you through wet cedar and hemlock forest to the jagged cliffs along McDonald Creek. These famous cascades are joined by a classic Glacier backdrop of steep mountains and pointed peaks.

See map on p. 65.
Stream: McDonald Creek
Height: McDonald Falls, 35 feet, Sacred Dancing Cascade, 15 feet
Distance: 2.1 miles out and back
Elevation gain: 30 feet
Difficulty: Easy
Trail surface: Dirt
Hiking time: 1–3 hours
Canine compatibility: Dogs are not allowed
Seasons: Apr to Oct
County: Flathead
Land status: National park

Fees and permits: National Park Pass is required to enter Glacier National Park, nps.gov/glac/planyourvisit/fees.htm
Trail contact: Glacier National Park, Park Headquarters, PO Box 128, West Glacier, MT 59936; (406) 888-7800; nps.gov/glac/
Maps: *DeLorme Atlas and Gazetteer Montana* Page 22, C5; *USGS Quad* Mount Cannon
Camping: Sprague Creek Campground is located along McDonald Lake and has twenty-five sites for a fee. Avalanche Creek Campground is located near the trailhead and has eighty-seven sites for a fee.

Finding the Trailhead: From the park entrance at West Glacier, drive east for 12 miles on Going-to-the-Sun Road, along Lake McDonald's eastern shoreline. A mile after passing Lake McDonald Hotel, turn left on North McDonald Road and drive for 0.3 mile to the trailhead. Catch a glimpse of McDonald Falls from the bridge just before reaching the parking pullout on the right. **GPS:** 48.6373, -113.8685 Elevation: 3,185 feet

The Hike

Black bears and grizzly bears frequent the deep woods and streams of this flat, forested canyon, so keep your bear spray handy just in case. The path leads north, through fairytale-like woods where moss covers just about every inch of the forest floor. The trail curves toward the stream, and you begin to see white cascades at some abrupt cliffs. Make a sharp turn onto a path diverging on the right and descend gradually to the edge of the canyon. Look for white pines growing in the sunny areas of McDonald Creek.

Hike along the top of the cliff until you reach the brink of McDonald Falls as it roars and launches mist into the air. Be careful as you explore the rim around the falls—the wet rock is more slippery than it seems. If you want to try another view,

McDonald Falls.

follow the path another tenth of a mile to a place where you can easily descend the cliffs to the water's edge. Although the distance is greater, it's a more direct angle of the waterfall from creek level.

To visit Sacred Dancing Cascade, retrace your way back to the junction and turn right on McDonald Trail heading northeast. Walk for a few minutes along a beautiful portion of the trail that follows the mighty stream through the vibrant forest. You soon reach a large footbridge and views of the small waterfall.

Miles and Directions

0.0 McDonald Trailhead

0.5 Make a sharp right on side trail to falls.

GPS: 48.6420, -113.8623 Elevation 2,955 feet

0.75 Brink of McDonald Falls

GPS: 48.6394, -113.8645 Elevation: 3,195 feet

0.85 Base of cliff with view of falls

1.2 Retrace your way back to McDonald Trail and follow it northeast.

1.4 Sacred Dancing Cascade near footbridge

GPS: 48.6418, -113.8569 Elevation: 3,150 feet

2.1 Arrive back at the trailhead.

16 Monument Falls and Avalanche Gorge

The beautiful waterfalls at Avalanche Lake, the emerald-green water, and the dense, old-growth forest along raging Avalanche Creek are what make this hike so popular. It's best to visit in the early morning or late afternoon to avoid crowds. Begin the hike in a thick grove of ancient cedars and follow the creek to a narrow gorge filled with raging whitewater. A climb to Avalanche Lake gives you a spectacular view of the 300-foot Monument Falls and two other gigantic waterfalls flowing down from the ridge between Little Matterhorn and Bearhat Mountain. There are several access points to the water so you can wade or fish while gazing at the beautiful cascades.

See map on p. 65.
Stream: Avalanche Creek
Height: 300 feet
Distance: 5.6 miles out and back
Elevation gain: 405 feet
Difficulty: Moderate
Trail surface: Dirt and rock
Hiking time: 4-5 hours
Canine compatibility: Dogs are not allowed
Seasons: June to Oct
County: Flathead
Land status: National park

Fees and permits: National Park Pass is required to enter Glacier National Park, nps.gov/glac/planyourvisit/fees.htm
Trail contact: Glacier National Park, Park Headquarters, PO Box 128, West Glacier, MT 59936; (406) 888-7800; nps.gov/glac/
Maps: *DeLorme Atlas and Gazetteer Montana* Page 23, C6; *USGS Quad* Mount Cannon
Camping: Sprague Creek Campground is located along McDonald Lake and has twenty-five sites for a fee. Avalanche Creek Campground is located near the trailhead and has eighty-seven sites for a fee.

Finding the Trailhead: From the park entrance at West Glacier, drive east for 16.2 miles on Going-to-the-Sun Road. From the park entrance at St. Mary, drive west for 33.9 miles. Park your vehicle at the Trail of the Cedars Trailhead on the south side of the road. You can also use the shuttle bus to avoid driving and parking issues.
GPS: 48.6806, -113.8188 Elevation: 3,475 feet

The Hike

The first portion of the hike is wheelchair accessible and follows the east side of the Trail of the Cedars loop trail. You pass through tall, shady forest of old-growth western red cedar and western hemlock. There are interpretive signs spread throughout the loop and places to access the sunlit creek. To vary your experience, hike the west side of the loop on your way back. The boardwalk curves west and crosses a bridge over the creek just below Avalanche Gorge. Here, the creek crashes through a narrow chasm, forming smoothly curved walls. Turn left on the trail to Avalanche Lake after the bridge and continue to explore the rim of the gorge.

Monument Falls behind Avalanche Lake.

As you start climbing to the lake, the tall headwall of Cannon Mountain comes into view to the northeast. The trail leaves the creek and passes through some steep sections with tall, shady trees. Very little undergrowth vegetation grows here due to lack of sunlight.

There is only the moss on the boulders and a few scattered ferns. The trail leads you over a rise to an open view of Hidden Creek flowing down a slope and into Avalanche Creek. Notice the evidence of avalanche destruction along the steep slopes.

The trail finally flattens after a couple of miles, and you start to glimpse three tall and elegant waterfalls and hear the thunderous sound of water in the basin. Sperry Glacier, nestled high in a basin over the ridge, is the source of these majestic cascades.

Walk to a large gravelly beach with spectacular views of the falls pouring into Avalanche Basin behind the gorgeous turquoise-colored waters of Avalanche Lake. Monument Falls to the left makes a 300-foot, near-vertical drop. The other two waterfalls on the right are unnamed but they rival Monument Falls in beauty. Keep following the trail to access a couple more beaches along the southwest shore.

Miles and Directions

0.0 Trail of the Cedars Trailhead

0.3 Base of Avalanche Gorge at footbridge
GPS: 48.6766, -113.8137 Elevation: 3,580 feet

0.4 Turn left at junction with Avalanche Lake Trail.

2.0 First beach access area at Avalanche Lake with views of Monument Falls and two unnamed falls
GPS: 48.6593, -113.7904 Elevation: 3,880 feet

2.4 Second beach access

2.8 End of trail and third beach access
GPS: 48.6517, -113.7841 Elevation: 3,840 feet

5.6 Arrive back at the trailhead.

17 Florence Falls and Deadwood Falls

This moderate hike takes you through the forests and marshlands of the St. Mary River valley to the base of Florence Falls, one of the tallest and most beautiful cascades in Glacier National Park. You also visit the small but forceful Deadwood Falls, which is an attractive destination for those looking for a shorter hike. Along the way, you pass occasional vistas of Jackson and Blackfoot Glaciers and a viewpoint of Mirror Pond with a spectacular mountain backdrop. There are excellent options to continue your trek to Gunsight Lake, where more glacier views, alpine scenery, and impressive waterfalls await you.

Stream: Florence Falls, tributary of St. Mary River, Deadwood Falls, Reynolds Creek
Height: Florence Falls, 800 feet; Deadwood Falls, 10 feet
Distance: 8.6 miles out and back
Elevation loss: 395 feet
Difficulty: Moderate
Trail surface: Dirt and rock
Hiking time: 4–5 hours
Canine compatibility: Dogs are not allowed
Seasons: June to Oct
County: Glacier
Land status: National park

Fees and permits: National Park Pass is required to enter Glacier National Park, nps.gov/glac/planyourvisit/fees.htm
Trail contact: Glacier National Park, Park Headquarters, PO Box 128, West Glacier, MT 59936; (406) 888-7800; nps.gov/glac/
Maps: *DeLorme Atlas and Gazetteer Montana* Page 23, C6; *USGS Quad* Logan Pass
Camping: Rising Sun Campground is located 6.3 miles east of St. Mary and has eighty-four sites for a fee. St. Mary Campground is located near the park entrance at St. Mary and has 148 sites for a fee.

Finding the Trailhead: From the park entrance at West Glacier, drive 36.3 miles east on Going-to-the-Sun Road. From the park entrance at St. Mary, drive 13.8 miles west. Park your vehicle at the Jackson Glacier Overlook on the south side of the road. You can also use the shuttle bus to avoid driving and parking issues.
GPS: 48.6774, -113.6523 Elevation: 5,230 feet

The Hike

The trail is marked Gunsight Pass Trail, but you actually follow Piegan Pass Trail for the first mile. You immediately start descending the slope through semi-open forests of Engelmann spruce and Douglas fir. The underbrush is dense and lush, and the sides of the trail are often overgrown. On warm days, the humidity produced by the thick vegetation can make the area feel like a jungle.

The path continues to drop to the valley floor until it reaches Reynolds Creek where Deadwood Falls tumbles with impressive force. Water spills vertically over a 10-foot wall, creating a foamy pool at the base. Downstream you might be enticed

Florence Falls.

by an ice-cold yet refreshing swimming hole—a foot soak is recommended at a minimum.

The small gorge in the woods is made up of smooth layers of pink, red, and gray-colored sedimentary rock. Take a right at the junction for Gunsight Pass Trail shortly after the falls. You cross a suspension bridge over the creek and then pass Reynolds Creek Campground. Make sure you get a permit in advance if you plan on camping.

After climbing over a hill, drop within sight of a willow marshland along the St. Mary River. You can hear the roar of an unnamed cascade that descends Dusty Star Mountain's high slopes. Later, the trail descends to the river with a view of its

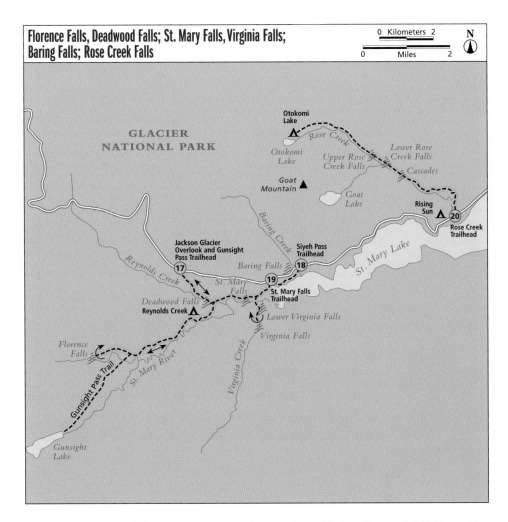

0   Kilometers   2

0   Miles   2

N

GLACIER
NATIONAL PARK

Otokomi
Lake

Rose Creek

Otokomi
Lake

Upper Rose
Creek Falls

Lower Rose
Creek Falls

Cascades

Goat
Mountain

Goat
Lake

Rising
Sun

1

20

Rose Creek
Trailhead

Jackson Glacier
Overlook and Gunsight
Pass Trailhead

Baring Creek

Siyeh Pass
Trailhead

17

Reynolds Creek

Baring Falls

18

St. Mary Lake

19

Deadwood Falls

St. Mary
Falls

St. Mary Falls
Trailhead

Reynolds Creek

Lower Virginia Falls

Florence
Falls

Virginia Creek

Virginia Falls

Gunsight Pass Trail

St. Mary River

Gunsight
Lake

gentle currents and deep, aqua-green pools. Continue skirting the north hillside until you reach a spectacular sight: parks of willow and grass surround a small body of blue water called Mirror Pond, with Citadel Mountain forming a dramatic alpine backdrop.

Watch for wildlife, too. The brushy waterway is an excellent habitat for moose, bear, and Canadian geese. Follow the river bottom and then cross a footbridge over a small tributary stream. Look closely at the peaks to the south for views of Jackson Glacier and Blackfoot Glacier clinging to the high, rocky slopes.

You soon begin to follow a large fork of the St. Mary River that originates at Twin Lakes. Turn right onto a small, less-worn trail that leads to the falls. The path cuts through a verdant understory of ferns, cow parsnip, devil's club, and thimbleberry.

The humidity can be intense here in the summer, but pools in the large creek offer more potential swimming opportunities for a hot traveler.

As the sound of gushing water gets louder, the trail gets rougher and overgrown with thick vegetation. Views of the majestic waterfall finally start to appear and the trail ends in a shady grove of Douglas fir. Your perch in the trees is a great place to view the enormous cascade. Florence Falls is one of the most graceful and scenic waterfalls in the state of Montana. Water descends a total of 800 feet in a series of slides and stair-steps that glisten in the sunshine. Since the upper portion is tucked out of view, you can only see the bottom 440 feet of the falls. Mount Jackson crowns the southern horizon, adding to the intensity of the experience. Sit on the grassy hilltop to get refreshed by the cool breeze and gentle mist generated by the splash.

To extend the hike, continue 2 miles to Gunsight Lake. Enjoy views along the way of Siksika Falls, whose name is derived from the words "Black" and "foot" in the Blackfoot language. This and several unnamed falls descend from Blackfoot and Jackson Glaciers. Once you reach Gunsight Lake, you have two options. Take a left after the bridge to explore the 1.7 mile challenging side trail to closer views of Jackson Glacier. Or, take a right and climb a few miles to Gunsight Pass, reveling in the excellent views of Gunsight Lake Falls and unnamed waterfalls that cascade down alpine terrain and into the lake. Bears are common in the area so carry bear spray and make noise as a precaution.

Miles and Directions

0.0 Gunsight Pass Trailhead

1.1 Base of Deadwood Falls
   GPS: 48.6667, -113.6371 Elevation: 4,835 feet

1.2 Turn right at junction with Gunsight Pass Trail. Cross suspension bridge.

3.6 Turn right at junction with Florence Falls Trail.

4.3 Base of Florence Falls
   GPS: 48.6506, -113.6923 Elevation: 4,850 feet

8.6 Arrive back at the trailhead.

18 Baring Falls

Baring Falls is a misty, wonderful waterfall near the shoreline of St. Mary Lake. The whole family will appreciate the sights along this easy downhill hike. The trail passes through lodgepole forest burned in the Reynolds Creek Fire of 2015. The landscape is rugged, rocky, and full of wildflowers. You'll be able to cool off by the spray of the falls and enjoy amazing mountain views from the lakeshore.

See map on p. 79.
Stream: Baring Creek
Height: 35 feet
Distance: 1.0 mile out and back
Elevation loss: 255 feet
Difficulty: Easy
Trail surface: Dirt and rock
Hiking time: 30–60 minutes
Canine compatibility: Dogs are not allowed
Seasons: May to Oct
County: Glacier
Land status: National park

Fees and permits: National Park Pass is required to enter Glacier National Park, nps.gov/glac/planyourvisit/fees.htm
Trail contact: Glacier National Park, Park Headquarters, PO Box 128, West Glacier, MT 59936; (406) 888-7800; nps.gov/glac/
Maps: *DeLorme Atlas and Gazetteer Montana* Page 23, C7; *USGS Quad* Rising Sun
Camping: Rising Sun Campground is located 6.3 miles east of St. Mary and has eighty-four sites for a fee. St. Mary Campground is located near the park entrance at St. Mary and has 148 sites for a fee.

Finding the Trailhead: From the park entrance at St. Mary, drive west on Going-to-the-Sun Road for 10.1 miles to the Siyeh Trailhead at Sunrift Gorge. There is limited parking. Take the shuttle to avoid driving and parking issues.
GPS: 48.6785, -113.5955 Elevation: 4,680 feet

The Hike

To begin the downhill descent on Siyeh Pass Trail, follow some stone steps down from the south side of the road. You encounter a chain of tumbling 5-foot cascades that fall where water emerges from the narrow, mossy gorge. You then leave the creek side and drop down a steep ravine of burned lodgepole pine. After a quarter mile, the trail intersects with Piegan Pass Trail. Turn right and walk a few minutes to a footbridge near the base of Baring Falls. Explore different views from the rocks along the creek and underneath an overhanging cliff. Baring Creek curves through a narrow chasm and then quickly plunges 35 feet to the creek bottom. You'll notice a temperature drop around the falls and a refreshing spray of mist. Several live spruce and fir that survived the fires of 2015 cling to the wet environment near the cascade. Watch for American dippers catching aquatic insects in the creek rapids. Before returning to the trailhead, walk the trail for another tenth of a mile to a pleasant spot on the north shore of St. Mary Lake.

Baring Falls.

Miles and Directions

0.0 Siyeh Pass Trailhead at Sunrift Gorge

0.25 Turn right at junction with Piegan Pass Trail.
   GPS: 48.6776, -113.5916 Elevation: 4,490 feet

0.4 Base of Baring Falls
   GPS: 48.6768, -113.5935 Elevation: 4,425 feet

0.5 North shore of St. Mary Lake

1.0 Arrive back at the trailhead.

19 St. Mary Falls and Virginia Falls

Many Falls Trail drops into the St. Mary River valley through lodgepole forest burned in the Reynolds Creek Fire of 2015. As you descend to the river through the charred landscape, enjoy views of the western arm of St. Mary Lake. Water-loving American dippers nest behind the silver curtains of St. Mary Falls. Leaving the St. Mary River, you begin to follow Virginia Creek and pass views of numerous waterfalls. While hiking up the southern slope, you enter a cool, wet spruce forest where the excitement culminates at the base of awe-inspiring Virginia Falls. Many hikers turn back too soon thinking they have reached Virginia Falls when they see the impressive preliminary cascades along Virginia Creek.

See map on p. 79.

Stream: St. Mary River, Virginia Creek

Height: St. Mary Falls, 50 feet; Lower Virginia Falls, 85 feet; Virginia Falls, 150 feet

Distance: 3.4 miles out and back

Elevation change: 375 feet loss, 295 feet gain, 670 feet total

Difficulty: Easy

Trail surface: Dirt and rock

Hiking time: 2–3 hours

Canine compatibility: Dogs are not allowed

Seasons: June to Oct

County: Glacier

Land status: National park

Fees and permits: National Park Pass is required to enter Glacier National Park, nps.gov/glac/planyourvisit/fees.htm

Trail contact: Glacier National Park, Park Headquarters, PO Box 128, West Glacier, MT 59936; (406) 888-7800; nps.gov/glac/

Maps: *DeLorme Atlas and Gazetteer Montana* Page 23, C7; *USGS Quad* Rising Sun

Camping: Rising Sun Campground is located 6.3 miles east of St. Mary and has eighty-four sites for a fee. St. Mary Campground is located near the park entrance at St. Mary and has 148 sites for a fee.

Finding the Trailhead: From the park entrance at St. Mary, drive west on Going-to-the-Sun Road for 10.6 miles to the St. Mary Falls parking area. There is limited parking. Take the shuttle to avoid driving and parking issues.

GPS: 48.6751, -113.6045 Elevation: 4,765 feet

The Hike

Begin the hike either at the parking area at mile 10.6 or at the shuttle stop at mile 10.8 of Going-to-the-Sun Road. Both trails drop down switchbacks and join at a small creek. If hiking from the parking area, keep right at the intersection with Piegan Pass Trail. After crossing the small creek, keep left to join St. Mary Lake Trail and continue through the burned lodgepole pine forest.

The trail winds to the St. Mary River at the valley floor and begins to advance upstream. You come to a large wooden footbridge at the base of spectacular St. Mary Falls, where water gushes down two tall shelves in the bedrock. Graceful white

St. Mary Falls.

curtains splash through a gorge of folded sedimentary rock and terminate in a foamy, clear pool that continues to bubble vigorously as it extends under the bridge.

The hike continues along a cliff of dripping wet moss and across stepping-stones over a small feeder stream. Soon, you come to Virginia Creek where Lower Virginia Falls descends beautifully over terraces of rosy-colored argillite. Advanced hikers can follow a rugged path down the rock shelves to the base. Stay clear of slippery wet rock surfaces in this potentially dangerous location.

You begin a moderate climb and suddenly enter a moist, unburned forest of Engelmann spruce. Keep going up the path past several small waterfalls until you

Virginia Falls.

arrive at a sign marking a trail to a viewpoint of Virginia Falls. Climb to a few bridges that lead to up-close vistas of the 150-foot waterfall, one of Montana's most amazing cataracts. Virginia Creek plunges vertically over a colorful cliff formed by water-eroded layers of sedimentary rock. As you approach, be prepared to experience a powerful gust of wind spraying billows of mist. Return to the main trail and hike down to a bridge for a different vantage point.

Miles and Directions

0.0 St. Mary Falls Trailhead

0.1 Keep right at junction with Piegan Pass Trail.
GPS: 48.6739, -113.6057 Elevation: 4,620 feet

0.4 Trail from shuttle stop trailhead merges on the right at creek crossing.

0.45 Turn left on St. Mary Lake Trail.
GPS: 48.6717, -113.6127 Elevation: 4,570 feet

0.95 Base of St. Mary Falls at footbridge
GPS: 48.6679, -113.6151 Elevation: 4,470 feet

1.2 Arrive at Virginia Creek at Lower Virginia Falls.
GPS: 48.6662, -113.6134 Elevation: 4,520 feet

1.6 Turn right at signed side trail to Virginia Falls.
GPS: 48.6614, -113.6138 Elevation: 4,710 feet

1.7 Base of Virginia Falls
GPS: 48.6603, -113.6132 Elevation: 4,845 feet

3.4 Arrive back at the trailhead.

20 Rose Creek Falls

Spectacular vistas of St. Mary Lake and surrounding peaks are a continuous reward as you climb over 1,000 feet along Rose Creek. Several sizable cascades rage during high water, and the largest and most beautiful of them all, Upper Rose Creek Falls, awaits you at the foot of Goat Mountain. Extend the hike a couple more miles to Otokomi Lake, nestled in a glacially carved basin. The landscape around Rose Creek Trail was affected by the Reynolds Creek Fire of 2015. Be aware of hazards when hiking in recently burned areas, such as falling trees, sliding rocks, and flash floods.

See map on p. 79.
Stream: Rose Creek
Height: Varying from 5 to 25 feet
Distance: 6.0 miles out and back
Elevation gain: 1,270 feet
Difficulty: Moderate
Trail surface: Dirt and rock
Hiking time: 3–5 hours
Canine compatibility: Dogs are not allowed
Seasons: June to Oct
County: Glacier
Land status: National park

Fees and permits: National Park Pass is required to enter Glacier National Park, nps.gov/glac/planyourvisit/fees.htm
Trail contact: Glacier National Park, Park Headquarters, PO Box 128, West Glacier, MT 59936, (406) 888-7800; nps.gov/glac/
Maps: *DeLorme Atlas and Gazetteer Montana* Page 23, C7; *USGS Quad* Rising Sun
Camping: Rising Sun Campground is located 6.3 miles east of St. Mary and has eighty-four sites for a fee. St. Mary Campground is located near the park entrance at St. Mary and has 148 sites for a fee.

Finding the Trailhead: From the park entrance at St. Mary, drive west on Going-to-the-Sun Road for 5.6 miles to Rising Sun. Turn right toward the Rising Sun Motor Inn and park near the trailhead located west of the General Store.
GPS: 48.6948, -113.5194 Elevation: 4,520 feet

The Hike

The trail follows the east side of Rose Creek through the Rising Sun cabins area and then comes to a junction with a second trailhead sign. Take a left and continue up the rocky drainage through the forest of fir, pine, spruce, cottonwood, aspen, and maple. Climb a few switchbacks to a bench overlooking the gorge. Proceed to make a moderate climb through partially scorched forest toward Goat Mountain to the west and Otokomi Mountain to the north. Bear grass, paintbrush, wild strawberry, and periwinkle-colored Rocky Mountain clematis line the sides of the path in May and June.

After the first mile of hiking, the trail returns to the edge of the narrow ravine, where you can hear the raging Rose Creek making its descent. As you skirt the burned ridge above the creek, enjoy fabulous views of St. Mary Lake with a majestic

Upper Rose Creek Falls and Goat Mountain.

backdrop of Curly Bear Mountain, Red Eagle Mountain, Mahtotopa Mountain, and Little Chief Mountain. Across the ravine, steep cliffs rise over several hundred feet in some sections. You come to a narrow section of the gorge where tree-obstructed waterfalls flow below you. After 2 miles of hiking, the trail approaches the creek again to a series of large unnamed cascades ranging from 5 to 10 feet. A side trail takes you to a delightful resting spot on rocks between a couple of impressive falls.

Continue upstream through mixed live and burned forest, passing more dynamic cascades. Keep an eye out for moose, elk, and bear as you amble along Rose Creek.

The grasses along the banks are spotted with glacier lily and dandelion. You reach a large avalanche chute with amazing views of some lower ridges of Goat Mountain.

Cross a wooden footbridge over a large tributary stream that originates at an unnamed lake near Otokomi Mountain. Shortly after the bridge, amble off trail for a couple of minutes toward the sound of falling water until you reach the base of Lower Rose Creek Falls, which pours over a 15-foot ledge into a narrow chasm. Since there is no side trail to this viewpoint, use caution near steep or wet areas of rock. A fall into the extremely cold stream could cause hypothermia.

Return to the trail and climb moderately back into lush, unburned forest of pine and spruce until you arrive at a lookout of Upper Rose Creek Falls. Two channels of water join at the top of the falls and then plummet about 25 feet to a foamy pool at the base. Moss clings to the layers of sedimentary rock. Snow-covered until July, Goat Mountain stands proudly behind the falls. To extend the walk, go another couple of miles to Otokomi Lake in the glacially carved Rose Basin. Backpackers can spend a night at Otokomi Lake Campground but will need to obtain a backcountry permit in St. Mary.

Miles and Directions

0.0 Rose Creek Trailhead

0.2 Keep left at second trail sign.

2.1 View from above a string of large cascades along Rose Creek
GPS: 48.7074, -113.5444 Elevation: 5,580 feet

2.5 Large avalanche chute

2.55 Cross footbridge over large tributary stream.

2.6 Base of Lower Rose Creek Falls
GPS: 48.7100, -113.5521 Elevation: 5,545 feet

3.0 Base of Upper Rose Creek Falls
GPS: 48.7129, -113.5578 Elevation: 5,790 feet

6.0 Arrive back at the trailhead.

21 Pyramid Falls, via Gros Ventre Falls and White Quiver Falls

This is an epic waterfall backpacking adventure that gives you a real appreciation of the lofty peaks and deep valleys of Glacier National Park. The 28-mile trek is best done in at least 3 days, and you will need to secure a camping permit from the backcountry office in St. Mary before venturing out on the trail. There are six backcountry campgrounds to choose from that are dispersed along the route. The trail takes you along the Belly River drainage for the first 6 miles and then proceeds to follow the Mokowanis River. Along this stream you pass Gros Ventre Falls, Cosley Lake, and Glen Lake. After Mokowanis Junction, the route takes you past White Quiver Falls and the subalpine Mokowanis Lake. The trek ends at the foot of tall and elegant Pyramid Falls, which gushes down from two large glaciers situated high up near the Continental Divide. Along the way you have a good chance of spotting an array of Rocky Mountain wildlife.

Stream: Mokowanis River and Pyramid Creek

Height: Gros Ventre Falls, 30 feet; White Quiver Falls, 20 feet; Pyramid Falls, 320 feet

Distance: 28.2 miles out and back in 3 or more days of overnight backpacking

Elevation change: 700 feet loss, 450 feet gain

Difficulty: Moderate due to length

Trail surface: Dirt and rock

Hiking time: 14–16 hours

Canine compatibility: Dogs are not allowed

Seasons: July to Oct

County: Glacier

Land status: National park

Fees and permits: Backcountry camping permit must be obtained in St. Mary. National Park Pass is required to enter Glacier National Park, nps.gov/glac/planyourvisit/fees.htm

Trail contact: Glacier National Park, Park Headquarters, PO Box 128, West Glacier, MT 59936; (406) 888-7800; nps.gov/glac/

Maps: *DeLorme Atlas and Gazetteer Montana* Page 23, A6; *USGS Quad* Gable Mountain

Camping: St. Mary Campground is located near the park entrance at St. Mary and has 148 sites for a fee.

Finding the Trailhead: From St. Mary, drive north on US 89 for 12.9 miles. Pass through the town of Babb and turn left on Chief Mountain Highway, County Highway 17. Drive for 14.2 miles to the trailhead parking area on the west side of the road just south of the US-Canadian International Border.
GPS: 48.9959, -113.6600 Elevation: 5,310 feet

The Hike

The trail immediately begins to drop toward the Belly River valley through thick stands of lodgepole pine. After a half mile, the forest diversifies, with aspen, cottonwood, fir, and spruce mingling with the pines. Most of the 700-foot descent to the

Pyramid Falls.

river is along gradual switchbacks. The long downhill walk is a leisurely way to start the trek, but it makes for a challenging finish.

After crossing the first tributary stream, you pass a series of open meadows with splendid views of Sentinel Mountain and Bear Mountain to the west. Look for beds and paths in the tall grass created by resident elk, moose, and bear. The trail finally comes to the gravelly banks of the Belly River. The river valley is lined with willow and aspen that envelop the meadows and conifer parklands. Because of the many broad-leaf trees, this is a spectacular hike to take in the fall.

The trail begins to follow the stream south along the eastern slope and then comes to a beautiful large meadow with a sweeping panorama of tall peaks. Chief Mountain towers on the left and Cosley Ridge and Natoas Peak rise between two drainages to the southwest. To the north, the Belly River flows into Alberta from Montana after passing below the slope of Bear Mountain. The willow-lined stream creates excellent habitat for birds and other wildlife. After almost 6 miles of hiking, a side trail to the first backcountry campsite, Gable Creek Campground, appears on your right at a gorgeous view of the colorful rock ridges of Gable Mountain.

At a junction with Cosley Lake Cutoff Trail, turn right and hike down to a large swinging bridge that takes you to the north side of the Belly River. Avoid the fisherman's trail leading to the right and head straight past the bridge through open spruce and aspen.

A short, steep climb takes you to a bench with a good view, and then you make a mile-long traverse through dense pine and spruce to the first lookout of the Mokowanis River. Later, you come to a sign for the first waterfall of the hike, Gros Ventre Falls, which is a must-see on the way up the Mokowanis River valley. Turn left and down a side trail, and in a few minutes, you arrive at the rocks below the 30-foot cascade. Its deep, round pool is a great swimming hole if the water isn't too cold for your liking.

Return to Cosley Lake Cutoff Trail and continue hiking west. Gorgeous views of the lake and its meandering outlet stream appear, and Cosley Ridge rises proudly from the south shore. You pass Bear Mountain Trail on the right, which is a 3.4-mile optional side trip to an observation point revealing the vast landscape. When you pass a junction for Ptarmigan Trail on the left, continue forward on what becomes Stoney Indian Pass Trail. The first half mile of shoreline is through open parkland, but the forest thickens as you arrive at Cosley Lake Campground.

Before leaving the lake, the trail accesses a lovely swimming beach on the west shore. Cross a footbridge over Kaina Creek, a medium-sized creek that flows out of a steep-walled canyon from Kaina Lake. You pass another campsite upon reaching the foot of Glenns Lake. A steady climb takes you to a flat bench where you begin to traverse the slope through tall montane forest of Engelmann spruce. For the next 3 miles you follow the long, slender Glenns Lake but rarely catch a glimpse of the water through the thick trees. You pass a campsite at the head of the lake and reach Mokowanis Junction less than half a mile later.

To continue your way to Pyramid Falls, turn left on Mokowanis Lake Trail.

Find a side trail on the right between the bridges over the Mokowanis River and Pyramid Creek, and amble to the sound of falling water. White Quiver Falls slides gracefully down a 20-foot-tall slab of rock. Head back to Mokowanis Lake Trail and take a right. You soon come to the shore of Glen Lake for some breathtaking views of crystal-clear waters shimmering beneath lofty peaks. Walk through dense spruce until you reach Mokowanis Lake and a campground located at its east shore. After passing through the camp, the trail begins to get more rocky and overgrown.

Pyramid Falls via Gros Ventre Falls and White Quiver Falls; Paiota Falls, Atsina Falls, and Raven Quiver Falls via Gros Ventre Falls and Mokowanis Cascade; Dawn Mist Falls

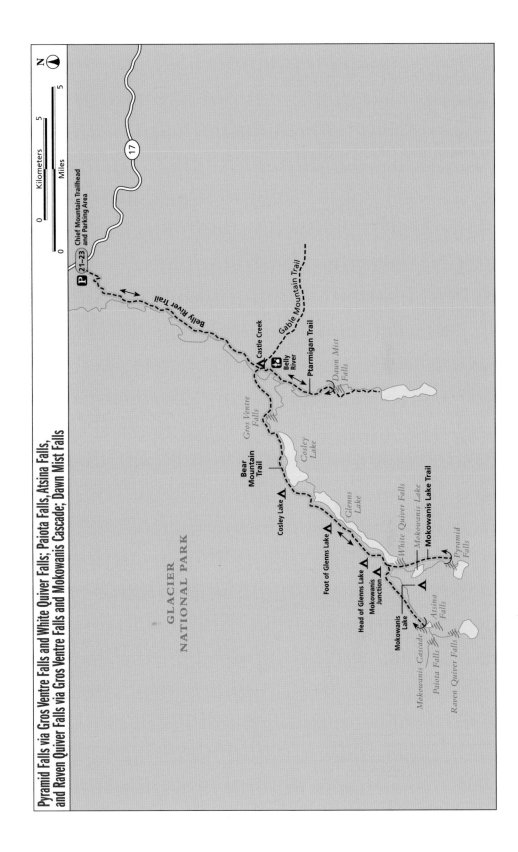

As the forest opens up and the landscape transitions into subalpine terrain, the 320-foot Pyramid Falls comes into view. It's surely one of the most beautiful waterfalls you will ever see. In the background, the Continental Divide straddles the ridge between Pyramid Peak to the west and Mount Merritt to the east. Ipasha and Chaney Glaciers are nestled out of view along the divide and form the headwaters of Pyramid Creek. A few small, stair-stepping cascades pour over the red argillite rocks of the creek as you make your way toward the large cataract. The brush thickens, and the trail peters out before reaching the base of the falls.

Miles and Directions

0.0   Chief Mountain Trailhead

3.0   Trail reaches Belly River.

4.2   Footbridge

5.8   Gable Creek Campground

5.9   Turn right at junction with Cosley Lake Cutoff Trail.
GPS: 48.9331, -113.7130 Elevation: 4,620 feet

7.4   Take side trail to Gros Ventre Falls on the left.
GPS: 48.9313, -113.7405 Elevation: 4,775 feet

7.5   Base of Gros Ventre Falls
GPS: 48.9307, -113.7404 Elevation: 4,745 feet

7.8   Stay left at junction with Bear Mountain Trail at view of Cosley Lake.

8.0   Stay right on Stoney Indian Pass Trail at junction with Ptarmigan Trail.

8.7   Cosley Lake Campground

9.0   Cosley Lake beach access

9.8   Cross bridge over Kaina Creek.

10.1   Foot of Glenns Lake Campground

12.4   Head of Glenns Lake Campground

12.8   Turn left onto Mokowanis Lake Trail at Mokowanis Junction.
GPS: 48.8879, -113.8149 Elevation: 4,830 feet

12.9   Base of White Quiver Falls
GPS: 48.8862-113.8146 Elevation: 4,850 feet

13.6   Mokowanis Lake Campground

14.2   Views of Pyramid Falls
GPS: 48.8696, -113.8116 Elevation: 5,080 feet

28.2   Arrive back at the trailhead.

22 Paiota Falls, Atsina Falls, and Raven Quiver Falls via Gros Ventre Falls and Mokowanis Cascade

The best way to get acquainted with Glacier National Park is to backpack deep into the heart of it and spend a few days walking among its deep, glacially carved valleys, towering peaks, dense forests, and abundant wildlife. This hike provides you with the opportunity to do just that. You're never far from water as you pass several lakes, cold rushing streams, and an array of waterfalls. The trek culminates at a trio of tall and powerful cascades above Atsina Lake. Water pours down from glaciers that hug the high ridges. You will need to secure a camping permit from the backcountry office in St. Mary before venturing out on the trail. There are five backcountry campgrounds to choose from that are dispersed along the route.

See map on p. 93.
Stream: Mokowanis River
Height: Gros Ventre Falls, 30 feet; Mokowanis Cascade, 480 feet; Paiota Falls, 320 feet; Atsina Falls, 320 feet; Raven Quiver Falls, 600 feet
Distance: 30.4 miles out and back in 3 or more days of overnight backpacking
Elevation change: 700 feet loss, 1,260 feet
Difficulty: Difficult due to length and steepness in the last 2 miles
Trail surface: Dirt and rock
Hiking time: 15–17 hours
Canine compatibility: Dogs are not allowed
Seasons: July to Oct

County: Glacier
Land status: National park
Fees and permits: Backcountry camping permit must be obtained in St. Mary. National Park Pass is required to enter Glacier National Park, nps.gov/glac/planyourvisit/fees.htm
Trail contact: Glacier National Park, Park Headquarters, PO Box 128, West Glacier, MT 59936; (406) 888-7800; nps.gov/glac/
Maps: *DeLorme Atlas and Gazetteer Montana* Page 23, A6; *USGS Quad* Gable Mountain
Camping: St. Mary Campground is located near the park entrance at St. Mary and has 148 sites for a fee.

Finding the Trailhead: From St. Mary, drive north on US 89 for 12.9 miles. Pass through the town of Babb, then turn left on Chief Mountain Highway, County Hwy. 17. Drive for 14.2 miles to the trailhead parking area on the west side of the road just south of the US-Canadian International Border.
GPS: 48.9959, -113.6600 Elevation: 5,310 feet

The Hike

The trail drops to the Belly River for a couple of miles and then heads up the valley through forests and occasional meadows. After almost six miles of hiking, a side trail

Mokowanis Cascade.

to the first backcountry campsite, Gable Creek Campground, appears on your right at a gorgeous view of the colorful rock ridges of Gable Mountain.

At a junction with Cosley Lake Cutoff Trail, turn right and hike down to a large swinging bridge that takes you to the north side of the Belly River. Avoid the fisherman's trail leading to the right and head straight past the bridge through open spruce and aspen. A short, steep climb takes you to a bench with a good view, and then you make a mile-long traverse through dense pine and spruce to the first lookout of the Mokowanis River. Later, you come to a sign for the first waterfall of the hike, Gros Ventre Falls, which is a must-see on the way up the Mokowanis River valley.

Turn left and down a side trail, and in a few minutes, you arrive at the rocks below the 30-foot cascade. Its deep, round pool is a great swimming hole if the water isn't too cold for your liking.

Return to Cosley Lake Cutoff Trail and continue hiking west. Gorgeous views of the lake and its meandering outlet stream appear and Cosley Ridge rises proudly from the south shore. You pass Bear Mountain Trail on the right, which is a 3.4-mile optional side trip to an observation point revealing the vast landscape. When you pass a junction for Ptarmigan Trail on the left, continue forward on what becomes Stoney Indian Pass Trail. The first half mile of shoreline is through open parkland, but the forest thickens as you arrive at Cosley Lake Campground.

Before leaving the lake, the trail accesses a lovely swimming beach on the west shore. Cross a footbridge over Kaina Creek, a medium-sized creek that flows out of a steep-walled canyon from Kaina Lake. You pass another campsite upon reaching the foot of Glenns Lake. A steady climb takes you to a flat bench where you begin to traverse the slope through tall montane forest of Engelmann spruce. For the next three miles you follow the long, slender Glenns Lake but rarely catch a glimpse of the water through the thick trees. You pass a campsite at the head of the lake and reach Mokowanis Junction less than half a mile later.

From the junction, take a short side trip down to Pyramid Creek for a view of White Quiver Falls. Find a side trail on the right between the bridges over Mokowanis

Raven Quiver Falls, Paiota Falls, and Atsina Falls behind Atsina Lake.

River and Pyramid Creek and amble to the sound of falling water. White Quiver Falls slides gracefully down a 20-foot-tall slab of rock.

To continue your way to Atsina Lake to see its trio of amazing waterfalls, head back to Mokowanis Junction and take a left on Stoney Indian Pass Trail. You soon reach Mokowanis Junction Campground, the last of the available backcountry camping options along this route. There is a mile of woods walking before you enter brushy hillside terrain. Mokowanis Cascade begins to appear as you make a steady climb up the slope. The waterfall tumbles for 480 feet over a long series of ledges at the foot of Pyramid Peak. The trail finally levels out as you approach Atsina Lake through parked-out spruce and willow. This area is a perfect example of a glacially formed hanging valley. These valleys occur at a higher elevation than the main valley floor and are a common geological phenomenon in Glacier National Park.

At the shoreline, you come to a view that's well worth the 15-mile trek to get there. Three spectacular waterfalls, Raven Quiver Falls, Paiota Falls, and Atsina Falls, plummet from Cathedral Peak and the out-of-view Shepard Glacier and make a magnificent backdrop for the alpine lake. Each falls is a treasure in itself.

Raven Quiver, the leftmost, falls near the headwaters of the Mokowanis River , which originates in Sue Lake. It drops for 600 feet like a string down a sheer cliff. Paiota, the middle waterfall, is also a section of the Mokowanis River, and it fans out over a 320-foot tall, terraced cliff face. Atsina is the rightmost waterfall, and it is part of a separate stream that falls about 320 feet in a mix of vertical drops and tiered cascades.

Meander up the trail to a spectacular vista below the lower two falls. To extend the hike, climb a few more miles on Stoney Indian Pass Trail and visit the pass and Stoney Indian Lake. You will have more waterfall views along the way and a decent chance of spotting mountain goats, grizzly bears, and other wildlife.

Miles and Directions

0.0 Chief Mountain Trailhead

3.0 Trail reaches Belly River.

4.2 Footbridge

5.8 Gable Creek Campground

5.9 Turn right at junction with Cosley Lake Cutoff Trail.
GPS: 48.9331, -113.7130 Elevation: 4,620 feet

7.4 Take side trail to Gros Ventre Falls on the left.
GPS: 48.9313, -113.7405 Elevation: 4,775 feet

7.5 Base of Gros Ventre Falls
GPS: 48.9307, -113.7404 Elevation: 4,745 feet

7.8 Stay left at the junction with Bear Mountain Trail at view of Cosley Lake.

8.0 Stay right on Stoney Indian Pass Trail at junction with Ptarmigan Trail.

8.7 Cosley Lake Campground

9.0 Cosley Lake beach access

9.8 Cross bridge over Kaina Creek.

10.1 Foot of Glenns Lake Campground

12.4 Head of Glenns Lake Campground

12.8 Mokowanis Junction. Turn left to take a short side trip to White Quiver Falls.
GPS: 48.8879, -113.8149 Elevation: 4,830 feet

12.9 Base of White Quiver Falls
GPS: 48.8862-113.8146 Elevation: 4,850 feet

13.0 Return to Mokowanis Junction. Turn left and hike west on Stoney Indian Pass Trail.

13.1 Mokowanis Junction Campground

14.5 Side views of Mokowanis Cascade
GPS: 48.8786, -113.8396 Elevation: 5,345 feet

15.1 Atsina Lake with backdrop view of Raven Quiver Falls, Paiota Falls, and Atsina Falls
GPS: 48.8765, -113.8441 Elevation: 5,745 feet

15.4 End of hike with view from below Paiota Falls and Atsina Falls
GPS: 48.8734, -113.8481 Elevation: 5,885 feet

30.4 Arrive back at Chief Mountain Trailhead.

23 Dawn Mist Falls

Without a doubt, Dawn Mist Falls is one of the most powerful and scenic waterfalls in Montana. It is situated in a beautiful and less-traveled region of Glacier National Park that abounds with wildlife and offers a variety of terrain. The hike from Chief Mountain Trailhead can be done as a very long day-hike or more comfortably as a backpacking trip with a night at Gable Creek Campground. Secure your camping permit in advance at the backcountry office in St. Mary. Remember that this is prime grizzly bear habitat, so keep your bear spray handy as you hike.

See map on p. 93.
Stream: Belly River
Height: 50 feet
Distance: 16.6 miles out and back; a very long day-hike or overnight backpacking trip
Elevation drop: 615 feet
Difficulty: Moderate due to length
Trail surface: Dirt and rock
Hiking time: 8–10 hours
Canine compatibility: Dogs are not allowed
Seasons: May to Oct
County: Glacier
Land status: National park

Fees and permits: Backcountry camping permit must be obtained in St. Mary. National Park Pass is required to enter Glacier National Park, nps.gov/glac/planyourvisit/fees.htm
Trail contact: Glacier National Park, Park Headquarters, PO Box 128, West Glacier, MT 59936; (406) 888-7800; nps.gov/glac/
Maps: *DeLorme Atlas and Gazetteer Montana* Page 23, A6; *USGS Quad* Gable Mountain
Camping: St. Mary Campground is located near the park entrance at St. Mary and has 148 sites for a fee.

Finding the Trailhead: From St. Mary, drive north on US 89 for 12.9 miles. Pass through the town of Babb, then turn left on Chief Mountain Highway, County Highway 17. Drive for 14.2 miles to the trailhead parking area on the west side of the road just south of the US-Canadian International Border.
GPS: 48.9959, -113.6600 Elevation: 5,310 feet

The Hike

The trail drops to the Belly River for a couple of miles and then heads up the valley through forests and occasional meadows. After almost six miles of hiking, a side trail to the first backcountry campsite, Gable Creek Campground, appears on your right at a gorgeous view of the colorful rock ridges of Gable Mountain.

At a junction with Cosley Lake Cutoff Trail, continue forward past the Belly River Ranger Station. When you pass Gable Pass Trail on the left, keep going straight along Belly River Trail. You enter diverse forests and proceed to hike over a few hills east of the river. Later, the trees get shorter and you glimpse gorgeous Gable Mountain. Its gold and blue bands of rock and towering headwall are often shrouded in

Dawn Mist Falls.

clouds. Cross a swinging bridge over the river to a junction where Belly River Trail merges with Ptarmigan Trail. Turn left and follow the river on its west shore.

A half mile later, a side trail on the left takes you a few hundred feet down to a gravel beach. As you turn toward the falls, prepare yourself for a shocking display of grace and beauty. Dawn Mist Falls spills over a wide ledge and forms a giant white curtain against the cliff. A large volume of water enters the pool forcefully, spraying plumes of mist into the air and showering the grassy hillside. Trees that spring from the moist rim of the canyon silhouette the horizon. To get another view from higher up, continue a short distance along Ptarmigan Trail to a side view near the brink of the falls.

Miles and Directions

0.0   Chief Mountain Trailhead

3.0   Trail reaches Belly River.

4.2   Footbridge

5.8   Gable Creek Campground

5.9   Continue forward on Belly River Trail at junction with Cosley Lake Cutoff Trail.
GPS: 48.9331, -113.7130 Elevation: 4,620 feet

6.0   Belly River Ranger Station. Continue forward on Belly River Trail at junction with Gable Pass Trail.

7.5   Swinging footbridge

7.6   Turn left at junction where Belly River Trail merges with Ptarmigan Trail.
GPS: 48.9162, -113.7289 Elevation: 4,650 feet

8.1   Turn left on side trail to Dawn Mist Falls.

8.2   Base of Dawn Mist Falls
GPS: 48.9082, -113.7221 Elevation: 4,695 feet

8.4   Cliff view of Dawn Mist Falls
GPS: 48.9084, -113.7229 Elevation: 4,700 feet

16.6   Arrive back at the trailhead.

24 Apikuni Falls

The hike to Apikuni Falls is the shortest waterfall hike in the Many Glacier area, but it climbs steadily for almost a mile and gains a quick 130 feet. The whole family can easily reach a good view of the falls, but the scramble to the base of the falls is much more of a challenge. The waterfall is tall and graceful as it descends a colorful rock wall below towering peaks. Highlights include scenic vistas of Lake Sherburne and a chance to spot mountain goats and other wildlife. Come in the early morning if you want to catch the sunlight on the falls.

Stream: Apikuni Creek
Height: 150 feet
Distance: 1.8 miles out and back
Elevation gain: 130 feet
Difficulty: Easy, except for the optional scramble to base
Trail surface: Dirt and rock
Hiking time: 30–60 minutes
Canine compatibility: Dogs are not allowed
Seasons: June to Oct
County: Glacier
Land status: National park

Fees and permits: National Park Pass is required to enter Glacier National Park, nps.gov/glac/planyourvisit/fees.htm
Trail contact: Glacier National Park, Park Headquarters, PO Box 128, West Glacier, MT 59936; (406) 888-7800; nps.gov/glac/
Maps: *DeLorme Atlas and Gazetteer Montana* Page 23, B7; *USGS Quad* Many Glacier
Camping: Many Glacier Campground is located near the end of Many Glacier Road and has 109 sites for a fee.

Finding the Trailhead: From Babb, drive west on Many Glacier Road for 10.4 miles to the parking area on the north side of the road.
GPS: 48.8054, -113.6346 Elevation: 4,905 feet

The Hike

Red Gap Pass Trail leaves the parking area to the northeast and Apikuni Falls Trail to the northwest. Start hiking on Apikuni Falls Trail, climbing gently up a brushy slope in open forest. You enter a second-growth forest of lodgepole and aspen and begin to climb more steadily. Along the way, several side trails lead to lookout points revealing the rugged Apikuni Creek drainage as well as Lake Sherburne and iconic peaks to the south.

As you gain elevation, the trees become a subalpine scrub forest and the sound of the falling water begins to call you onward. Apikuni Falls comes into view as you arrive at the headwalls of Altyn Peak to the west and Apikuni Mountain to the north.

Falling over 150 feet, the slender and elegant waterfall makes a vertical drop and then slides gracefully down a steep crevice of red, orange, and purple rock.

The trail levels out with good views of the falls as you approach. Leaving the trees, you enter a rocky amphitheater and follow Apikuni Creek almost to the foot of the

Apikuni Falls; Morning Eagle Falls, via Hidden Falls; Grinnell Falls, and Feather Plume Falls; Ptarmigan Falls; Redrock Falls

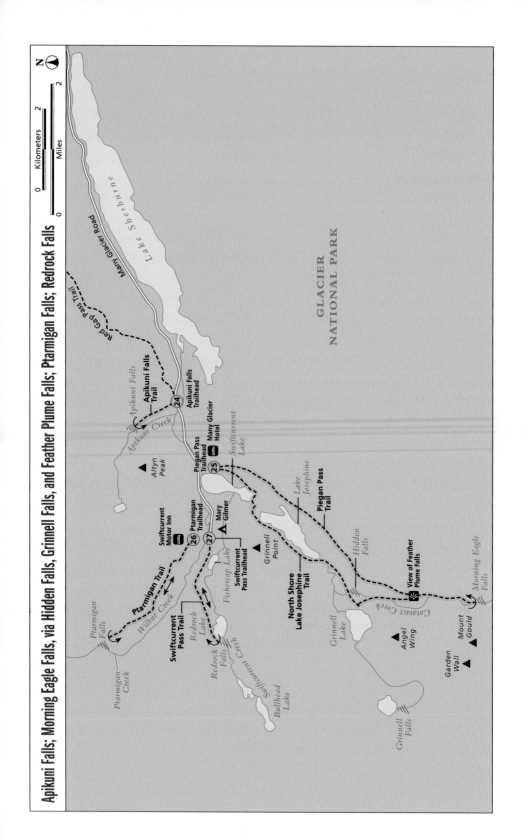

Apikuni Falls.

cascade. Beginner hikers should stop and enjoy the spectacle from this point because the final stretch of the trail requires some difficult rock scrambling. If you can make it to the base, it's definitely worth the effort. Look up on the grassy slopes below Altyn Peak to see if you can spot grazing mountain goats or perhaps a lumbering grizzly bear.

Miles and Directions

0.0 Apikuni Falls Trailhead

0.8 First view of Apikuni Falls

0.9 Base of Apikuni Falls
    GPS: 48.8141, -113.6427 Elevation: 5,035 feet

1.8 Arrive back at the trailhead.

25 Morning Eagle Falls, via Hidden Falls, Grinnell Falls, and Feather Plume Falls

This is one of the most rewarding waterfall day-hikes in Montana for its abundance of great scenery and watchable wildlife. If you complete the route described here, you can see three lakes and four waterfalls. In addition to water features, the hike offers classic views of tall peaks and deep glacial valleys, and there are good opportunities to observe moose, bear, bighorn sheep, and mountain goats.

See map on p. 104.

Stream: Cataract Creek
Height: Hidden Falls, 50 feet; Grinnell Falls, 960 feet; Feather Plume Falls, 800 feet; Morning Eagle Falls, 220 feet
Distance: 11.0-mile loop
Elevation gain: 550 feet
Difficulty: Moderate due to length
Trail surface: Dirt and rock
Hiking time: 6–8 hours
Canine compatibility: Dogs are not allowed
Seasons: June to Oct
County: Glacier

Land status: National park
Fees and permits: National Park Pass is required to enter Glacier National Park, nps.gov/glac/planyourvisit/fees.htm
Trail contact: Glacier National Park, Park Headquarters, PO Box 128, West Glacier, MT 59936; (406) 888-7800; nps.gov/glac/
Maps: *DeLorme Atlas and Gazetteer Montana* Page 23, B7; *USGS Quad* Many Glacier
Camping: Many Glacier Campground is located near the end of Many Glacier Road and has 109 sites for a fee.

Finding the Trailhead: From Babb, drive west on Many Glacier Road for 11.5 miles to the turn-off for Many Glacier Hotel. Turn left and drive for 0.1 mile. Turn left again at a sign for the trailhead. After 0.2 mile you arrive at the Piegan Pass Trailhead.
GPS: 48.7956, -113.6559 Elevation: 4,920 feet

The Hike

There are many trails and junctions in the area, so finding the right route can be a bit tricky. A simpler alternative to avoid confusion is to just follow Piegan Pass Trail directly to Morning Eagle Falls. However, taking this more complex route with little extra distance allows you to visit many other amazing sights along the way, such as Swiftcurrent Lake, Lake Josephine, Hidden Falls, Grinnell Lake, and Grinnell Falls.

The trail begins with a Y-junction, at which you take a right and follow the signs for Piegan Pass. Walk another tenth of a mile until the trail empties into a gravel road.

Follow this road to its end at a couple of large cabins near the shore of Swiftcurrent Lake. Grinnell Point reaches to the sky like a large triangle behind the lake. Find a wide path and head left (south) along the west shore of the lake. When you reach a split in the trail, take North Shore Josephine Lake Trail on the right to a bridge over

Morning Eagle Falls.

the inlet stream. The trail slowly curves west and arrives at a boat dock. (You can opt to take the ferry from Many Glacier Hotel to this location to shorten your total hike by 2 miles.) Take a left at the junction at the boat dock to continue on North Shore Josephine Lake Trail. Climb a paved path over a hill through Engelmann spruce to reach another boat dock at the north end of Lake Josephine. (The same ferry service can get you across this lake as well, if you want to reduce the total hike by another 2.6 miles.)

As you walk along the shore, the scenery opens up offering terrific vistas of Cataract Mountain behind the turquoise-colored lake. During your gentle stroll along the shimmering waters, you pass a trail to Grinnell Glacier on the right. Stay left along the shore until you arrive at the outlet stream at the south end of the lake. Pass a second foot trail on the right and head straight to a boardwalk that leads to a bridge over Cataract Creek.

Wooden walkways continue to take you easily across the marshlands of the inlet area to the south shore of Lake Josephine. Take a right at a junction that leads to another boat dock for arriving ferries, and start walking through the wooded valley. The trail passes through great habitat for bear and moose: dense spruce forest enveloping small clearings and a willow-lined stream. Pass a couple of pit toilets on the left and then make your way to a swinging bridge over Cataract Creek. Just before the bridge, take a left on a side path heading up the hill to Hidden Falls. You wind along the rim of a concealed gorge in the forested valley. After a couple hundred feet, you arrive at an overlook of the 25-foot plunge of whitewater. The creek empties into a deep pool and then flows into a narrow slot canyon of smooth, rounded rock. Majestic Mount Gould creates a nice backdrop to this pretty cascade and beckons you in the direction of the next waterfall.

Return to the bridge, cross Cataract Creek, and walk a few minutes to Grinnell Lake. At the shore, you can view from a distance one of the largest and most beautiful waterfalls in Montana—Grinnell Falls. This 960-foot cascade descends the cliffy terrain from Grinnell Glacier all the way to the Grinnell Lake basin. Hopefully, the weather cooperates to give you enough visibility to glimpse this amazing waterfall.

Rest for a while on the gravel beach, and take in the incredible views and cool breeze coming in off the lake. Tall peaks and ridges surround you in every direction.

From Grinnell Lake, follow the trail sign pointing to Piegan Pass Trail. After climbing a short hill, the path levels out and follows Cataract Creek on its west side through tall brush.

Make some noise in these areas of low visibility to alert bears of your presence. Angel Wing is the peak at the top of the headwall to your right. You soon reach another swinging bridge over Cataract Creek, and then the trail borders the gently meandering stream.

Enjoy the views of subalpine forest leading up to grassy slopes below the high walls of rock. When the trail bisects Piegan Pass Trail, turn right and hike to a ford over a medium-sized creek. The crossing is easy at normal water level but could be difficult during high water. After crossing the stream, look for a dark spot on the rock wall above you. If you come early in the season, you might see Feather Plume Falls leaping out over a ledge and showering the cliff for over 800 feet. Late in the season it is either dried up or barely visible.

After walking another half mile through tall spruce, you emerge from the trees to your first glimpse of the 220-foot-tall Morning Eagle Falls in the distance. Keep walking toward the scenic waterfall, crossing a footbridge to the east side of the creek.

Huge snowfields hug the base of the rock wall, and small streams of water descend from each one. These are the remnants of the glaciers that had once carved this valley.

When you reach the location where the trail suddenly climbs away from the stream, you have arrived at the best place to rest and enjoy the falls. Cataract Creek pours vertically like a curtain over a high ledge and then continues falling in a series of cascades. The Garden Wall rises behind the falls, with peaks such as Mount Gould, Bishop's Cap, and Pollock Mountain crowning the jagged ridges. Below the falls, the gentle and winding Cataract Creek flows through brushy terrain and scrub forest.

Keep an eye out for mountain goats, bighorn sheep, and grizzly bears in the falls area.

You can wander up the creek drainage a bit closer to the falls (if the water conditions aren't hazardous), or you can follow Piegan Pass Trail another half mile to a scenic side view of Morning Eagle Falls. Along the way, you might be treated to dense patches of huckleberry nestled in pockets of subalpine fir. To extend the hike even more, Piegan Pass is located several grueling miles past the falls. To return to the trailhead, retrace your steps for about a mile back to the junction near the creek ford. Take a right to stay on Piegan Pass Trail, and then begin a 4-mile traverse across the spruce-forested slopes of Allen Mountain until you return to the Many Glacier Hotel area.

Miles and Directions

0.0 Keep right at Y-junction near Piegan Pass Trailhead.

0.1 Follow gravel road.

0.5 Reach cabin at Swiftcurrent Lake. Turn left and follow path along lake.

0.8 Turn right on North Shore Josephine Lake Trail at Y-junction.

1.0 Keep left at boat dock on west end of Swiftcurrent Lake.

1.2 Boat dock on east end of Lake Josephine

1.9 Stay left on North Shore Josephine Lake Trail at junction with Grinnell Glacier Trail.

2.2 Keep left when passing merging trail on the right.

2.5 Take a right at junction to boat dock.

3.2 Pit toilet

3.3 Side trail to Hidden Falls

3.3 Overlook of Hidden Falls
GPS: 48.7664, -113.6951 Elevation: 5,035 feet

3.7 Turn left upon returning to main trail.

3.7 Grinnell Lake with view of Grinnell Falls
GPS: 48.7650, -113.7005 Elevation: 4,890 feet

4.3 Cross swinging bridge over Cataract Creek.

4.8 Turn right onto Piegan Pass Trail.
GPS: 48.7519, -113.6974 Elevation: 5,125 feet

4.9 View to the west of seasonal Feather Plume Falls at creek crossing

5.4 First view of Morning Eagle Falls at footbridge

5.9 Closest viewpoint of Morning Eagle Falls from trail
GPS: 48.7380, -113.6989 Elevation: 5,470 feet

11.0 Complete loop hike by taking Piegan Pass Trail all the way back to the parking area.

26 Ptarmigan Falls

Ptarmigan Falls is a pretty location to visit while on the way to other nearby destinations like Iceberg Lake and Ptarmigan Tunnel. The easy day-hike offers spectacular vistas of the lofty peaks and glacier-cut valleys of the Many Glacier area. The popular trail traverses a subalpine landscape that gives you good opportunities to view wildlife. While the falls are partially visible from the trail, a little scrambling down a steep path gets you a much clearer view.

See map on p. 104.
Stream: Ptarmigan Creek
Height: 40 feet
Distance: 4.8 miles out and back
Elevation gain: 775 feet
Difficulty: Easy
Trail surface: Dirt and rock
Hiking time: 2–4 hours
Canine compatibility: Dogs are not allowed
Seasons: June to Oct
County: Glacier
Land status: National park

Fees and permits: National Park Pass is required to enter Glacier National Park, nps.gov/glac/planyourvisit/fees.htm
Trail contact: Glacier National Park, Park Headquarters, PO Box 128, West Glacier, MT 59936; (406) 888-7800; nps.gov/glac/
Maps: *DeLorme Atlas and Gazetteer Montana* Page 23, B6; *USGS Quad* Many Glacier
Camping: Many Glacier Campground is located near the end of Many Glacier Road and has 109 sites for a fee.

Finding the Trailhead: From Babb, drive west on Many Glacier Road for 12.6 miles to the Swiftcurrent Motor Inn. Turn right at a sign for Ptarmigan Trailhead and follow a narrow road for a tenth of a mile to the parking area on the left.
GPS: 48.7995, -113.6791 Elevation: 4,900 feet

The Hike

For the first quarter mile, you climb steadily up steep and lush forests of pine, spruce, and aspen and then come to a bench of tundra with a spectacular view. Grinnell Point, Mount Grinnell, and Mount Wilbur rise up from the wide glacial valleys where Wilbur Creek and Swiftcurrent Creek flow. The trail then traverses a grassy slope on the lower flanks of Mount Henkel for almost a mile. Later, you enter a subalpine forest of pine and spruce and continue winding along the hillside. Listen for a low cooing sound to help you spot ptarmigan in their preferred tundra habitat. Also, keep an eye out for bighorn sheep, mountain goats, and grizzly bears as you pass along the rocky slope.

After crossing a small tributary stream, the trail passes a path to a pit toilet up the hill. Soon after, you arrive at a view of the 40-foot Ptarmigan Falls through the trees. Water slides vigorously down colorful rock in a pristine-forested ravine, and the alpine splendor of the 8,900-foot Crowfeet Mountain rises in the background.

Bighorn sheep on Ptarmigan Trail.

You can follow the rim of the small canyon to the top of the falls. For a clearer view and a bit of solitude, skilled hikers can scramble down a steep footpath through thick spruce to the base area.

To extend your hike a few more miles from the junction near the falls, you have two fantastic options: turn right to hike to Ptarmigan Tunnel via Ptarmigan Lake, or turn left to hike to famous Iceberg Lake, which often holds large chunks of floating ice until well into summer.

Miles and Directions

0.0 Ptarmigan Trailhead

2.3 View of Ptarmigan Falls

2.3 Base of Ptarmigan Falls
GPS: 48.8213, -113.7118 Elevation: 5,675 feet

2.4 Top of Ptarmigan Falls

4.8 Arrive back at the trailhead.

27 Redrock Falls

Redrock Falls is the easiest waterfall to access in the Many Glacier area of Glacier National Park. The route crosses second-growth pine, spruce, and aspen forests and passes two scenic mountain lakes. You have a very good chance of seeing moose near the waterways and black bears and deer in the forests. The waterfall makes its descent at a reddish outcropping of boulders and ledges with a perfect mountain backdrop. It takes its name from the layers of red argillite, a sedimentary rock common in the Belt Supergroup of western Montana.

See map on p. 104.
Stream: Swiftcurrent Creek
Height: 20 feet
Distance: 3.8 miles out and back
Elevation gain: 220 feet
Difficulty: Easy
Trail surface: Dirt and rock
Hiking time: 2–3 hours
Canine compatibility: Dogs are not allowed
Seasons: June to Oct
County: Glacier
Land status: National park

Fees and permits: National Park Pass is required to enter Glacier National Park, nps.gov/glac/planyourvisit/fees.htm
Trail contact: Glacier National Park, Park Headquarters, PO Box 128, West Glacier, MT 59936, (406) 888-7800; nps.gov/glac/
Maps: *DeLorme Atlas and Gazetteer Montana* Page 23, B6; *USGS Quad* Many Glacier
Camping: Many Glacier Campground is located near the end of Many Glacier Road and has 109 sites for a fee.

Finding the Trailhead: From Babb, drive west on Many Glacier Road for 12.6 miles to the Swiftcurrent Motor Inn. Swiftcurrent Pass Trailhead is located at the far west side of the parking area.
GPS: 48.7975, -113.6786 Elevation: 4,840 feet

The Hike

Swiftcurrent Pass Trail immediately comes to a bridge over gently meandering Wilbur Creek and then climbs easily to a side trail to Fishercap Lake. Take a left and head down the path to the shore, where you might see a moose wading in the lake and feeding on aquatic plants. If there are no moose present, this is a good place to take a refreshing swim on a hot day.

Back on Swiftcurrent Pass Trail, continue west through second-growth forest that has regenerated since the Heaven's Peak Fire of 1932. Climb a gentle rise toward the distant sound of falling water and then amble through a pretty blend of coniferous and deciduous trees. Later, you reach an aspen grove at the foot of Mount Wilbur, which retains snow patches on its high walls throughout the year. Iconic Glacier Peak stands majestically between the Wilbur and Swiftcurrent valleys.

You soon come to a small gravel beach on Redrock Lake. This area is also prime moose habitat, so stop here and scan the shorelines for Glacier National Park's largest

Redrock Falls. Photo by Martha Gunsalam.

mammal before continuing along the spruce-lined north shore. Just beyond the west end of the lake, you arrive at a spur trail on the left to Redrock Falls. Walk downhill for a few hundred feet to Swiftcurrent Creek and to the accumulation of red boulders that form the waterfall. Whitewater tumbles for about 20 feet and then settles into a gentle, winding stream that empties into Redrock Lake. The multiterraced waterfall is especially scenic thanks to its backdrop of horn-shaped Mount Grinnell.

Be sure to make your way to the top of the falls, either by following dirt paths or by scrambling along the reddish argillite ledges. You can peek into pristine pools of water deposited between the slabs of rock. From the top of the outcropping, enjoy a fabulous view to the east of Redrock Lake and Mount Henkel. If you want to extend your hike, Swiftcurrent Pass Trail continues on to Bullhead Lake and then ascends in several long switchbacks to the top of Swiftcurrent Pass.

Miles and Directions

0.0 Swiftcurrent Pass Trailhead

0.1 Cross bridge over Wilbur Creek.

0.2 Take spur trail on the left for short side trip to Fishercap Lake.

1.6 Redrock Lake

1.8 Take side trail on the left to Redrock Falls.

1.8 Base of Redrock Falls
GPS: 48.7951, -113.7124 Elevation: 5,060 feet

1.9 Top of Redrock Falls

3.8 Arrive back at the trailhead.

28 Atlantic Falls

The beauty is extreme in the less-visited Cut Bank area of Glacier National Park, and the hike to Atlantic Falls features a balance of scenic open areas and lush covered terrain. You follow the creek through numerous small meadows bursting with color during wildflower season. Aspen, cottonwood, and mountain maple put on a vibrant display in the fall. Watch for wildlife in the willow flats and forest edges as you gaze at tall peaks of the Hudson Bay Divide and the Continental Divide. You pass views of a couple of unnamed waterfalls flowing out of high glacial valleys and arrive at the 20-foot Atlantic Falls at the foot of the peaks.

Stream: Atlantic Creek
Height: 20 feet
Distance: 8.0 miles out and back
Elevation gain: 140 feet
Difficulty: Moderate
Trail surface: Dirt and rock
Hiking time: 4–6 hours
Canine compatibility: Dogs are not allowed
Seasons: June to Oct
County: Glacier
Land status: National park

Fees and permits: National Park Pass is required to enter Glacier National Park, nps.gov/glac/planyourvisit/fees.htm
Trail contact: Glacier National Park, Park Headquarters, PO Box 128, West Glacier, MT 59936; (406) 888-7800, nps.gov/glac/
Maps: *DeLorme Atlas and Gazetteer Montana* Page 23, D8; *USGS Quad* Cut Bank Pass
Camping: Cut Bank Campground is located near the trailhead at the end of Cut Bank Road. There are fourteen campsites for a fee.

Finding the Trailhead: From St. Mary, drive south on US 89 for 13.9 miles. Turn right on gravel Cut Bank Road. The road enters Glacier National Park at 4 miles and reaches the Cut Bank Trailhead at 4.9 miles.
GPS: 48.6025, -113.3837 Elevation: 5,155 feet

The Hike

Pitamakan Pass Trail begins to cross grassy meadows surrounded by groves of aspen and stands of lodgepole pine. The route follows North Fork Cut Bank Creek as it flows through wooded bottomlands of thick willow and spruce. The trail stays along the north side of the valley in shady forest with dense foliage. You come to an open view at a ridge looking down at the large creek where Mad Wolf, Eagle Plume, and Bad Marriage Mountains rise to the southwest. The path takes you back to the edge of an eroded slope and view of the crystal-clear waters of the stream. A tall waterfall flows down from between two of the peaks in the distance.

You descend a hill through small meadows full of diverse wildflowers. For the next half mile, you proceed to border a giant willow flat that provides excellent habitat for moose, beaver, and a variety of other animals. The trail then leaves the stream and winds through forests of mostly spruce, pine, and willow to a large tributary

Atlantic Falls.

stream flowing down from Kupunkamit Mountain to the north. You can glimpse a waterfall gushing out from the hanging valley below the massive peak. The shady cottonwood-lined gravel bar, gentle stream, and views of regal mountains make this an excellent midway resting spot.

The trail climbs steeply for a short distance until you are rewarded with a glorious view of a whitewater section of North Fork Cut Bank Creek and lofty Medicine Grizzly Peak in the background. A short side trail takes you to a lookout on a windswept ridge next to white bark pines. Next, the trail drops slowly back to the stream banks and resumes its course through mostly flat wooded terrain. You pass a

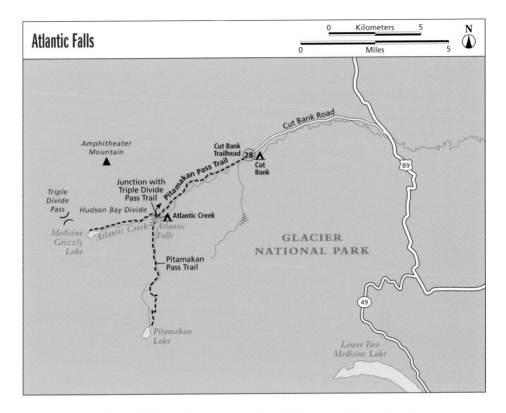

Atlantic Falls

0 — Kilometers — 5

0 — Miles — 5

N

Amphitheater Mountain

Cut Bank Road

Cut Bank Trailhead 28

Cut Bank

89

Junction with Triple Divide Pass Trail

Pitamakan Pass Trail

Triple Divide Pass

Hudson Bay Divide

Atlantic Creek

Atlantic Creek

Atlantic Falls

GLACIER NATIONAL PARK

Medicine Grizzly Lake

Pitamakan Pass Trail

Pitamakan Lake

49

Lower Two Medicine Lake

medium-sized pond below the headwall of Bad Marriage Mountain where you are likely to spot ducks or other waterfowl. Looking up toward Pitamakan Pass, you can see two perfect cone-shaped peaks tower in the distance—Flinsch Peak and Mount Morgan.

After crossing three footbridges over a braided tributary stream, you come to a junction with Triple Divide Pass Trail. Keep left to stay on Pitamakan Pass Trail and hike a final quarter mile to a close-up view of Atlantic Falls from a footbridge. The medium-sized Atlantic Creek pours over a 20-foot-tall ledge and flows into a spruce bog below. Mount James and Amphitheater Mountain loom behind the falls to the north. If you'd like to spend a night near the falls, Atlantic Creek Campground lies just a quarter mile up Triple Divide Pass Trail. Be sure to secure your backcountry permit in St. Mary before you camp. To extend the hike, you can reach Morning Star Lake a few more miles up Pitamakan Pass Trail or Medicine Grizzly Lake several miles up Triple Divide Pass Trail.

Miles and Directions

0.0 Cut Bank Trailhead

0.4 Open view of stream and peaks

0.9 Trail meets Atlantic Creek

2.2 Cross footbridge over large tributary in gravel bar.

2.6 Side trail viewpoint of Atlantic Creek and Medicine Grizzly Peak

3.2 Pond below Bad Marriage Mountain

3.5 Three footbridges over braided stream

3.7 Keep left on Pitamakan Pass Trail at junction with Triple Divide Pass Trail.
GPS: 48.5757, -113.4481 Elevation: 5,275 feet

4.0 Atlantic Falls
GPS: 48.5728, -113.4503 Elevation: 5,295 feet

8.0 Arrive back at the trailhead.

29 Running Eagle Falls

Running Eagle Falls is a beautifully unique waterfall where Two Medicine Creek pours at two separate levels—a lower underground channel gushes out of a cave while an upper channel spills vertically over a high ledge. The aspect of the waterfall changes drastically with the seasons. Situated only a mile from the park entrance at the foot of tall peaks, Running Eagle Falls is a great way to commence your Glacier visit. Even though it's located in a less-crowded region of Glacier, its attractiveness and easy access make it a very popular destination. It is one of the two wheelchair-accessible trails in the park.

Stream: Two Medicine Creek
Height: 70 feet total; upper drop, 50 feet; lower drop from sinkhole, 20 feet
Distance: 0.6 mile out and back
Elevation gain: 15 feet
Difficulty: Very easy
Trail surface: Dirt
Hiking time: 20-30 minutes
Canine compatibility: Dogs are not allowed
Seasons: Apr to Oct
County: Glacier
Land status: National park

Fees and permits: National Park Pass is required to enter Glacier National Park, nps.gov/glac/planyourvisit/fees.htm
Trail contact: Glacier National Park, Park Headquarters, PO Box 128, West Glacier, MT 59936; (406) 888-7800; nps.gov/glac/
Maps: *DeLorme Atlas and Gazetteer Montana* Page 23, D8; *USGS Quad* Dancing Lady Mountain
Camping: Two Medicine Campground is located near Pray Lake and has one hundred campsites for a fee.

Finding the Trailhead: From the park entrance on Two Medicine Road, drive 1.1 miles to the trailhead on the right.
GPS: 48.4961, -113.3482 Elevation: 4,920 feet

The Hike

The wide, flat trail passes through thick spruce and cottonwood and soon reaches the banks of Two Medicine Creek. A straight-on view of Running Eagle Falls appears as you walk out onto the rock bar. Rising Wolf Mountain looms at 9,510 feet and creates a picturesque backdrop. To get a closer look, cross the footbridge to the other side and hike to the edge of the pool at the base of the falls. If you come in the early season, chances are the bridge will have been washed away by the forces of nature during high water. It is reconstructed annually to allow visitors safe crossing over the swift creek in the summer.

Running Eagle Falls is fed by an underground sinkhole as well as by a ground-level stream. During spring runoff, Two Medicine Creek's large volume of water makes the two sources indistinguishable—both combine into one grand 70-foot descent of whitewater. At normal flow, however, it's easier to appreciate the natural

Running Eagle Falls; Appistoki Falls; Twin Falls; Aster Falls; Rockwell Falls

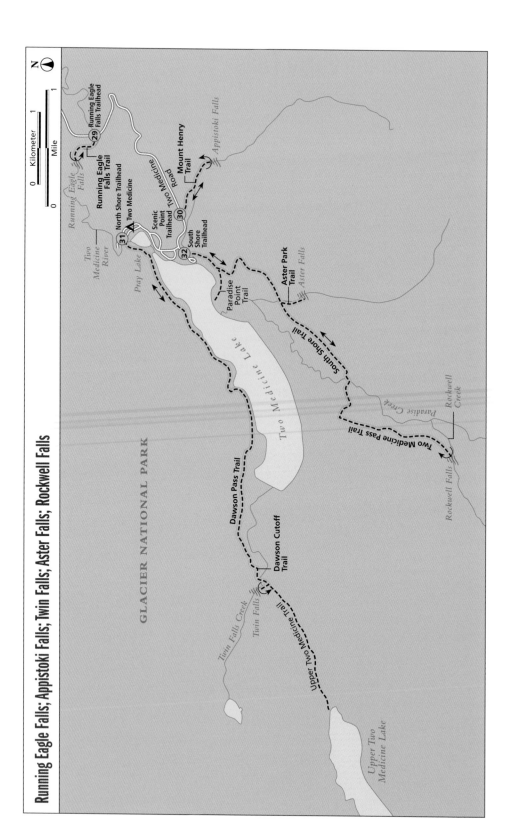

Running Eagle Falls at normal water level.

bridge formation where water emerges mysteriously from a cave. Due to the unusual natural phenomenon, this cascade is also often referred to as Trick Falls.

Miles and Directions

0.0 Running Eagle Falls Trailhead

0.2 View of Running Eagle Falls from rock bar
GPS: 48.4972, -113.3499 Elevation: 4,930 feet

0.3 Base of Running Eagle Falls
GPS: 48.4983, -113.3515 Elevation: 4,935 feet

0.6 Arrive back at the trailhead.

30 Appistoki Falls

Appistoki Falls is a beautiful destination for a short family hike, but for an added challenge, you can also continue on to a panoramic vista atop Scenic Point. The trail takes you into a classic hanging valley where the waterfall is tucked deep in a ravine.

See map on p. 120.

Stream: Appistoki Creek
Height: 40 feet
Distance: 1.4 miles out and back
Elevation gain: 105 feet
Difficulty: Easy
Trail surface: Dirt and rock
Hiking time: 30–45 minutes
Canine compatibility: Dogs are not allowed
Seasons: June to Oct
County: Glacier
Land status: National park

Fees and permits: National Park Pass is required to enter Glacier National Park, nps.gov/glac/planyourvisit/fees.htm
Trail contact: Glacier National Park, Park Headquarters, PO Box 128, West Glacier, MT 59936; (406) 888-7800; nps.gov/glac/
Maps: *DeLorme Atlas and Gazetteer Montana* Page 23, D8; *USGS Quad* Dancing Lady Mountain
Camping: Two Medicine Campground is located near Pray Lake and has one hundred campsites for a fee.

Finding the Trailhead: From the park entrance on Two Medicine Road, drive 6.9 miles to Scenic Point Trailhead on the left.
GPS: 48.4852, -113.3615 Elevation: 5,320 feet

The Hike

Mount Henry Trail climbs gently through a thick forest of fir, spruce, and lodgepole pine. As you emerge into the more open and sunny forest, enjoy views to the south of Scenic Point and its high ridges that connect with Medicine Mountain, Mount Henry, and Appistoki Peak. After about a half mile, you come to a sign marking a side trail to Appistoki Falls. Turn right and walk carefully along a canyon rim above a steep vertical drop. Climb for a few hundred feet to reach a lateral view of Appistoki Falls, which winds and splashes through a forested ravine. Appistoki Peak forms a gorgeous backdrop with its green, grassy slopes and jagged ridgeline. To extend the hike, follow Mount Henry Trail for a few miles to the top of Scenic Point for unforgettable views.

Miles and Directions

0.0 Scenic Point Trailhead
0.6 Take a side trail on the right to Appistoki Falls.
0.7 Top of Appistoki Falls
GPS: 48.4824, -113.3525 Elevation: 5,425 feet
1.4 Arrive back at the trailhead.

Appistoki Falls.

31 Twin Falls

The easy hike to Twin Falls follows the scenic north shore of Two Medicine Lake, with gorgeous views of the waterway and surrounding mountains. The trail passes through grassy meadows with abundant wildflowers and enters cool forests with a thick understory. Twin Falls descends a rocky slope in two parallel cascades that join at the base. The ice-cold water invites you for a refreshing dip on a hot day. Many hikers also visit this popular destination by taking a 45-minute ferry across the lake and then walking the remaining distance to the falls. Watch for wildlife including grizzly bears throughout the hike.

See map on p. 120.
Stream: Twin Falls Creek
Height: 80 feet
Distance: 6.8 miles out and back
Elevation gain: 75 feet
Difficulty: Easy
Trail surface: Dirt and rock
Hiking time: 4–5 hours
Canine compatibility: Dogs are not allowed
Seasons: June to Oct
County: Glacier
Land status: National park

Fees and permits: National Park Pass is required to enter Glacier National Park, nps.gov/glac/planyourvisit/fees.htm
Trail contact: Glacier National Park, Park Headquarters, PO Box 128, West Glacier, MT 59936; (406) 888-7800; nps.gov/glac/
Maps: *DeLorme Atlas and Gazetteer Montana* Page 23, D8; *USGS Quad* Mount Rockwell
Camping: Two Medicine Campground is located near Pray Lake and has one hundred campsites for a fee.

Finding the Trailhead: From the park entrance on Two Medicine Road, drive 7.1 miles to the turnoff to the campground and picnic area. Turn right and drive for 0.2 mile until you reach North Shore Trailhead near a footbridge.
GPS: 48.4921, -113.3656 Elevation: 5,165 feet

The Hike

The hike begins by crossing a footbridge over Two Medicine Creek where it flows out of Pray Lake, a small lake attached to the east end of Two Medicine Lake. You then approach a clearing at a junction with Pitamakan Pass Trail. Keep left on what becomes Dawson Pass Trail and advance along the north shore below the flanks of Rising Wolf Mountain. Weaving in and out of open meadows and patches of dense spruce, fir, and pine, the trail offers splendid views of Two Medicine Lake as it passes just above its shoreline. Look up to spot raptors soaring along the high cliffs and big-horn sheep and mountain goats grazing on steep grassy slopes.

After almost a mile, you reach a large grassy meadow with a great vantage point of the surrounding peaks and basins. From right to left you see Rising Wolf Mountain, Pumpelly Pillar, Sinopah Mountain, Painted Tipi Peak, Never Laughs Mountain, and

Twin Falls.

Scenic Point, just to name a few. Several small seasonal waterfalls rage down the north face in June. As you come to the west end of the lake, the headwall of Rising Wolf Mountain appears close to your right. You cross stepping-stones over a good-sized stream and then climb a bluff that offers a stunning glimpse of the peaks farther up toward Two Medicine Pass and Dawson Pass.

When you reach a signed junction with Dawson Cutoff Trail, take a left and drop down a hill into a timbered valley. South Shore Trail soon merges on the left. (You can add a few miles to your hike by taking this route back to the trailhead along the opposite side of Two Medicine Lake.) To reach Twin Falls, keep right on what becomes Upper Two Medicine Lake Trail, and walk toward the roar of the falls. Cross a footbridge over a large tributary stream and then turn onto a path on the right that leads to the base of the Twin Falls. Just as the name suggests, two distinct cascades tumble side by side down the bedrock. They split into two channels at the brink of the falls and rejoin again at the base. Brave souls can jump from the rocks into the ice-cold water, and adventurous hikers can ascend small footpaths to explore the upper areas of the 80-foot waterfall.

Miles and Directions

0.0 North Shore Trailhead

0.8 Clearing with views of peaks to the south and seasonal waterfalls on Rising Wolf Mountain

2.1 Cross large tributary.

3.0 Turn left at junction with Dawson Cutoff Trail.

3.2 Turn right at junction with Upper Two Medicine Lake Trail.

3.3 Take a right on spur trail after crossing footbridge.

3.4 Base of Twin Falls

      GPS: 48.4759, -113.4262 Elevation: 5,240 feet

6.8 Arrive back at the trailhead.

32 Aster Falls and Rockwell Falls

This popular hike gives you a good idea of the spectacular beauty of the Two Medicine area. This less-crowded part of Glacier National Park has abundant wildlife, lush vegetation, and scenic waterways that pass through glacially carved valleys. You follow Aster Creek and Paradise Creek over flat terrain through forest and marshlands. Aster Falls offers a nice breaking point along the way and a chance to swim in a pristine pool. Rockwell Falls makes for a scenic final destination with its multiple sections of plunging whitewater.

See map on p. 120.
Stream: Aster Creek, Rockwell Creek
Height: Aster Falls, 20 feet; Rockwell Falls, 40 feet
Distance: 6.2 miles out and back
Elevation loss: 25 feet
Difficulty: Easy
Trail surface: Dirt and rock
Hiking time: 4–5 hours
Canine compatibility: Dogs are not allowed
Seasons: June to Oct
County: Glacier

Land status: National park
Fees and permits: National Park Pass is required to enter Glacier National Park, nps.gov/glac/planyourvisit/fees.htm
Trail contact: Glacier National Park, Park Headquarters, PO Box 128, West Glacier, MT 59936; (406) 888-7800; nps.gov/glac/
Maps: *DeLorme Atlas and Gazetteer Montana* Page 23, E8; *USGS Quad* Mount Rockwell
Camping: Two Medicine Campground is located near Pray Lake and has one hundred campsites for a fee.

Finding the Trailhead: From the park entrance on Two Medicine Road, drive 7.1 miles to the turnoff to the campground and picnic area. Continue straight for another 0.1 mile to South Shore Trailhead at the end of the road.
GPS: 48.4833, -113.3695 Elevation: 5,180 feet

The Hike

South Shore Trail begins in a dense spruce forest on the east side of Two Medicine Lake and soon arrives at a junction with Paradise Point Trail. Keep left and start to amble along small meadows and ponds. Rising Wolf Mountain towers beside you, and the majestic Sinopah Mountain beckons you forward. You cross a footbridge over Aster Creek and then come to a junction with Aster Park Trail. Turn left and climb gently through lodgepole pine and spruce to a path on the left that leads to the base of Aster Falls. Water cascades from side to side down sheaves of stone in a narrow ravine. Cool off in the shimmering pools before resuming your hike to Rockwell Falls.

Back at the main trail, head left and continue your way up South Shore Trail. You cross a small wooden bridge and then drop into a marshy area that is excellent moose habitat. Later, you cross a rickety swinging bridge over Paradise Creek—hold on

Aster Falls.

tight to your belongings. The trail then climbs gently to a T-junction. Take a left onto Two Medicine Pass Trail and start walking up Paradise Creek through lush, green parklands. Magnificent mountain views appear as you ascend. You come to a small footbridge over Rockwell Creek where you first glimpse the falls. Turn at the signed junction and follow the path to a closer viewpoint. Rockwell Falls tumbles down several drops in a forested ravine at the foot of Sinopah Mountain.

The closest section is a perfectly formed, 40-foot-tall curtain of falling water. Small footpaths on the north side of the creek will guide your explorations of the upper sections of the falls.

Rockwell Falls.

Miles and Directions

0.0   South Shore Trailhead

0.2   Keep left on South Shore Trail at junction with Paradise Point Trail.

0.9   Footbridge over Aster Creek

1.0   Turn left on Aster Park Trail.

1.1   Turn left on path to Aster Falls.

1.2   Base of Aster Falls

        GPS: 48.47141, -113.3757 Elevation: 5,155 feet

1.4 Backtrack to South Shore Trail and continue left.

2.3 Swinging bridge over Paradise Creek

2.5 Turn left at the T-junction with Two Medicine Pass Trail.

3.2 Bridge over Rockwell Creek with first view of Rockwell Falls

3.3 Base of Rockwell Falls.
   GPS: 48.4531, -113.4023 Elevation: 5,170 feet

6.2 Arrive back at the trailhead.

Flathead Range

The Flathead Range is a group of rugged mountains that forms a critical ecological link with Glacier National Park. The range encompasses the Great Bear Wilderness, which has some of the densest populations of grizzly bears in the lower forty-eight states. The range is bordered by the Swan Range to the west, and it is drained by the South Fork and Middle Fork of the Flathead River. There are over 300 miles of trails throughout these mountains, though many are not well maintained.

The 120-foot Silver Staircase Falls along US 2.

33 Dean Falls

The hike to Dean Falls is a great overnight backpacking trip that features much more than just a waterfall. If you're willing to drive the 60 miles of back roads, this adventure will give you solitude, beautiful scenery, and a good chance to see wildlife. Trek along the wild Spotted Bear River into the Great Bear and Bob Marshall Wildernesses to a spacious campsite at the river below the Limestone Wall. A difficult scramble on a small path leads to a nice pool at the base of Dean Falls. There are many options for extending your backpacking trip deeper into the largest wilderness area in Montana. Bear spray and bug spray are both a must for hiking in this area.

Stream: Spotted Bear River
Height: 30 feet
Distance: 12.2 miles out and back
Elevation gain: 275 feet
Difficulty: Moderate
Trail surface: Dirt and rock
Hiking time: 8–10 hours
Canine compatibility: Dogs are allowed
Seasons: May to Oct
County: Flathead
Land status: Wilderness area, national forest

Fees and permits: No fees required
Trail contact: Flathead National Forest, 650 Wolfpack Way, Kalispell, MT 59901; (406) 758-5208; fs.usda.gov/flathead/
Maps: *DeLorme Atlas and Gazetteer Montana* Page 39, C9; *USGS Quad* Trilobite Peak
Camping: Beaver Creek Campground is located a few miles before Silvertip Trailhead on Spotted Bear River Road and has four no-fee sites near the river.

Finding the Trailhead: From Hungry Horse, take West Reservoir Road #895 southeast for 55.7 miles. The first 15 miles are paved, but the washboard surface and sharp curves of the remaining miles of gravel road will keep you going slow. After crossing the South Fork of the Flathead River, you come to a T-junction. Turn right onto FR 38 and travel 1.4 miles. Turn left on Spotted Bear River Road and drive 14.2 miles to Silvertip Trailhead.
GPS: 47.9363, -113.3086 Elevation: 4,455 feet

The Hike

A connector trail drops toward the river and enters thick forest. You soon merge left onto Spotted Bear River Trail and proceed to walk along the hillside overlooking a few ponds between the pines. In a thick understory of Rocky Mountain maple, you cross a small tributary. Make noise when hiking through dense spots like these to alert bears of your presence. Keep going straight on Spotted Bear River Trail at the junction with Gunsight Peak Trail. You come to another junction, this time with Silvertip Creek Trail, which leads down to the river on the right. Stay left and walk up the hill past Silvertip Forest Service Cabin. As you peer through the trees to the south, you'll start to notice wide bands of exposed limestone on the mountains to the southwest.

Dean Falls. Photo by Luke Kratz.

These yellowish–white outcroppings are part of the Limestone Wall that will form the backdrop of the rest of the hike.

You come to a couple of small lakes called the Blue Lakes that are perched atop a bench surrounded by tall trees. This is a beautiful spot to take a break to enjoy the scenery and the unusual aqua color of the water. As the trail passes right between the two bodies of water, look for waterfowl or other animals that may come for a drink. The river finally comes into view after two and a half miles of hiking when you enter a section of burned forest. Spears of pink fireweed spring up along the sides of the trail, and the 100-foot-tall Limestone Wall extends along the southern ridge that parallels the river. Watch for wildlife at the forest edges.

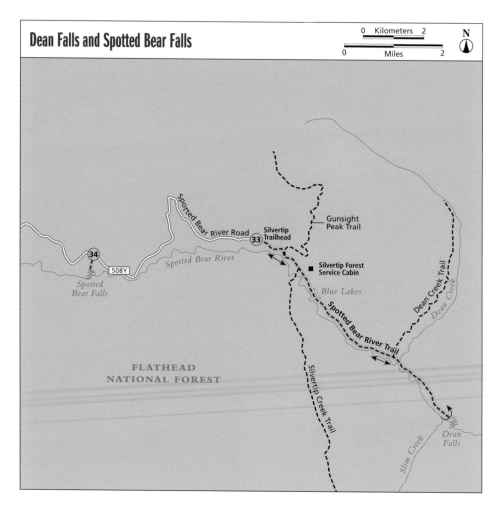

Dean Falls and Spotted Bear Falls

Spotted Bear River Road

Silvertip Trailhead

33

34

508Y

Spotted Bear River

Spotted Bear Falls

Gunsight Peak Trail

Silvertip Forest Service Cabin

Blue Lakes

Spotted Bear River Trail

Dean Creek Trail

Dean Creek

FLATHEAD NATIONAL FOREST

Silvertip Creek Trail

Slim Creek

Dean Falls

After reentering green forest, you pass a sign marking the entrance to the Great Bear Wilderness and arrive at a junction with Dean Creek Trail. Keep right and walk to a Y-junction. The trail to the right leads to an excellent campsite by the river. Take a left to continue to the falls. A short distance ahead you ford Dean Creek, which may be too difficult during spring runoff season. The trail climbs out of the Dean Creek drainage to a flat bench in the forest. You pass a sign indicating entrance into the Bob Marshall Wilderness and continue through forests loaded with huckleberries in the summer and fall.

Finally you reach the edge of a sudden canyon with the sound of Dean Falls gushing below. Be careful not to get too close to the edge at the lookout point. If you're an experienced hiker, a rugged path leads to the bottom of the canyon. Use rocks, trees, and bushes to guide you as you descend. You come to a view of the 10-foot lower portion of Dean Falls, which rages through the gorge. The deep green pool between the walls of rock is a great place for swimming, but the water is ice cold.

Watch closely and you can see schools of 14-inch westslope cutthroat trout cruising around the edges of the pool. Thick carpets of moss grow on the rocky shelves of the cliff and Limestone Peak crowns the horizon.

Miles and Directions

0.0 Silvertip Trailhead

0.1 Merge left onto Spotted Bear River Trail #83.

0.9 Keep going straight on Spotted Bear River Trail at junction with Gunsight Peak Trail #43.

1.1 Keep left on Spotted Bear River Trail at junction with Silvertip Creek Trail #89.

1.3 Silvertip Forest Service Cabin

1.6 Blue Lakes

4.0 Sign marking entrance into Great Bear Wilderness

4.0 Keep right on Spotted Bear River Trail at junction with Dean Creek Trail #87.

4.1 Keep left on Spotted Bear River Trail at junction with trail to campsite.

4.2 Ford Dean Creek

4.7 Sign marking entrance into Bob Marshall Wilderness

6.1 Top of Dean Falls
GPS: 47.8779, -113.2126 Elevation: 4,730 feet

12.2 Arrive back at the trailhead.

34 Spotted Bear Falls

The Spotted Bear River cuts a deep gorge in the valley, forming numerous cascades and deep pools. Spotted Bear Falls is a unique water feature located in a far-off region of the Flathead National Forest where you'll definitely find some solitude, but you have to drive over 60 miles on back roads to get there. The whole family can manage the short but steep hike down into this wild and pristine location.

See map on p. 134.
Stream: Spotted Bear River
Height: 10 feet
Distance: 0.5 mile out and back
Elevation loss: 240 feet
Difficulty: Easy
Trail surface: Dirt and rock
Hiking time: 30–45 minutes
Canine compatibility: Dogs are allowed
Seasons: May to Oct
County: Flathead

Land status: National forest
Fees and permits: No fees required
Trail contact: Flathead National Forest, 650 Wolfpack Way, Kalispell, MT 59901; (406) 758-5208; fs.usda.gov/flathead/
Maps: *DeLorme Atlas and Gazetteer Montana* Page 39, C8; *USGS Quad* Trilobite Peak
Camping: Beaver Creek Campground is located a few miles before Silvertip Trail on Spotted Bear River Road and has four no-fee sites near the river.

Finding the Trailhead: From Hungry Horse, take West Reservoir Road #895 southeast for 55.7 miles. The first 15 miles are paved, but the washboard surface and sharp curves of the remaining miles of gravel road will keep you going slow. After crossing the South Fork of the Flathead River, you come to a T-junction. Turn right onto FR 38 and travel 1.4 miles. Turn left on Spotted Bear River Road and drive 8.4 miles. Turn right on road 568Y at the sign marked "Outfitter Corrals." Drive 0.3 mile and park at the end of the road.
GPS: 47.9272, -113.3902 Elevation: 4,240 feet

The Hike

Follow the old roadbed at the end of the turnaround into a forest of lodgepole pine, Douglas fir, and western larch. After passing a primitive campsite, you drop steeply toward the river. The trail splits and rejoins a few times in a series of switchbacks. The river curves west when you reach its rocky banks in the middle of the valley. After crossing a tiny tributary stream, you begin hiking downstream toward the falls.

Numerous 5-foot cascades tumble in a braided pattern through the white and gray rock formations of the deep gorge. Beautifully smoothed and sculpted walls of stone line the river. Look into the water at the end of the gorge to spot large cutthroat trout circling the edges of the deep pools. If you're lucky you'll even see trout jumping the falls. There is good access to the pools for swimming if you can bear the ice-cold water. With a number of campsites in the area and good river access, Spotted Bear Falls is an excellent destination to spend some time in the outdoors.

Spotted Bear Falls. Photo by Luke Kratz.

Miles and Directions

0.0 Spotted Bear Falls Trailhead
0.2 Spotted Bear Falls
        GPS: 47.9240, -113.3913 Elevation: 4,000 feet
0.5 Arrive back at the trailhead.

Swan Range

The Swan Range lies east of the Missions and the densely forested Swan Valley. The well-loved Bob Marshall Wilderness extends along the range's east slope and many hikers enter its vast backcountry via the Swan's excellent trail system. The highest peak in the range, Holland Peak, can be observed on the hike to Big Salmon Falls.

Holland Peak at sunrise from Necklace Lakes.

35 Graves Creek Falls

This scenic area is located between the Hungry Horse Reservoir, Jewel Basin, and Pioneer Ridge. A brief stroll takes you to a pretty cascade surrounded by lush forests. The falls are within minutes of the shores of Graves Bay. Come on a weekday to get maximum solitude at this popular location.

Stream: Graves Creek
Height: 30 feet
Distance: 0.1 mile out and back
Elevation gain: 60 feet
Difficulty: Very easy
Trail surface: Dirt
Hiking time: 5–10 minutes
Canine compatibility: Dogs are allowed
Seasons: May to Oct
County: Flathead

Land status: National forest
Fees and permits: No fees required
Trail contact: Flathead National Forest, 650 Wolfpack Way, Kalispell, MT 59901; (406) 758-5208; fs.usda.gov/flathead/
Maps: *DeLorme Atlas and Gazetteer Montana* Page 39, A6; *USGS Quad* Pioneer Ridge
Camping: Graves Creek Campground is located at the trailhead and has ten lightly used, no-fee campsites near the creek.

Finding the Trailhead: From Hungry Horse, take West Reservoir Road for 33.2 miles. The first 15 miles are paved and then it becomes a wide gravel road. The washboard surface and sharp curves will keep you going slow. Turn right onto road #10187 to Graves Creek Campground and drive 0.1 mile to the end of the road. If the campground area is congested, you can park in the reservoir access parking across the road.
GPS: 48.1276, -113.8111 Elevation: 3,580 feet

The Hike

Follow a short path that climbs over a rise through a forest of Douglas fir, western larch, Engelmann spruce, Rocky Mountain maple, and western white pine. After only a couple hundred feet, you come to a wooden railing with a dynamic view of Graves Creek Falls.

Water descends multiple terraces of bedrock and passes around boulders and deadfall before landing in a foamy pool. Hike to the end of the trail at the edge of the rocky outcropping that forms the falls. Watch for waterfowl and other wildlife in

Graves Creek Falls. Photo by Luke Kratz.

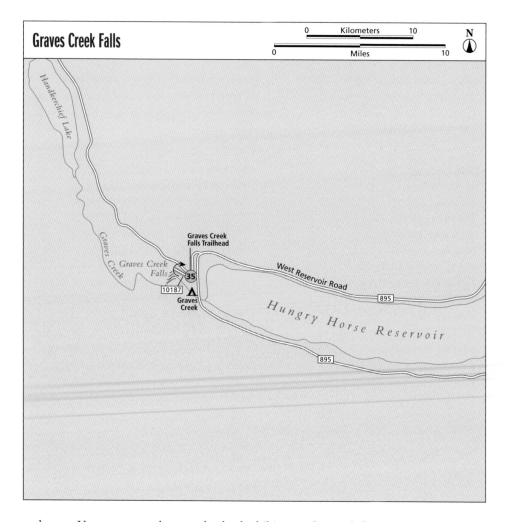

Graves Creek Falls

Kilometers 0 — 10

Miles 0 — 10

N

the area. You can access the water's edge by hiking up the creek from the campground along placid pools and rapids.

Miles and Directions

0.0 Graves Creek Falls Trailhead

0.05 Viewpoint of Graves Creek Falls

0.05 Graves Creek Falls

GPS: 48.1280, -113.8128 Elevation: 3,640 feet

0.1 Arrive back at the trailhead.

36 Bond Creek Falls

The trail to Bond Creek Falls enters one of the most inland temperate rainforests of the continent, an area of rich biodiversity. Tree species such as paper birch, western larch, Rocky Mountain maple, and grand fir abound, and all North American apex predators are present. Take the hike in May and June to enjoy raging falls and a colorful display of wildflowers. The easy, maintained trail makes the hike suitable for beginners and families. Beyond the falls you can access backcountry lakes, the crest of the Swan Range, and trails entering the Bob Marshall Wilderness.

Stream: Bond Creek
Height: Two 20-foot waterfalls
Distance: 3.8 miles out and back
Elevation gain: 605 feet
Difficulty: Easy
Trail surface: Dirt
Hiking time: 2–3 hours
Canine compatibility: Dogs are allowed
Seasons: May to Oct
County: Lake

Land status: National forest
Fees and permits: No permits required
Trail contact: Flathead National Forest, 650 Wolfpack Way, Kalispell, MT 59901; (406) 758-5208; fs.usda.gov/flathead/
Maps: *DeLorme Atlas and Gazetteer Montana* Page 39, C6; *USGS Quad* Swan Lake
Camping: Swan Lake Campground is located a few miles north on Highway 83.

Finding the Trailhead: From Bigfork: Take Highway 209 for about 10 miles to the junction of Highway 83. Drive south on Highway 83 for about 13 miles. Turn east on Lost Creek Road #680 and drive 1.5 miles. Turn left onto Road #9507 and drive 0.7 mile. Keep left twice to stay on road #9507 and then drive a final 1.6 miles to Upper Bond Creek Trailhead at the end of the road. Alternatively, you can start the hike at Lower Bond Creek Trailhead, located at a marked road on Highway 83, just north of Lost Creek Road. This trailhead is easier to access but adds a few miles to the hike.
Upper Bond Creek Trailhead: GPS: 47.9179, -113.8166 Elevation: 3,285 feet
Lower Bond Creek Trailhead: GPS: 47.9096, -113.8339 Elevation: 3,180 feet

The Hike

The hike starts out in a forest opened up by windstorms. You drop for a half mile to a wooden footbridge over medium-sized Bond Creek. The trail proceeds to traverse the north slope within earshot of the creek. Watch for calypso orchids, trilliums, and violets as you pass through lush forest. After a couple of miles, you approach the creek at the falls. A side trail drops to a nice viewing area that is ideal for a picnic. There are two main 20-foot drops that plunge over large mossy boulders. The green of the moss makes the location vibrant even on cloudy days. A steep path goes to the base of the lower waterfall.

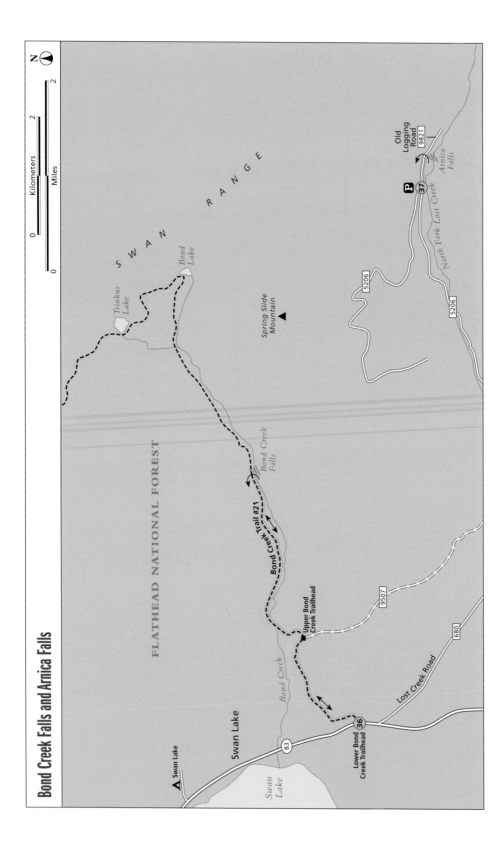

Bond Creek Falls and Arnica Falls

Bond Creek Falls. Photo by Ted Muhs.

You can extend the hike another 4 miles to Bond Lake, 5 miles to Trinkus Lake, and 6 miles to meet the Alpine Trail at the Swan Crest. Keep going to join a vast network of trails to explore the western region of the Bob Marshall Wilderness.

Miles and Directions

0.0 Upper Bond Creek Trailhead, Trail #21

0.5 Footbridge

1.9 Bond Creek Falls

       GPS: 47.9242, -113.7851 Elevation: 3,890 feet

3.8 Arrive back at the trailhead.

37 Arnica Falls

Located a few miles east of Swan Lake in the North Fork Lost Creek drainage, Arnica Falls is a scenic waterfall that few people visit. A brief hike takes you within view of the 125-foot waterfall from the trail. An unobstructed view of the falls requires a fairly steep bushwhack up a couple hundred feet. Be sure to carry bear spray as the Swan Mountains are home to a large population of grizzly bears.

See map on p. 142.
Stream: Tributary of North Fork Lost Creek
Height: 125 feet
Distance: 0.7 mile out and back
Elevation gain: 210 feet
Difficulty: Easy to limited trail view, difficult final scramble to base
Trail surface: Roadbed, dirt, rock
Hiking time: 1 hour
Seasons: May to Nov
Canine compatibility: Dogs are allowed
County: Lake

Land status: National forest
Fees and permits: No fees required
Trail contact: Flathead National Forest, 650 Wolfpack Way, Kalispell, MT 59901; (406) 758-5208; fs.usda.gov/flathead/
Maps: *DeLorme Atlas and Gazetteer Montana* Page 39, C6; *USGS Quad* Connor Creek
Camping: Swan Lake Campground is located across the highway from Swan Lake on the north side of town. There are thirty-six heavily used sites for a fee.

Finding the Trailhead: From the town of Swan Lake, drive south on Highway 83 for 1.0 mile to Lost Creek Road #680. Turn left and drive east for 2.4 miles. Turn left on road #5206 after crossing a bridge and drive for 4.5 miles. Park your vehicle near old logging road #9821, which begins on the right before reaching a switchback.
GPS: 47.8999, -113.7180 Elevation: 4,260 feet

The Hike

As you stroll along the old logging road, you can appreciate the beauty of Thunderbolt Mountain and other high peaks of the Swan Range towering to the east. You walk above North Fork Lost Creek through paper birches that brighten the forests with their silky white exteriors. After scrambling over a section of trees collapsed by a recent avalanche, you reach a tributary to the North Fork and can glimpse the cascades up the steep ravine to the north. The views of Arnica Falls are much better if you hike off-trail up the steep hillside for another tenth of a mile. Stay close to the trees and avoid the loose scree as you climb. Once you get within view, take a seat and enjoy the sight. A precipitous drop followed by a long run of cascading torrents forms the 125-foot Arnica Falls.

Arnica Falls.

Miles and Directions

0.0 Trailhead to Arnica Falls

0.2 Limited view of falls from trail
GPS: 47.8999, -113.7120 Elevation: 4,275 feet Arnica Falls.

0.3 Base of Arnica Falls
GPS: 47.90035, -113.7122 Elevation: 4,470 feet

0.7 Arrive back at the trailhead.

38 Rumble Creek Falls

Like other Swan Range hikes, the route to Rumble Creek Falls is strenuous, but worthwhile. You gain over three thousand feet in a couple of miles and are rewarded with splendid views of alpine peaks, lakes, and waterfalls. The return trip is also a delight, with a westward view of the Mission Mountains.

Stream: South Fork Rumble Creek
Height: Lower falls about 50 feet; Upper falls about 200 feet
Distance: 6.8 miles out and back
Elevation gain: 3,100 feet
Difficulty: Difficult
Trail surface: Dirt
Hiking time: 6–8 hours
Canine compatibility: Dogs are allowed
Seasons: June to Oct
County: Missoula

Land status: National forest
Fees and permits: No permits required
Trail contact: Flathead National Forest, 650 Wolfpack Way, Kalispell, MT 59901, (406) 758-5208, fs.usda.gov/flathead/
Maps: *DeLorme Atlas and Gazetteer Montana* Page 39, F7; *USGS Quad* Condon and Holland Peak
Camping: A primitive campsite is available at the trailhead.

Finding the Trailhead: Take MT Highway 83 north for 25 miles from Seeley Lake or 2 miles south from Condon. Turn east on Rumble Creek Road #560. Continue for 3.7 miles on this gravel road to the East Foothills Trailhead at the end of the road.
GPS: 47.523602, -113.640897 Elevation: 4,460 feet

The Hike

At the trailhead there is a sign stating there is no official, maintained route to Rumble Creek Lakes and a chance of dangerous conditions. Except for extreme steepness during a mile, the trail is currently in decent condition all the way to the falls.

Follow East Foothills Trail #192 and head north up a steadily climbing trail for a quarter mile. The path curves right and gently traverses the mountain through pine and fir. Next, you cross a series of small bridges over Rumble Creek and arrive at an unmarked junction. Take a left and head north on a small path. Here you begin the grueling ascent that is popular with peak baggers looking to add Holland Peak to their list of summit achievements.

The very steep trail climbs through thick lodgepole pine forest that opens up occasionally to stunning views of the Swan Valley and the snowy Mission Mountains to the west. Continue scaling the ridge high above South Fork Rumble Creek. After about 2 miles and over 2,800 feet of climbing, you reach the top of the ridge and the trail levels out. Stay right when you reach a Y-junction with an old path.

The trail traverses a slope and then comes to a dangerous rock slide. At this location, fabulous views of Swan Range appear before you, with Holland Peak looming

Rumble Creek Falls. Photo by Ted Muhs.

Rumble Creek Falls; Holland Falls; Big Salmon Falls; Upper Holland Falls

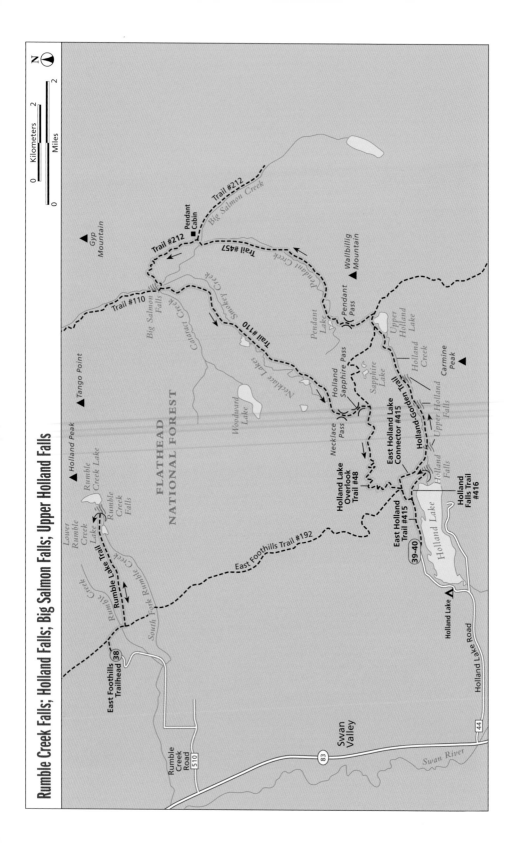

in the distance. The mountains invite you onward. Be sure to take a sharp right on the steep path that has been rerouted downhill and away from the slide. Drop carefully to the base of the rocks and then continue east along the open slope. Watch for wildlife such as mountain goats and grizzly bears in this subalpine landscape. The trail finally comes close to the creek while climbing over a hill of burned forest. These remains of the Holland Peak Fire of 2006 lead you to the final distance to the first lake. But first, don't miss the small waterfall that appears just before reaching the lake basin. It flows gracefully off the lip of the glacially formed hanging valley.

At Lower Rumble Creek Lake, you are greeted with a vivid display of waterfalls that originate in the upper lake and tumble down a steep slope of spruce and fir all the way to the shoreline. The final cascade rumbles loudly as it plunges into the lake. There are a few primitive campsites at the first lake.

Cross the outlet stream to the east and follow the path along the shore to the shale slope and begin to climb again toward the upper falls. Vertical walls of rock tower above. Be alert for falling rocks that rumble down from the cliffy heights. After about 3.5 miles you come to the base of the upper section of Rumble Creek Falls. This fan-shaped cascade changes drastically with the seasons. During spring runoff, water rages through the mountains with impressive force and is even visible with binoculars from the valley floor. By the end of the season, only a gentle trickle remains.

To extend the hike, experienced hikers can reach Upper Rumble Lake by climbing up either side of the falls. The easier route is to cross the stream below the falls and follow the vegetation up a steep ravine to the west shore. Watch out for loose dirt and gravel as you make the steep descent back to the trailhead.

Miles and Directions

0.0 East Foothills Trailhead #192

0.7 Bridges over Rumble Creek

0.8 Unmarked junction. Take a left on unofficial Holland Peak Trail.
GPS: 47.5227, -113.6314 Elevation: 4,795 feet

2.0 Y-junction. Stay right.

2.3 Stay right on rerouted downhill trail.

2.7 Lower Rumble Creek Lake with view of lower falls. Turn right and cross outlet stream.

3.4 Base of upper section of Rumble Creek Falls.
GPS: 47.5282, -113.5911 Elevation: 7,550 feet

6.8 Arrive back at the trailhead.

39 Holland Falls

The popular hike to Holland Falls takes you along the north shore of Holland Lake to the foothills of the Swan Range. The Swan Valley is thick with wildlife, and many observable species live in the lake's shoreline habitat. Surrounding forests are a fine example of a Crown of the Continent ecosystem in which towering ponderosa pines and western larch dominate the landscape. At the falls, you'll enjoy magnificent views of the Mission Mountains' tallest peaks across the lake and valley.

On a hot day, you can approach within a few feet of the cascade to be showered by its refreshing mist.

See map on p. 148.
Stream: Holland Creek
Height: 50 feet
Distance: 2.8 miles out and back
Elevation gain: 725 feet
Difficulty: Easy
Trail surface: Dirt and rock
Hiking time: 2-3 hours
Seasons: Apr to Nov
Canine compatibility: Dogs are allowed
County: Missoula

Land status: National forest
Fees and permits: No fees required
Trail contact: Flathead National Forest, 650 Wolfpack Way, Kalispell, MT 59901; (406) 758-5208; fs.usda.gov/flathead/
Maps: *DeLorme Atlas and Gazetteer Montana* Page 39, F7; *USGS Quad* Holland Lake
Camping: Holland Lake Campground consists of two loops near the lakeshore along the drive to the trailhead. There are forty heavily used sites for a fee.

Finding the Trailhead: From Seeley Lake, drive north on MT 83 for 21.7 miles. Turn right on Holland Lake Road #44 and drive 3.8 miles to the trailhead at the end of the road.
GPS: 47.4558, -113.6037 Elevation: 3,540 feet

The Hike

Follow Trail #415 / #416 for a few hundred feet to a Y-junction. Stay right on trail #416 and begin following the lakeshore through forests of Douglas fir, western larch, and ponderosa pine. If you listen and look closely you will notice the diverse wildlife that inhabits the shoreline area. You are likely to encounter whitetail and mule deer as well as waterfowl like Canada geese, mergansers, and buffleheads. Bears, mountain lions, wolves, and coyotes are also close by.

The trail heads east toward Wolverine Peak and Carmine Peak, which rise abruptly in front of you. You can occasionally glimpse the waterfall at the far end of the lake as you pass openings in the forest. After crossing a small wooden bridge over a creek lined with paper birch, the trail begins a steep climb along a rocky slope. Postcard views of celestial-blue Holland Lake and the white-capped Mission Mountains appear to the west.

Holland Falls.

You come to the foot of Holland Falls, with its impressive whitewater spilling for 50 feet over a couple of massive rock benches. The 360° view in all directions is breathtaking. If you scramble closer to the falls, you'll delight in the sensation of "waterfall wind" that blasts with increasing force as you approach.

Miles and Directions

0.0 Holland Trailhead #415 and #416

0.1 Keep right on Holland Falls Trail #416 at the Y-junction.
GPS: 47.4521, -113.6026 Elevation: 4,065 feet

0.6 View of falls across lake in distance

1.0 Small bridge over creek

1.4 Holland Falls
GPS: 47.4510, -113.5763 Elevation: 4,265 feet

2.8 Arrive back at the trailhead.

40 Big Salmon Falls, via Upper Holland Falls

This challenging route takes you into the spectacular backcountry of the Swan Range and the Bob Marshall Wilderness, where you can get away from civilization and experience the beauty of diverse and changing terrain. Find relaxing lakeside campsites at Upper Holland Lake, Pendant Lakes, and Necklace Lakes and inspiring vistas at three mountain passes along the way. Waterfall lovers will especially enjoy the many dynamic cascades of Upper Holland Falls as well as the remoteness and force of Big Salmon Falls. Be prepared for multiple stream fords and log crossings and take all necessary precautions for safe backcountry camping in bear country.

See map on p. 148.
Stream: Big Salmon Creek, Holland Creek
Height: Big Salmon Falls, 60 feet; Upper Holland Falls, 10–25 feet
Distance: 19.8-mile lollipop loop
Elevation change: 5,120 feet gain, 1,115 feet loss
Difficulty: Strenuous
Trail surface: Dirt and rock
Hiking time: 15–25 hours in three or more days of overnight backpacking
Seasons: July to Oct
County: Missoula

Land status: National forest
Fees and permits: No fees required
Trail contact: Flathead National Forest, 650 Wolfpack Way, Kalispell, MT 59901; (406) 758-5208; fs.usda.gov/flathead/
Maps: *DeLorme Atlas and Gazetteer Montana* Page 39, F7; *USGS Quad* Holland Lake and Holland Peak
Camping: Holland Lake Campground consists of two loops near the lakeshore along the drive to the trailhead. There are forty heavily used sites for a fee.

Finding the Trailhead: From Seeley Lake, drive north on MT 83 for 21.7 miles. Turn right on Holland Lake Road #44 and drive 3.8 miles to the trailhead at the end of the road.
GPS: 47.4558, -113.6037 Elevation: 3,540 feet

The Hike

Begin hiking on a flat trail through tall larches and pines, a short distance from the shoreline of Holland Lake. You immediately make a left onto East Holland Trail #415 after a few hundred feet. The path climbs gradually over the foothills of the Swan Range, with occasional views of lofty Carmine Peak looming ahead of you. In Swan Valley you might encounter ripe huckleberries among the understory as early as late June.

After almost a mile, you begin to climb steep switchbacks and arrive at a flat bench and a junction with East Foothill Trail #192. Keep right and proceed to climb until you meet another junction, where you pass Holland Lake Overlook Trail #42 on the left. You will eventually use this trail to complete the loop on the return descent from Necklace Lakes.

Continue toward the sound of a cascading stream and make an easy crossing. The trail cuts onto an open slope with stunningly big views of the Mission Mountains to the east across Swan Valley. Traverse the slope above steep cliffs on a hot trail until you reach shadier terrain along Holland Creek. As soon as you meet the stream, you come across the first in a series of many sections of Upper Holland Falls. You can take a short but challenging side trail that's covered in deadfall to the base of the 20-foot double waterfall. Hike a few minutes upstream to a sketchy footbridge and large campsite. Here, a couple more scenic falls tumble down the ravine. Farther up the trail, there is an excellent swimming hole beneath a 10-foot waterfall. Stay to the left at an unmarked junction, where you merge onto Holland-Gordon Trail #35, and proceed to follow Holland Creek along the southern slope.

Continue past another section of Upper Holland Falls and a view of an open avalanche chute to the north, where a large tributary makes its rapid descent. Follow switchbacks through tall spruce and larch while enjoying the sight of Carmine Peak to the south. Colorful plants like paintbrush and purple aster cling to the mossy earth along the side of the trail. A nameless waterfall descends along a tributary in another avalanche chute to the south. Up ahead, you arrive at a cascade that slides down angled rock into a deep pool. It's a tough but doable scramble to the bottom if you're looking to cool off. You pass a plunging horsetail-type cascade in a rocky ravine, and then farther ahead, round a switchback at the sight of a 15-foot waterfall in a sunny spruce forest.

After crossing a small tributary that flows down from Sapphire Lake to the north, you climb up onto a flat basin and arrive at the foot of Upper Holland Lake. This is a good place to spend the first night. There are a few campsites along the north shore and a rocky point for swimming and fishing. You pass two junctions as you round the talus and forested slopes north of the lake. Bear right when passing the trail to Sapphire Lake, but a quarter mile later, turn left onto Trail #457 toward Pendant Pass. A short but steep stretch of switchbacks takes you to a flat area at the pass where you pass a sign marking entrance to the Bob Marshall Wilderness.

As you descend into the Pendant Lakes basin, look for moose feeding on aquatic plants in the waterways. At the first lake, carefully cross an outlet pond where Columbia spotted frogs swim on warm days. Waldbillig Mountain rises to the south, and several steep cascading streams descend the layered cliffs. Hike down the eastern slope through brushy, open terrain to Pendant Cascade, a pretty place where Pendant Creek glides down an angled slab of rock. The path continues past a few brushy avalanche chutes and then comes to a thigh-deep ford across Pendant Creek. Continue downstream on the west side of the creek through an open forest of tall Engelmann spruce for about a mile and a half. You reach the confluence area and make another thigh-deep ford at a wide place in Big Salmon Creek. Climb to a T-junction near Pendant Cabin and turn left onto Trail #212 below some steep gray cliffs.

Big Salmon Falls. Photo by Juan Esteban Hudorovich.

Go up and down switchbacks through tall, thick timber until you start to hear the sound of Big Salmon Falls. As you come around the bend, the sight of the tall and elegant waterfall will instantly put a smile on your face. Big Salmon Creek gushes over ledges at a rocky outcropping in the forest and plummets over 60 feet. Take a cold dip in a gentle part of the pool next to a dripping wall of layered rock. You're bound to see an active family of American dippers that nest in the wet cliff near the falling water. On a knoll next to the falls there is a campsite, making this a great place to rest up for the return trip, spending a night close to the crashing water.

When you're ready to leave the falls area, continue along the trail to a challenging ford over Big Salmon Creek. Find a large stick to help you balance your weight in the fast current. After crossing, there is a meadow that's a good option for camping if the falls campsite is too loud for your liking. Just beyond the campsite, you turn left on Trail #110 at an unmarked junction. This critical junction for your return trip is easy to miss, so look carefully. Begin to climb steep switchbacks, with the sound of Cataract Creek flowing on your right. After almost a quarter mile, you start to gain views of scenic Gyp Mountain to the northeast. You pass some rocky clearings and come to the sound of Smokey Creek in the wooded ravine. You circle a pond and ford Smokey Creek to the south side below some tumbling cascades. Watch for wildlife in the meadows along the creek.

After passing the first Necklace Lake, which can be accessed via a spur trail, the landscape starts to transition into subalpine forest and Holland Peak and Tango Point appear to the northwest. Soon, you come to a side trail on the right that leads a short distance down to the second Necklace Lake. The third lake has excellent alpine views, and campsites are easily accessible from the trail. Very old white bark pines reach their branches out like arms over the water. You climb into another set of lakes with spur trails leading to shoreline campsites. Look for rare alpine larch with tiny needles that are bright green in the summer and a vibrant orange in the fall. The Necklace Lakes is an ideal area to camp for the final night.

Climb through open subalpine country, passing a few ponds formed by annual snowmelt. Be prepared to cross scattered snowfields at this high elevation until well into July. You finally reach Necklace Pass, the highest point on the route, and a sign telling you you're leaving the Bob Marshall Wilderness. After taking in the spectacular alpine views, continue down the other side of the pass toward Sapphire Lake. Just when you begin to glimpse the lake through the trees, turn right at a junction with Holland-Sapphire Trail #48. As you climb a couple hundred feet over Holland-Sapphire Pass, familiar vistas of the Mission Mountains and Swan Valley spread out before you. These expansive views provide an exhilarating grand finale to your multiday journey.

Keep left when you come to a junction with Holland Lake Overlook Trail #42. The descent to your final destination at Holland Lake is a 3-mile, 4,000-foot drop down switchbacks through changing forest. After passing a tall cascade over yellowish cliffs, you finally merge back onto East Holland Trail #415 and complete the loop. Turn right to hike the last mile back to the trailhead.

Miles and Directions

0.0 Trailhead #415 and #416

0.1 Turn left onto East Holland Trail #415 at Y-junction.
GPS: 47.4519, -113.6024 Elevation: 3,970 feet

0.6 Keep right on East Holland Trail at junction with East Foothill Trail #192.
GPS: 47.4564, -113.5865 Elevation: 4,430 feet

1.2 Keep right on East Holland Trail at junction with Holland Lake Overlook Trail #42.
GPS: 47.4568, -113.5838 Elevation: 4,670 feet

2.1 First section of Upper Holland Falls
GPS: 47.4508, -113.57 Elevation: 4,745 feet

2.2 Second and third sections of Upper Holland Falls at campsite
GPS: 47.4510, -113.5689 Elevation: 4,750 feet

2.3 Fourth section of Upper Holland Falls at swimming hole

2.3 Turn left to merge onto Holland-Gordon Trail #35 at unmarked Y-junction.
GPS: 47.4509, -113.5683 Elevation: 4,825 feet

2.7 Fifth section of Upper Holland Falls

2.9 Sixth section of Upper Holland Falls
GPS: 47.4530, -113.5547 Elevation: 5,245 feet

3.0 Footbridge

3.6 Seventh section of Upper Holland Falls
GPS: 47.4564, -113.5461 Elevation: 5,795 feet

3.8 Eighth section of Upper Holland Falls

4.2 Ninth section of Upper Holland Falls

4.5 Foot of Upper Holland Lake

4.7 Keep right on Holland-Gordon Trail at junction with Trail #110.
GPS: 47.4633, -113.5282 Elevation: 6,205 feet

4.9 Turn left at junction with Trail #457.
GPS: 47.4654, -113.5248 Elevation: 6,140 feet

5.6 Pendant Pass and sign marking entrance to Bob Marshall Wilderness Area
GPS: 47.4700, -113.5271 Elevation: 6,600 feet

5.9 First Pendant Lake

6.1 Large pond

6.3 Third Pendant Lake

6.8 Pendant Cascade

7.5 Ford over Pendant Creek

8.9 Ford over Big Salmon Creek

9.0 Turn left at junction with Trail #212 near Pendant Cabin.
GPS: 47.5058, -113.4985 Elevation: 5,815 feet

10.4 Big Salmon Falls
GPS: 47.5136, -113.5137 Elevation: 5,675 feet

10.5 Ford over Big Salmon Creek

10.5 Turn left at junction with Trail #110 at large campsite.
GPS: 47.5143, -113.5160 Elevation: 5,485 feet

11.9 Pond

12.1 Cross Smokey Creek.

12.4 View of first Necklace Lake

13.0 Side trail to second Necklace Lake

13.8 Campsites at third Necklace Lake

14.0 Fourth Necklace Lake

14.2 Side trail to largest and uppermost Necklace Lake

15.1 Necklace Pass and sign marking exit from Bob Marshall Wilderness
GPS: 47.4696, -113.5589 Elevation: 7,545 feet

15.5 Turn right at junction with Trail #48.
GPS: 47.4660, -113.5543 Elevation: 7,255 feet

15.7 Holland-Sapphire Pass
GPS: 47.4647, -113.5551 Elevation: 7,535 feet

16.2 Keep left at junction with Holland Overlook Trail #42.
GPS: 47.4638, -113.5643 Elevation: 7,120 feet

18.4 Glimpse waterfall through trees.

18.7 Turn right at junction with East Holland Trail #415.

19.8 Arrive back at the trailhead.

41 Morrell Falls

Located at the foot of Crescent Mountain in the southern end of the Swan Range, Morrell Falls is one of the most popular waterfalls in Montana. The hike offers spectacular views of the Swan Range and passes Morrell Lake on the way to the falls. Much of the hike passes through forest damaged by the Rice Ridge Fire of 2017, but nonetheless, the destination still attracts a crowd.

Stream: Morrell Creek
Height: 90 feet
Distance: 4.8 miles out and back
Elevation gain: 50 feet
Difficulty: Easy
Trail surface: Dirt and rock
Hiking time: 2–3 hours
Canine compatibility: Dogs on leash
Seasons: May to Nov
County: Powell

Land status: National forest
Fees and permits: No fees required
Trail contact: Lolo National Forest, 24 Fort Missoula Road, Missoula, MT 59804; (406) 329-3750; fs.usda.gov/lolo/
Maps: *DeLorme Atlas and Gazetteer Montana* Page 55, A8; *USGS Quad* Morrell Lake
Camping: Backpackers can enjoy the primitive sites at Morrell Lake.

Finding the Trailhead: From Seeley Lake, take MT 83 to the north end of town and turn right (east) onto Morrell Creek Road. Drive 1.2 miles until you see a sign for Morrell Falls Trail and Pyramid Pass Trail just past Seeley Creek Trailhead. Turn left onto FR 4352 and drive 6.5 miles to the trailhead. The road curves to the right at 5.7 miles and becomes FR 4381. At 5.9 miles, keep left on FR 4364 when the road splits one last time. Overflow parking is available along the side of the road before entering the parking loop. Camping is not allowed at the trailhead.
GPS: 47.2735, -113.4509 Elevation: 4,730 feet

The Hike

You begin the hike by crossing a bridge over a tributary to Morrell Creek and then start skirting the base of the Swan Mountains. The trail is wide and level and passes through burned forest of lodgepole pine. After a short climb to a bench, you advance through the charred snags of larch and spruce, where the new growth of trees and understory emerges. The Rice Ridge Fire destroyed more than 150,000 acres but new life is taking hold as the forest begins to regenerate.

When you come to an unnamed lake tucked into the forest and bordered by banks of grass and reeds, look for mergansers or buffleheads swimming solo or with their mates. A short distance later, Morrell Lake appears on your right. This lake is much larger, and its irregular arms stretch into different parts of the forest. A path leads down to a few primitive campsites near one of the extensions of the lake. Behind the lake, steep flanks of Crescent Mountain rise up to rocky cliffs.

Morrell Falls. Photo by Martha Gunsalam.

Morrell Falls; Monture Falls; Lodgepole Falls

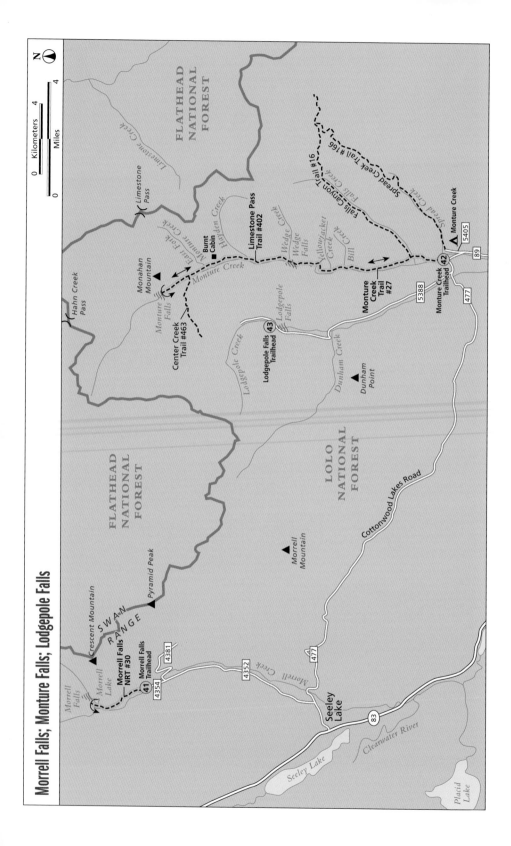

As you begin the final approach, you'll surely hear the unmistakable thunder of the falls ahead. After crossing a bridge over Morrell Creek, you arrive at the base of the awesome cascade. Morrell Falls tumbles ferociously down a 90-foot cliff and makes an intense landing onto rocks and small pools. The creek then flattens and splits into two channels. Although the wide creek is too shallow for swimming, wading is delightful. In the late afternoons and early evenings of spring and summer, rainbows often appear as blasts of sun penetrate the rising mist.

Miles and Directions

0.0 Morrell Falls National Recreation Trailhead

1.7 Unnamed lake

2.0 Morrell Lake

2.2 Bridge

2.4 Base of Morrell Falls
GPS: 47.3006, -113.4644 Elevation: 4,680 feet

4.8 Arrive back at the trailhead.

42 Monture Falls

Monture Falls is a small but pretty cascade where you'll certainly find space and seclusion. The first mile of the hike passes through healthy and diverse trees. Then you cross a landscape scorched by the Rice Ridge Fire of 2017 for several miles, followed by a swath scarred by the Monture Creek Fire of 2000 for the final miles. It is interesting to compare the recovery of the forest from two wildfires almost 20 years apart. Shade is rare, so this hike is best in cooler weather. Be prepared to make several creek crossings, including the Hayden Creek ford, which can be too difficult during spring runoff.

See map on p. 160.
Stream: Monture Creek
Height: 15 feet
Distance: 23.2 miles out and back
Elevation gain: 1,010 feet
Difficulty: Difficult due to length and fords
Trail surface: Dirt and rock
Hiking time: 10-12 hours
Canine compatibility: Dogs are allowed
Seasons: Late June to Nov
County: Powell

Land status: National forest
Fees and permits: No fees required
Trail contact: Lolo National Forest, 24 Fort Missoula Road, Missoula, MT 59804; (406) 329-3750; fs.usda.gov/lolo/
Maps: *DeLorme Atlas and Gazetteer Montana* Page 55, B9; *USGS Quad* Hahn Creek Pass
Camping: Monture Creek Campground is located near the trailhead and has six no-fee sites.

Finding the Trailhead: Once you reach the turnoff for Ovando on MT 200, look for unmarked Monture Creek Road #89 on the north side of the highway. Take this gravel road north for 7.0 miles. Just before a bridge, turn right on FR 5405. Drive 0.6 mile to the trailhead at the end of the road.
GPS: 47.1264, -113.1452 Elevation: 4,185 feet

The Hike

You enter a broad valley east of the creek on a wide trail worn by heavy equestrian use. Cross Spread Creek and continue ahead on Monture Creek Trail through a rare forest of primarily western larch trees that are present in all shapes and sizes—from tiny new saplings to century-old giants almost 200 feet tall. You reach the edge of a scree slope to the east that gives you open views of rocky crags.

After less than a mile from the trailhead, you enter a zone of the Rice Ridge Fire that burned at intense heat in 2017. Finding shade is challenging for the next four miles.

You arrive at a bridge over Falls Creek and a junction with Falls Creek Trail #16. Fires have opened up views of a scenic cascade that rolls out of the canyon. Taller drops of Falls Creek Falls are nestled up the gorge. As an optional side trip, you could take a right onto Falls Creek Trail, hike up three switchbacks, and then follow a small path to a lookout. Otherwise, keep left at the junction and continue your hike toward

Monture Falls. Photo by Martha Gunsalam.

Monture Falls. You start to stroll along an almost perfectly level and straight path for over a mile. The trail finally approaches Monture Creek and a side trail leads to a large campsite scorched by the fire. After crossing Bill Creek, the path gradually climbs the east slope of the drainage and gains views of the mountains to the west.

On the mountainside above Monture Creek, you come to a ford across Yellow-jacket Creek below a pretty cascade over moss-covered rocks. Continue along the slope until you arrive at a canyon area. Before crossing a footbridge over Wedge Creek, take a peek into the rugged ravine at Wedge Falls. The 10-foot vertical waterfall spills under a large boulder wedged between the steep walls of the gorge. It's an intriguing place to stop for a midway rest.

Further up the trail, you thankfully enter a short stretch of unburned forest before crossing an old burn with open views of the 8,130-foot Monahan Mountain. You soon reach a more difficult ford over Hayden Creek. During runoff season, the water is knee-deep and fast, so exercise caution. A mile later you pass Burnt Cabin at Burnt Cabin Creek, and there is a junction with Limestone Pass Trail on the right. Keep hiking straight on Monture Creek Trail toward Hahn Creek Pass.

After crossing a footbridge over East Fork Monture Creek at the foot of Monahan Mountain, you begin to cross a section of forest burned by the Monture Fire of 2000. A new generation of lodgepole, willow, and aspen is taking hold. After a right turn at a junction with Center Creek Trail, you finally arrive at views of Monture Falls from the trail. The creek slides out of a narrow ravine in the valley and gushes over a 15-foot ledge into a large pool. The Monture Creek Fire opened up the views significantly in the drainage, and a clear shot of the waterfall now delights travelers who pass through the area on the way to Hahn Creek Pass. To extend the hike, make your way another 5 miles to the pass and drop down the other side to explore the headwaters of the South Fork Flathead River. Monture Falls is a great starting point for long expeditions into the Bob Marshall Wilderness.

Miles and Directions

- **0.0** Monture Creek Trailhead #27
- **0.3** Cross Spread Creek.
- **1.4** Cross bridge over Falls Creek.
- **1.4** Keep left on Monture Creek Trail at Y-intersection with Falls Canyon Trail #16.
  GPS: 47.1434, -113.1494 Elevation: 4,180 feet
- **3.7** Cross Bill Creek.
- **4.5** Cross Yellowjacket Creek below pretty cascade.
- **6.3** Footbridge at base of Wedge Falls
- **8.5** More challenging ford over Hayden Creek
- **9.5** Cross footbridge over Burnt Cabin Creek at Burnt Cabin. Keep left at junction with Limestone Pass Trail #402.
  GPS: 47.2382, -113.1543 Elevation: 5,180 feet
- **10.0** Footbridge over East Fork Monture Creek
- **10.9** Keep right on Monture Creek Trail at junction with Center Creek Trail #463.
  GPS: 47.2557, -113.1668 Elevation: 5,155 feet
- **11.6** Monture Falls
  GPS: 47.2640, -113.1751 Elevation: 5,195 feet
- **23.2** Arrive back at the trailhead.

43 Lodgepole Falls

Located just south of the Bob Marshall Wilderness Complex, the hike to Lodgepole Falls is easy, except for the final descent to viewpoints below the cascade. The final scramble to this waterfall could prove too difficult for some hikers, especially small children. Three 20- to 30-foot drops of water plunge from right to left down a cliffy gorge. The forests of most of the Lodgepole Creek drainage, including the hike to the falls, were burned by the Rice Ridge Fire of 2017. Watch for danger like falling snags when hiking in burned terrain. Also, both black bears and grizzly bears are numerous in this area, so carry bear spray as a precaution.

See map on p. 160.

Stream: Lodgepole Creek
Height: 75 feet
Distance: 0.8 mile out and back
Elevation loss: 230 feet
Difficulty: Easy except for a steep and difficult final descent
Trail surface: Dirt and rock
Hiking time: 30-60 minutes
Canine compatibility: Dogs are allowed
Seasons: May to Nov

County: Powell
Land status: National forest
Fees and permits: No fees required
Trail contact: Lolo National Forest, 24 Fort Missoula Road, Missoula, MT 59804; (406) 329-3750; fs.usda.gov/lolo/
Maps: *DeLorme Atlas and Gazetteer Montana* Page 55, B9; *USGS Quad* Dunham Point
Camping: There are a couple of primitive sites at the beginning of the trail.

Finding the Trailhead: Once you reach the turnoff for Ovando on MT 200, look for unmarked Monture Creek Road #89 on the north side of the highway. Take this gravel road north for 7.0 miles. Take a left onto FR 477 (marked as #44) and drive 1.1 miles to the junction with Dunham Creek Road #4388. Turn right and drive for another 7.3 miles. After crossing the second bridge over the creek, park your vehicle near the gate of FR 4397.
GPS: 47.2101, -113.1986 Elevation: 5,280 feet

The Hike

Follow the old logging road south, traversing the slope of burned trees east of Lodgepole Creek. It's an easy and scenic stroll among the remnant snags of spruce, larch, and pines. Fireweed and lush green grass emerge in the open forest and there are views of cliff outcroppings that dot the surrounding mountains. You soon approach a gorge that snakes through the mountain and is too deep to see the stream roaring through it.

Look for a hard-to-find path that takes you down to the base of the falls when the gorge curves to the west. The steep and winding descent takes you to a perfect view of Lodgepole Falls in all its glory. The force of the three tall splashes creates a misty breeze, and small rainbows appear when sunlight is present. Even on a warm summer

Lodgepole Falls.

Rainbow at base of Lodgepole Falls.

day, you might want to wear a jacket in this cool, wet environment. Visit during high water to see the waterfall in full rage.

Miles and Directions

- **0.0** Begin hike at gated road #4397.
- **0.3** Locate the steep path leaving the logging road and head west just after the gorge curves.
- **0.4** Base of Lodgepole Falls
  GPS: 47.2061, -113.2009 Elevation: 5,050 feet
- **0.8** Arrive back at the trailhead.

44 North Fork Falls

This trail follows the North Fork Blackfoot River into the Scapegoat Wilderness. North Fork Falls forces its way through a narrow portion of the rugged canyon. The devastation from the Canyon Creek Fire of 1988 is evident along the hike, but young forests of aspen, cottonwood, pine, and larch are starting to make a comeback. Shade is scarce, so wear sunscreen or try to take this hike on a cooler day.

While certainly doable in a full day of hiking, many hikers prefer to break the distance into two days and stay a night in the backcountry. The waterfall is located in an area of vertical walls and sheer drops. A fall off the canyon rim could be fatal, so exercise extreme caution.

Stream: North Fork Blackfoot River
Height: Upper section, 20 feet; lower section, 40 feet
Distance: 14.2 miles out and back
Elevation gain: 700 feet
Difficulty: Moderate
Trail surface: Dirt and rock
Hiking time: 10–12 hours
Canine compatibility: Dogs are allowed
Seasons: May to Oct
County: Lewis and Clark

Land status: Wilderness area, national forest
Fees and permits: No fees required
Trail contact: Lolo National Forest, 24 Fort Missoula Road, Missoula, MT 59804; (406) 329-3750; fs.usda.gov/lolo/
Maps: *DeLorme Atlas and Gazetteer Montana* Page 56, B1; *USGS Quad* Lake Mountain
Camping: In addition to primitive camping along the hike, several primitive camping sites are available at North Fork Trailhead.

Finding the Trailhead: From Ovando, drive 6.8 miles east on MT 200. Turn left (north) on Kleinschmidt Flat Road and drive 2.8 miles on this gravel road. Turn right on unmarked Upper Dry Gulch Road. After 2 miles, this road curves left and becomes FR 5550. Follow this gravel road for a total of 7.5 miles to the trailhead.
GPS: 47.1189, -112.9674 Elevation: 4,730 feet

The Hike

Hobnob Tom Trail begins in a small valley surrounded by mountains where Lake Creek flows into the North Fork Blackfoot River from the west. You climb the forested ridge and immediately notice an unusual slope with steep chutes of white colored rock. The trail then flattens into a forest of regrowth lodgepole pine. At the junction with Lake Creek Trail on the left, keep right and climb to a flat spot with a great open view up the canyon of the raging whitewater river below.

Carpets of quarter century–old lodgepole and larch upholster the mountainsides and tall dead snags scorched in the blaze are scattered throughout the landscape. Continue to traverse the slope above the stream, enjoying the bluebells and wild rose as you go.

North Fork Falls. Photo by Christian Baker.

During mid- to late summer, you may come upon an abundance of strawberries, raspberries, and huckleberries along the side of the trail. You arrive at another beautiful lookout and then advance through more new pines that are now tall enough to offer a bit of shade.

A mile past the sign marking entrance into the Scapegoat Wilderness Area, you cross the first pack bridge to the east side of the river. Water passes swiftly through here, but at normal water level, you may find a pool for a cool dip. Cliffs appear to the west, where golden eagles soar above you and runoff streams forge ravines down the steep slopes from the cathedral-like ridgeline. In this interesting geological site, named Big Slide, notice how these seasonal creeks descend the mountain both above and below the ground.

In the next stretch, the trail often splits into two parallel one-way tracks due to heavy stock traffic. Keep right to stay on Hobnob Tom Trail when you reach the junction with Cutoff Trail on the left. Spectacular views of the mountains continue as the trail passes through occasional groves of young aspen, whose leaves flutter in the breeze. There is a small inconspicuous side trail exiting the main trail to the left and leading down to a flat campsite in the Sourdough Flats near the river. This is an ideal spot to stay a night in the wilderness if you wish to divide the long trek into 2 days of hiking. You might also decide to test your luck fishing the North Fork Blackfoot River in this portion of the drainage.

You then reach the second pack bridge at the North Fork Guard Station. At this location, the North Fork curves east, leaving the wide-open drainage and entering a much more narrow and rugged canyon. Although camping is not permitted in the guard station vicinity, this is a great spot for a rest because of a small beach area on the north bank of the river. You can soak your tired body and cool off in the shade of small cottonwood and aspen trees.

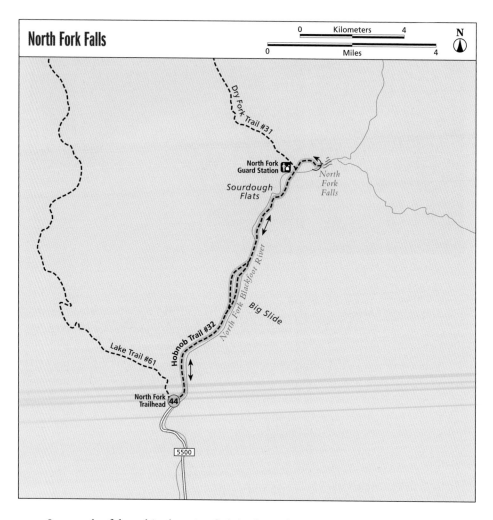

Just north of the cabin there is a fork in the trail. Keep right on Hobnob Tom Trail until you reach another split in the trail, and then veer right again. The grade steepens significantly during the last mile up the hill to where the trail rejoins the river. At a sign indicating the North Fork Falls area, find the path that leads to the right and follow it carefully along the rim of the canyon. There is a sheer drop into the deep canyon, so be sure to keep away from the dangerous edge.

Climb safely to a view of the upper portion of the falls, which is a 20-foot drop of water into a large, bubbling pool. Don't attempt to swim here because the water subsequently drops into the main waterfall, a raging 40-foot vertical plunge over the precipice. With limited visibility, you can glimpse this feature from the brink or from the canyon rim a few hundred feet downstream. In spite of the limited views, a visit to this dynamic spectacle is a rewarding experience.

The Canyon Creek Fire of 1988, which consumed 249,000 acres of forest in the Scapegoat Wilderness, was one of the largest wildfires in Montana since 1910. Photo by Christian Baker.

Miles and Directions

0.0 North Fork Trailhead

0.6 Keep right to stay on Hobnob Tom Trail #32 at junction with Lake Creek Trail #61.
GPS: 47.1257, -112.9632 Elevation: 4,785 feet

1.7 Side path for river access

2.5 Enter Scapegoat Wilderness.

3.6 Cross first pack bridge.

4.4 Keep right to stay on Hobnob Tom Trail at junction with Cutoff Trail #364.
GPS: 47.1708, -112.9262 Elevation: 5,030 feet

5.9 Side trail on the left to campsite near the river

6.2 Cross second pack bridge at North Fork Guard Station. Keep right to stay on Hobnob Tom Trail at Y-junction with Dry Fork Trail #31.
GPS: 47.1931, -112.9080 Elevation: 5,050 feet

7.0 Turn right on marked path to North Fork Falls.

7.1 Overlook of North Fork Falls
GPS: 47.1945, -112.8949 Elevation: 5,435 feet

14.2 Arrive back at the trailhead.

Mission Mountains

Located to the west of the Mission Valley and Flathead Lake, the Missions are a group of thickly forested mountains with alpine lakes and prominent, snow-capped peaks. Some of the range's roughly 45 miles of official trails pass through land belonging to the Confederated Salish-Kootenai Tribes, and nontribal members need to obtain a permit before entry.

Mission Mountains rising beyond Holland Lake and the Swan Valley.

45 North Crow Creek Falls

North Crow Creek Falls is located in the Mission Mountains south of Flathead Lake, and it's an easy hike through changing terrain to the foot of the unique waterfall. Massive round boulders form a 20-foot curtain of cool water that splashes gently into a calm pool. Definitely bring your swimsuit to this one.

Stream: North Crow Creek
Height: 20 feet
Distance: 1.8 miles out and back
Elevation gain: 270 feet
Difficulty: Easy
Trail surface: Dirt path
Hiking time: 2-3 hours
Seasons: Apr to Oct
Canine compatibility: Dogs are allowed
County: Lake
Land status: Native reservation

Fees and permits: Recreation permit required for nontribal members to access land and camp. http://www.cskt.org/
Trail contact: Confederated Salish & Kootenai Tribes, 42487 Complex Blvd., PO Box 278, Pablo, MT 59855; (406) 675-2700; http://www.cskt.org/
Maps: DeLorme Atlas and Gazetteer Montana Page 38, E5; USGS Quad Piper-Crow Pass
Camping: Nontribal members must acquire a permit in advance to camp at the trailhead or at backcountry sites.

Finding the Trailhead: From Ronan, drive north on US 93 for 0.7 mile and turn right onto Old Highway 93. Drive north for 1.5 miles and turn west onto Canyon Mill Road. Continue for 3.6 miles while the gravel road curves north and meets North Crow Road. Turn right at the unmarked junction and head east for 1.3 miles to North Crow Creek Trailhead at the end of the road.
GPS: 47.57723, -114.0169 Elevation: 3,680

The Hike

The trail begins on the north side of North Crow Creek and climbs the slope to a large scree field sweeping down from the cliffs. Make sure you carry bear spray. The Mission Mountains are home to a high concentration of black bears and grizzly bears.

You pass through lush forests and along giant boulders until you come to a fork in the trail. Turn left if you prefer an easier switchback, right for the quicker route up a steep hill. Both reunite at a nice resting spot on a bluff with a scenic view.

The stream rages below you as you climb to a bench on the mountainside. Turn right onto a side trail leading down to the creek toward the sound of crashing water. After a few hundred feet, you arrive at the base of North Crow Creek Falls. Water descends abruptly over a smooth overhanging cliff and splashes into a shallow pool about 20 feet wide. This is an excellent place to get in and fully experience the waterfall. There's nothing better than a shower of cold mountain water on a hot day.

North Crow Creek Falls.

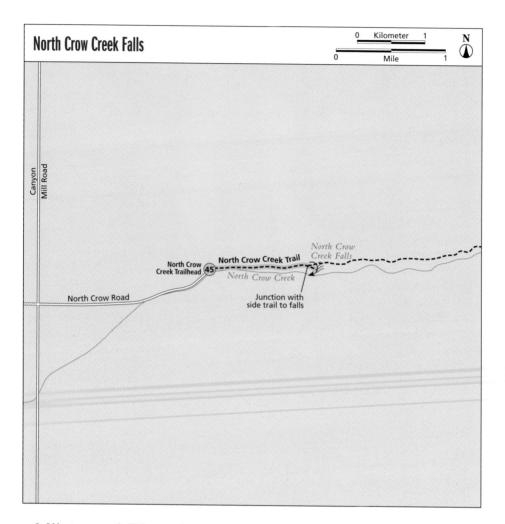

North Crow Creek Falls

Canyon Mill Road

North Crow Creek Trailhead **45**

North Crow Creek Trail

North Crow Creek

North Crow Creek Falls

North Crow Road

Junction with side trail to falls

0 Kilometer 1

0 Mile 1

N

Miles and Directions

0.0 North Crow Creek Trailhead

0.8 Turn right onto side trail to falls.
GPS: 47.5782, -113.9857 Elevation: 3,950

0.9 Base of North Crow Creek Falls
GPS: 47.5773, -113.9979 Elevation: 3,900

1.8 Arrive back at the trailhead.

46 Mission Falls

This is a fantastic hike for cascade lovers. Begin the tour with the delightful Lower Mission Falls near the trailhead. During the steep climb along Mission Creek, you pass views of South Fork Mission Falls to the north and Elizabeth Falls to the east. Mission Falls is a string of terraced cascades that's too tall to view all at once. But the trail approaches a spectacular section that's over 100 feet tall. The afternoon sun bathes the falls in light, and sometimes rainbows form above the misty terraces.

Stream: Mission Creek
Height: 600 feet
Distance: 4.0 miles out and back
Elevation gain: 1,075 feet
Difficulty: Moderate
Trail surface: Dirt and rock
Hiking time: 3–5 hours
Seasons: Apr to Oct
Canine compatibility: Dogs are allowed
County: Lake
Land status: Native reservation

Fees and permits: Recreation permits are required for nontribal members to hike or camp. http://www.cskt.org/
Trail contact: Confederated Salish & Kootenai Tribes, 42487 Complex Blvd., PO Box 278, Pablo, MT 59855; (406) 675-2700; http://www.cskt.org/
Maps: *DeLorme Atlas and Gazetteer Montana* Page 54, A5; *USGS Quad* St Mary's Lake
Camping: Mission Reservoir Campground has several no-fee sites. Nontribal members must acquire a camping permit in advance.

Finding the Trailhead: From St. Ignatius, drive south on US 93 for 1.5 miles. Turn west onto Old Highway 93, which soon becomes South Main, and drive 1.1 miles. Turn right onto paved Mission Creek Road and drive west for 3.5 miles. Turn left onto paved Foothill Road and drive 0.7 mile. Turn right onto Mission Dam Road, a bumpy road with numerous potholes. Drive 3.6 miles along Mission Reservoir to the unmarked trailhead at the end of the road.
GPS: 47.3241, -113.9747 Elevation: 3,480

The Hike

After stopping to enjoy the small but elegant Lower Mission Falls, start hiking up the north slope of Mission Canyon through tall semi-open forest of cedar and fir. The Mission Creek drainage teems with wildlife. Look for woodpeckers in the treetops and mountain goats on the cliff faces to the south. After a quarter mile of grueling climbing, you reach a ledge with an outstanding view of the mountains that tower over the canyon.

When passing a marshy fen on the right, look up the canyon to catch a glimpse of Mission Falls and Elizabeth Falls in the distance. Later, you come to a curious little spring in the forest where water trickles out from under a mossy boulder. The trail levels out again and then reaches a campsite in a shady grove of cedars. After passing

Mission Falls.

briefly near the swift waters of Mission Creek, you turn abruptly to the north and proceed to follow a dry streambed.

A short but very steep and strenuous climb takes you high up on the north wall of the canyon with breathtaking views. Look for the whitewater of South Fork Mission Falls shimmering through the tops of the trees and cheering you onward with its roar.

Tread carefully along the narrow trail as you skirt the steep cliffs that lead to Mission Falls.

You soon arrive at a perfect place to stop and feel the power of nature. A long chain of tall white cascades descends gracefully down the rocky slope. You can take

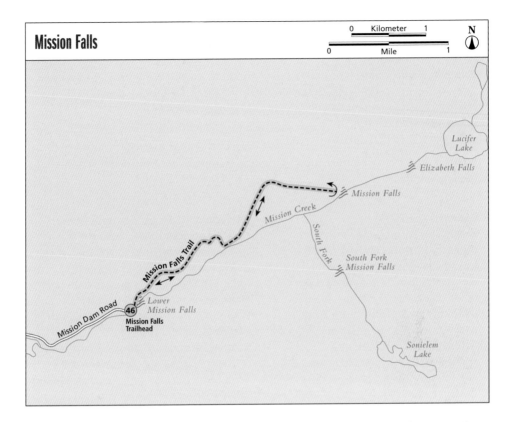

Mission Falls

a small path down to the boulders below the falls, but be careful near the wet rocks. As you hike back down to the valley, enjoy a clear view of cone-shaped Ch-paa-qn Peak to east.

Miles and Directions

0.0 Mission Falls Trailhead and Lower Mission Falls

0.4 Large fen and distant views up the canyon of Elizabeth Falls and Mission Falls

0.5 Spring

1.2 Primitive campsite in grove of cedars

1.6 View of South Fork Mission Falls across canyon

2.0 Trail reaches Mission Falls.
        GPS: 47.3363, -113.9416 Elevation: 4,555

4.0 Arrive back at the trailhead.

47 Glacier Creek Falls

This hike displays the scenic value of the Mission Mountain Wilderness. You first pass Little Glacier Creek Falls and then hike to a viewpoint of Glacier Creek Falls from Glacier Lake. The 3-mile, round-trip hike to the lake view is a good option for most hikers. But, if you're feeling adventurous, you can follow rugged paths around the lake and then make a difficult climb to the falls. Glacier Creek is an excellent place to find huckleberries in the summer months. Be sure to carry your bear spray when hiking in these mountains.

Stream: Glacier Creek
Height: 300 feet
Distance: 3.2 miles out and back to lake; 5.2 miles out and back to base of falls
Elevation gain: 460 feet to Glacier Lake; 665 feet to base of falls
Difficulty: Easy to Glacier Lake, difficult to base of falls
Trail surface: Dirt and rock
Hiking time: 2–3 hours to Glacier Lake; 3–4 hours to base of falls
Canine compatibility: Dogs are allowed
Seasons: June to Oct
County: Missoula

Land status: Wilderness area, national forest
Fees and permits: No fees required
Trail contact: Flathead National Forest, 650 Wolfpack Way, Kalispell, MT 59901; (406) 758-5208; fs.usda.gov/flathead/
Maps: *DeLorme Atlas and Gazetteer Montana* Page 55, A6; *USGS Quad* Hemlock Lake and Gray Wolf Lake
Camping: Backcountry camping is not allowed at Glacier Lake, but you can find sites at the nearby Heart and Crescent Lakes. Lindbergh Lake Campground is located at the end of Lindbergh Lake Road to the south, and there are eleven heavily used, no-fee campsites.

Finding the Trailhead: From Seeley Lake, drive north on MT 83 for 23 miles. Turn left on Kraft Creek Road #561, a well-maintained gravel road, and follow the signs for Glacier Creek Trail. Keep left on FR 561 at a junction with FR 9590 at 4.0 miles and left again at a junction with FR 9576 at 6.4 miles. After a total of 11.3 miles, you arrive at Glacier Creek Trailhead at the end of the road.
GPS: 47.3816, -113.7932 Elevation: 4,840 feet

The Hike

The trail climbs gradually through tall, old-growth forest dominated by western larch, alpine fir, and Engelmann spruce. The trees in the area have never been logged and were also spared by the nearby Crazy Horse Fire of 2003. After a couple hundred feet, you approach Glacier Creek at a small, scenic cascade and pool named Little Glacier Creek Falls. From here the trail leaves the main stem of the creek and proceeds to cross wooden footbridges over two large tributary streams, Horse Creek and Crescent Creek. In between the water crossings you see a sign marking entrance into the Mission Mountain Wilderness.

Glacier Creek Falls.

Just over a mile from the trailhead, you come to a spur trail that takes you to the base of Lower Glacier Creek Falls. This pretty location offers a secluded place to relax next to the series of 5- to 10-foot cascades. Most hikers walk right by without noticing. Turn left at the junction up the trail and hike the last quarter mile to Glacier Lake. The trail ends at a gravelly beach with a colorful wilderness vista. Across the shimmering blue lake, Glacier Creek Falls cascades down large slabs of rock on a partially forested slope.

Advanced hikers can access the foot of the falls by way of a challenging bushwhack.

There are some game trails along the north shore to help you through the thickets of Pacific yew. Cross the grassy meadow surrounding the inlet stream and begin climbing steeply through thick Engelmann spruce forest. You reach the bottom of the 70-foot lower portion of Glacier Creek Falls where whitewater slides and stair-steps down colorful sandstone. To access the upper portion, scramble upstream another couple hundred feet through difficult terrain to a clear view of a majestic cascade plummeting over a wall of sedimentary rock.

Miles and Directions

0.0 Glacier Lake Trailhead #690

0.1 Little Glacier Creek Falls

1.2 Lower Glacier Creek Falls

1.3 Turn left to Glacier Lake at Y-junction.
  GPS: 47.3766, -113.8150 Elevation: 5,210 feet

1.6 Glacier Lake and Glacier Creek Falls viewpoint
  GPS: 47.3758, -113.8204 Elevation: 5,300 feet

3.2 Arrive back at the trailhead.

Glacier Creek Falls

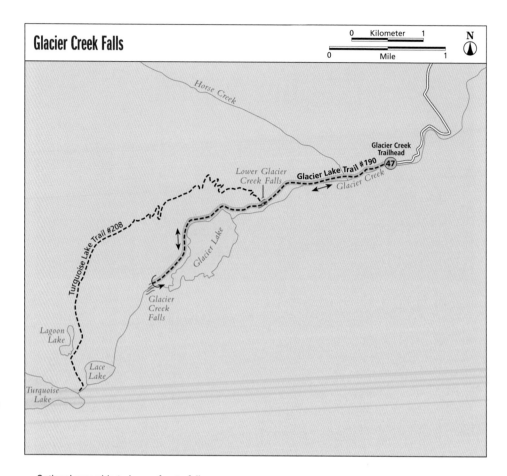

Optional scramble to base of waterfall:

2.5 Base of lower portion of Glacier Creek Falls

2.6 Glacier Creek Falls

GPS: 47.3672, -113.8344 Elevation: 5,505 feet

5.2 Arrive back at the trailhead.

Ninemile Divide

The Ninemile Divide is small range of low, forested mountains surrounded by the Clark Fork and Flathead Rivers on the west and the Reservation Divide to the east. Ponderosa pine dominates the forested landscape. The highest point is Stark Mountain, with a summit of 7,350 feet.

The Clark Fork River winding through the Ninemile Divide.

48 Cascade Falls

"The hike to Cascade Falls is a mild and relaxing climb. The area surrounding the trail is speckled with brightly colored moss and you are rewarded at the top with the quintessential western vista: a large meandering river cutting through the Rocky Mountains outlined by winding railroad tracks carrying a slow-moving train. The waterfall, viewed from the trail, is not an epic sight, but it is a pleasant spot for a picnic with plenty of space to sit and reflect while listening to the healing sounds of falling water." (Anne Kratz)

Stream: Cascade Creek
Height: 30 feet
Distance: 2.6 miles out and back
Elevation gain: 395 feet
Difficulty: Easy
Trail surface: Dirt and rock
Hiking time: 1-2 hours
Canine compatibility: Dogs are allowed
Seasons: Mar to Nov
County: Sanders

Land status: National forest
Fees and permits: No fees required
Trail contact: Lolo National Forest, 24 Fort Missoula Road, Missoula, MT 59804; (406) 329-3750; fs.usda.gov/lolo/
Maps: DeLorme Atlas and Gazetteer Montana Page 53, A10; USGS Quad Quinn Hot Springs
Camping: Cascade Campground is located at the trailhead, and there are ten sites for a fee.

Finding the Trailhead: From Plains, drive southeast on US 200 for 9.2 miles to the junction with MT 135. Turn right and drive south for about 5 miles to Cascade Campground on the left. Alternatively, you can take Interstate 90 to St. Regis, and then take MT 135 north for 16.5 miles. The trailhead is located within the campground loop. If you hike off-season, you can park at the gate.
GPS: 47.3054, -114.8251 Elevation: 2,580 feet

The Hike

There is plenty to look at while climbing the wide and nicely groomed trail: rounded hills and mountains, the twisting Clark Fork River, and tiny, orange larch needles strewn across the forest floor. The sounds of civilization fade away as you wind around the first big hill and come to a small stream lined with huge cedars. The trail opens up to views of the creek drainage and then crosses a slate outcropping.

After leveling out and reentering the forest, the trail comes to a marked junction with a side trail to the falls on the left. The overlook is positioned about 30 feet above the brink of the waterfall, so the view is somewhat limited. Bushwhacking down the cliff for a better view is an option for experienced hikers, but it must be done carefully so as to not to fall or damage the fragile vegetation.

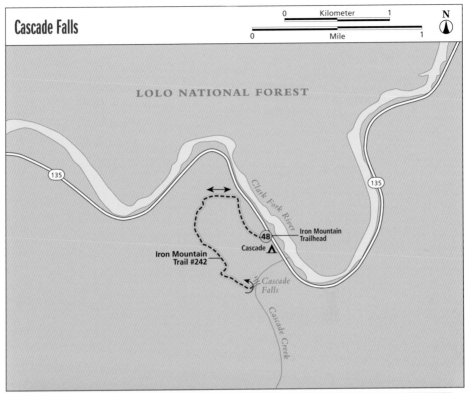

Cascade Falls

LOLO NATIONAL FOREST

135

Clark Fork River

48

Cascade

Iron Mountain Trailhead

Iron Mountain Trail #242

135

Cascade Falls

Cascade Creek

0   Kilometer   1

0   Mile   1

N

Cascade Falls.

Miles and Directions

0.0 Iron Mountain Trailhead #242

0.4 First overlook of Clark Fork River

1.2 Turn left at side trail to falls.

1.3 Cascade Falls

GPS: 47.3024, -114.8265 Elevation: 2,975 feet

2.6 Arrive back at the trailhead.

Bitterroot Mountains

Shared with Idaho to the west, the crest of the Bitterroot Range extends south and east for approximately 470 miles, forming Montana's longest mountain range. The Continental Divide follows along the southern half of the range, draining a large amount of water to both the Gulf of Mexico and the Pacific Ocean. These mountains are known for their granite spires and rugged terrain. Trapper Peak, rising to 10,155 feet, is the tallest peak in the Bitterroots.

Looking down toward the Bitterroot Valley from Canyon Falls.

49 Dipper Falls

Dipper Falls gets its name from the American dipper, commonly seen bobbing up and down and flittering its feathers near cascading water. The falls makes a splendid place to rest on this popular trail to Hub and Hazel Lakes. Moose and other wildlife are sometimes seen in the area. The summits of Ward Peak and Eagle Peak are accessible by trail to extend your adventure. This rewarding jaunt offers diverse natural features that can be enjoyed by many levels of hikers.

Stream: Ward Creek
Height: 50 feet
Distance: 2.5 miles out and back to Dipper Falls; 7.2 miles out and back to Hub Lake
Elevation gain: 605 feet to falls; 1,735 feet to Hub Lake
Difficulty: Easy to moderate
Trail surface: Dirt
Hiking time: 1–2 hours to falls; 5–7 hours to Hub Lake
Canine compatibility: Dogs are allowed
Seasons: May to Oct

County: Mineral
Land status: National forest
Fees and permits: No permits required
Trail contact: Lolo National Forest, 24 Fort Missoula Road, Missoula, MT 59804; (406) 329-3750, fs.usda.gov/lolo/
Maps: *DeLorme Atlas and Gazetteer Montana* Page 53, A6; *USGS Quad* De Borgia South and McGee Peak
Camping: One no-fee campsite is located near the trailhead.

Finding the Trailhead: From St. Regis: Drive 8 miles on I-90 west and take exit 25. Drive on I-90 eastbound for one mile and then take exit 26. Drive west on Ward Creek Road #889 for 6.2 miles to the trailhead.
GPS: 47.2868, -115.3388 Elevation: 3940 feet

The Hike

You begin the hike to Dipper Falls by ascending a cool and shady temperate rainforest dominated by large western red cedar. Halfway to the waterfall you pass a campsite near Ward Creek and then cross a small tributary. After a mile and a quarter, you reach an overlook of 50-foot Dipper Falls. Water descends a jagged and mossy wall in an open glade of towering trees. A steep and challenging scramble to the base provides solitude and a more impressive view. Stay on the main trail if conditions seem unsafe.

After enjoying some time at the falls, keep walking up the main trail toward Hub and Hazel Lakes. You soon arrive at a junction and turn right onto trail #280. As you climb a long switchback, the music of the waterfall behind you slowly fades and views of Ward Peak and Eagle Peak gradually appear above you. The forest of the south-facing slope transforms into mainly Engelmann spruce and western larch. Thankfully, the ascent becomes less steep as the path crisscrosses the mountainside.

Dipper Falls. Photo by Martha Gunsalam.

You come to a pretty cascade and cross the stream. A short distance ahead, a steep side trail drops to Hazel Lake. There is a campsite at this scenic blue haven below the cliffs. A path along the west shore approaches the sound of hidden falls at the inlet.

Return to the main trail and continue less than a mile to Hub Lake. The landscape is now a mix of montane and subalpine scrub forest. After a steep climb you come

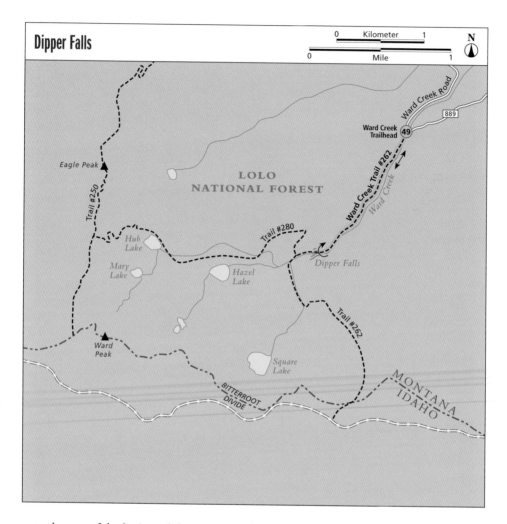

Dipper Falls

to the top of the basin and drop to cross the stream one more time. You finally reach Hub Lake, which has forest on the east shore and open terrain on the west shore. There are several nice campsites on the northwest shore. From the lake, the trail climbs to an interesting old mine shaft that is fun to explore with a flashlight.

Ambitious hikers can continue on trail #280 to the top of the Bitterroot Divide. From the junction with trail #250, you have the option to head north to summit Eagle Peak or south to the top of Ward Peak. Both mountains stand at about 7,300 feet and offer outstanding views of Montana and Idaho backcountry.

Miles and Directions

0.0 Ward Creek Trailhead #262
0.8 Campsite

Hub Lake. Photo by Martha Gunsalam.

1.2 View of Dipper Falls from trail
GPS: 47.2752, -115.3530 Elevation: 4,625 feet
1.4 Junction. Turn right onto trail #280.
GPS: 47.2749, -115.3544 Elevation: 4,635 feet
2.6 Side trail to Hazel Lake
3.4 East shore of Hub Lake
3.6 Campsites at northwest shore of Hub Lake
GPS: 47.2763, -115.3765 Elevation: 5,675 feet
7.2 Arrive back at the trailhead.

50 Lost Creek Falls

The trip to Lost Creek Falls begins with a long drive on rough gravel roads and ends at the foot of a gorgeous and secluded waterfall. The 2-mile-long trail is surprisingly uncrowded and ideal for families and beginner hikers. It borders Lost Meadows and then enters a lush, temperate rainforest. Beyond the falls, there is an option to hike an additional 5 miles to Lost Lake, or an additional 8.6 miles to the Bitterroot Divide at the Idaho border. The full hike to the ridge gains you panoramic views in all directions of mountain ranges and several subalpine lakes.

Stream: Lost Creek
Height: 50 feet
Distance: 2.4 miles out and back to Lost Creek Falls; 7.2 miles out and back to Lost Lake, and 11.0 miles out and back to the Bitterroot Divide
Elevation gain: 75 feet to falls; 1,165 feet to Lost Lake
Difficulty: Easy to falls, moderate to lake, difficult to ridge
Trail surface: Dirt and rock
Hiking time: 1–3 hours to falls; 4–6 hours to lake; 5–7 hours to ridge
Canine compatibility: Dogs are allowed

Seasons: June to Oct
County: Mineral
Land status: National forest
Fees and permits: No fees required
Trail contact: Lolo National Forest, 24 Fort Missoula Road, Missoula, MT 59804; (406) 329-3750; fs.usda.gov/lolo/
Maps: *DeLorme Atlas and Gazetteer Montana* Page 53, C8; *USGS Quad* Illinois Peak
Camping: There are primitive campsites for backpackers at Lost Meadows and Lost Lake. Dispersed camping is allowed along Cedar Creek Road.

Finding the Trailhead: From Superior, take River Street to the south side of I-90 and turn left (east) on Diamond Match Road. Drive 1.1 miles and turn right on Cedar Creek Road. This road is paved for the first 2.7 miles and then becomes a good gravel road. At mile 5.7, turn right on Oregon Gulch Road #7865. A high-clearance vehicle is recommended but not required. Be careful and take it slow at rough parts to avoid tire damage. Drive 8.1 miles to the trailhead just before the gate at the end of the road.
GPS: 47.1276, -115.1019 Elevation: 4,845 feet

The Hike

Lost Meadows appears at the beginning of the hike and a side trail leads down to a campsite in a grove of Engelmann spruce. Western larch trees surround the meadow and put on a radiant display of orange in October. Keep right on Lost Creek Trail and walk along the edge of the meadow to the entrance to a thick, fairy-tale-like forest. Large boulders covered in green moss are scattered among the massive cedar, hemlock, and spruce.

Lost Creek Falls.

You cross a series of tributary streams and climb uphill through the woods to a split in the trail. Take the path to the left and walk toward the sound of the falls. After a tenth of a mile, you reach an open slope of rocky bluffs. The trail diverges into a network of paths you can use to explore the waterfall. Stay on the paths and be careful not to slip on a wet rock. At the base you can see the multiple terraces that form the 50-foot cascade. The tallest drop in the waterfall is at the top, and there is a path to the right of the creek that leads to it.

To continue hiking to Lost Lake, return to the main trail and turn left. The route is easy for the first mile and then gets considerably steeper at a series of switchbacks.

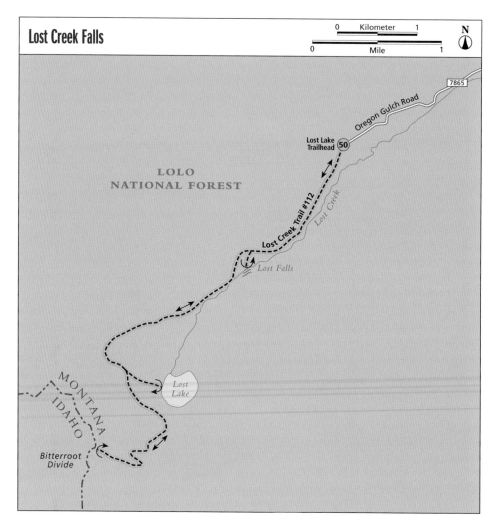

Cross a large clearing of subalpine terrain where the trail flattens out. At the junction, take a left to the lake. Lost Lake sits in a forested basin of pine and spruce. There is a small campsite in the alders near the shoreline.

You can extend the trek a few more miles by hiking to the top of the ridge at the Idaho border, but you'll want to bring a good topographical map. Return to the main trail and take a left to another junction. Keep right on the wide path and walk along a small ridge that offers views of the lake and creek drainage from above. Look for a faint trail on the right at a small clearing and climb up the slope for over a mile. From the Bitterroot Divide, enjoy panoramic views of mountains and lakes. Bonanza Lakes lie to the south, Frog Lake to the west, and Lost Lake and some alpine ponds to the north.

Miles and Directions

0.0 Lost Creek Trailhead #112

1.0 Turn left on side trail to falls.
GPS: 47.1165, -115.1158 Elevation: 4,790 feet

1.1 Base of Lost Creek Falls
GPS: 47.1152, -115.1170 Elevation: 4,920 feet

1.2 Return to junction. Turn left to hike to lake and ridge or right to return to trailhead.

2.4 Arrive back at the trailhead.

Optional miles to Lost Lake and Bitterroot Divide:

3.3 Turn left at junction to reach Lost Lake.
GPS: 47.1040, -115.1355 Elevation: 6,100 feet

3.7 Campsite at Lost Lake
GPS: 47.1019, -115.1301 Elevation: 6,010 feet

4.1 Return to junction. Turn left to continue to Bitterroot Divide.

4.3 Keep right at trail junction.

4.5 View of Lost Lake from trail

4.7 Turn right onto the inconspicuous side trail in clearing.

6.0 Top of the ridge at Bitterroot Divide

11.0 Arrive back at the trailhead.

51 Emerald Sun Falls and Trout Creek Cascades

This hike takes you to a secluded waterfall haven nestled in a shady old-growth forest. It is perfect for adventurous hikers who enjoy searching for hidden waterfalls off the beaten path. You follow an old overgrown logging road up a slope to North Fork Trout Creek and then scramble off-trail toward the stream banks to locate the cascades. Emerald Sun Falls is the easiest to access and provides a nice swimming hole. Angle Falls and Geometry Falls are great rewards for those willing to scramble downstream.

Stream: North Fork Trout Creek
Height: Emerald Sun Falls, 15 feet; Angle Falls, 15 feet; Geometry Falls, 20 feet
Distance: 1.9 miles lollipop hike
Elevation gain: 280 feet
Difficulty: Easy trail hike, difficult scramble to falls
Trail surface: Dirt, rock, forest floor
Hiking time: 1–2 hours
Canine compatibility: Dogs are allowed
Seasons: June to Nov

County: Mineral
Land status: National forest
Fees and permits: No fees required
Trail contact: Lolo National Forest, 24 Fort Missoula Road, Missoula, MT 59804; (406)-329-3750; fs.usda.gov/lolo/
Maps: *DeLorme Atlas and Gazetteer Montana* Page 53, C9; *USGS Quad* Landowner Mountain
Camping: Trout Creek Campground has sites by the creek for a fee.

Finding the Trailhead: From Superior, take River Street to the south side of I-90 and turn left (east) on Diamond Match Road. Drive on this paved road for about 5 miles until it curves to the southwest. At 6.2 miles it becomes Trout Creek Road #250. Follow this gravel road for 12.4 miles to an intersection with FR 7815 on the right. Park on the side of Trout Creek Road and look for an abandoned logging road heading southwest.
GPS: 47.0114, -114.9896 Elevation: 4,240 feet

The Hike

The old logging road takes you to a rocky opening with a gorgeous view up the South Fork Trout Creek drainage toward Heart Lake. Traverse the forested slope along a rock field for about a mile until you reach North Fork Trout Creek. Emerald Sun Falls is partly visible through the thick trees down the slope to the left. Head down a steep, rough path for about 50 feet to a big round pool below the 15-foot cascade.

The waterfall makes a loud and abrupt fall that lifts mist into the air. Cool off in the deep and refreshing waters surrounded by groves of very large old-growth cedars.

Head downstream past the place where Hoodoo Creek empties into the North Fork to discover a series of water features called the Trout Creek Cascades. Scramble

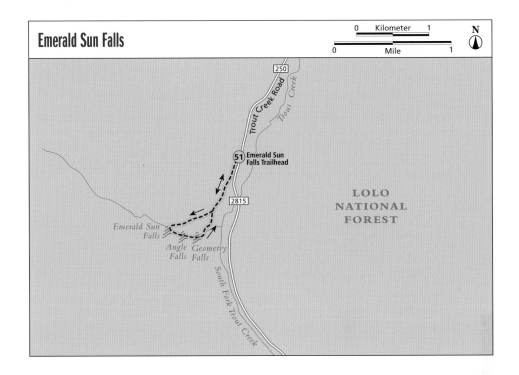

Emerald Sun Falls

0 Kilometer 1

0 Mile 1

N

250
Trout Creek Road
Trout Creek

51 Emerald Sun
Falls Trailhead

2815

LOLO
NATIONAL
FOREST

Emerald Sun
Falls

Angle Geometry
Falls Falls

South Fork Trout Creek

Geometry Falls.

through the forest for a tenth of a mile to the 15-foot Angle Falls that splashes down next to a moss-covered overhanging cave. Cedars and spruce soar to great heights along the banks, and a few old snags have fallen over the creek. Farther downstream there is perhaps the most impressive water formation of them all. Geometry Falls drops around a huge trapezoid-shaped rock in the middle of the creek bed, and water flows past deeply colored walls of mossy rock.

Given the tucked-away aspect of these waterfalls, you almost certainly won't encounter other visitors. To finish the lollipop-shaped hike, climb north away from the creek until you encounter the old logging road. Turn right and walk back to the trailhead.

Miles and Directions

0.0 Trailhead at start of old logging road

0.9 Descend the ravine along a rugged path on the left to base of Emerald Sun Falls.
GPS: 47.0025, -115.0015 Elevation: 4,515 feet

1.0 Scramble downstream to Angle Falls.
GPS: 47.0018, -114.9979 Elevation: 4,370 feet

1.1 Scramble downstream to Geometry Falls.
GPS: 47.0017, -114.9967 Elevation: 4,260 feet

1.2 Scramble uphill and turn right on old logging road.

1.9 Arrive back at the trailhead.

52 Stepladder Falls, via Chelsea Falls and Goldenrod Falls

The lush forests of Straight Creek give you a sense of what the Great Burn looks like a century after the two-day blaze of 1910 consumed this part of the Bitterroots. There are several tucked-away waterfalls to find on your way to Stepladder Falls. The route crosses the medium-sized stream a few times, so plan this hike for the late season, when the water is low.

Stream: Straight Creek
Height: 25 feet
Distance: 11.2 miles out and back
Elevation gain: 1,360 feet
Difficulty: Moderate
Trail surface: Dirt
Hiking time: 6-8 hours
Canine compatibility: Dogs are allowed
Seasons: Aug to Oct
County: Mineral
Land status: National forest

Fees and permits: No fees required
Trail contact: Lolo National Forest, 24 Fort Missoula Road, Missoula MT 59804; (406) 329-3750, fs.usda.gov/lolo/
Maps: *DeLorme Atlas and Gazetteer Montana* Page 53, D10; *USGS Quad* St. Patrick Peak and Straight Peak
Camping: Clearwater Crossing Campground has several no-fee campsites near West Fork Fish Creek.

Finding the Trailhead: From Alberton: Drive 8 miles east on I-90 and take exit 66. Drive 1 mile and turn right at junction. Continue for 1.5 miles and then take a left onto Fish Creek Road 343. Drive 7.7 miles. Turn right onto Forest Road 7750 and drive 6.7 miles to Clearwater Crossing Trailhead at the end of the road.
GPS: 46.9089, -114.8031, Elevation: 3,430 feet

The Hike

Just past the corrals and to the right, there is a wooden sign that marks the beginning of North Fork Fish Creek Trail #103. You enter a diverse forest that hosts most native Montana tree species. The trail follows North Fork Fish Creek through an understory of thick foliage. After less than a mile, you reach a junction and take a left onto Straight Creek Trail #99. This trail immediately leads to the first and most difficult ford, at the Straight Creek confluence. A second crossing comes shortly after.

Climb gently for almost 2 miles until you reach the third ford. Straight Creek Falls roars unmistakably down in a gorge, but off-trail exploration reveals only partial views of the falls. It is better to continue ahead to discover better options. Just before the fourth crossing, catch a glimpse of the unnamed waterfall that makes a 15-foot slide into a large pool. Find a resting spot near this peaceful display of nature.

Stepladder Falls in autumn. Photo by Martha Gunsalam.

After another mile, open views appear of Straight Peak to the south and Crater Mountain to the north. The ridgeline of the Bitterroot Divide rises due east. Twenty-foot Chelsea Falls sits just a short scramble down a large slab of rock. Less than a mile ahead you arrive at a primitive campsite. Nearby Goldenrod Falls requires a short bushwhack. Here, a curtain of water plunges vertically for 20 feet into a dark pool.

Stepladder Falls is next, and the trail leads straight to the brink. Scramble downstream along either side of the creek to the views from the base. Mountain slopes provide a verdant backdrop to the 25-foot, fan-shaped waterfall. Upstream, shelves of rock form terrace-style cascades and pools. To extend the hike, continue climbing to Chilcoot Pass, and then follow trail #510 east to Siamese Lakes.

Miles and Directions

0.0 Clearwater Crossing Trailhead. Head east on North Fork Fish Creek Trail #103.

0.7 Turn left onto Straight Creek Trail #99 at junction.
GPS: 46.9105, -114.8147

0.8 First ford

1.0 Second ford

2.7 Third ford

3.0 Obstructed views of Straight Creek Falls

3.4 Short bushwhack to unnamed falls
GPS: 46.9054, -114.8595

3.5 Fourth ford

4.6 Short scramble to Chelsea Falls
GPS: 46.9047, -114.8819

5.4 Short scramble to Goldenrod Falls
GPS: 46.9022, -114.8952

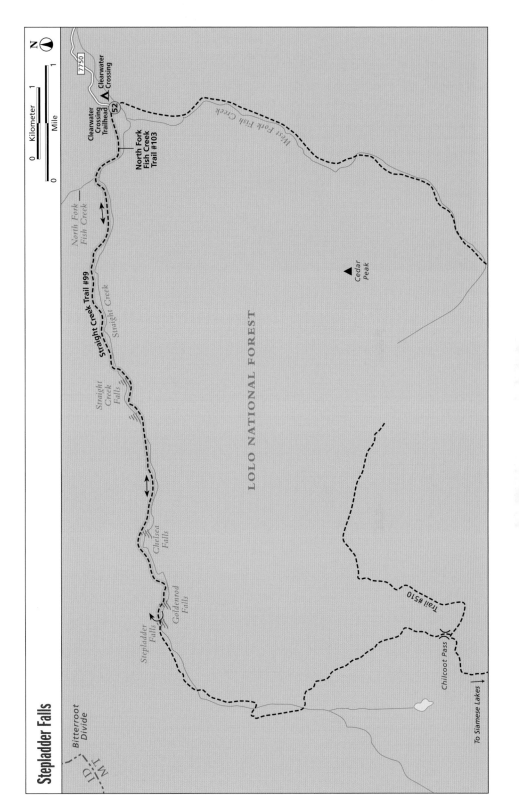

Stepladder Falls

Goldenrod Falls. Photo by Martha Gunsalam.

5.6   Stepladder Falls

GPS: 46.9022, -114.8980 Elevation: 4,790 feet

11.2   Arrive back at the trailhead.

53 Abha Falls

Abha Falls is the closest waterfall hike to Missoula, and Bass Creek Trail is very popular with hikers. However, you probably won't have too much company at the waterfall because it's tucked away in dense woods about 500 feet from the trail. This is an easy route that follows Bass Creek through rocky forest, passes a large pond, and arrives at a section of the canyon near a steep cliff wall.

Stream: Bass Creek
Height: 40 feet
Distance: 5.8 miles out and back
Elevation gain: 940 feet
Difficulty: Easy
Trail surface: Dirt and rock
Hiking time: 2–4 hours
Canine compatibility: Dogs are allowed
Seasons: Apr to Nov
County: Ravalli

Land status: Wilderness area, national forest
Fees and permits: No fees required
Trail contact: Bitterroot National Forest, 1801 North 1st, Hamilton, MT 59840; (406) 363-7100; fs.usda.gov/bitterroot/
Maps: *DeLorme Atlas and Gazetteer Montana* Page 68, A3; *USGS Quad* Saint Mary Peak
Camping: Charles Waters Campground is adjacent to the trailhead and has twenty-six sites for a fee.

Finding the Trailhead: From Missoula, drive 20 miles south on US 93. Turn right on Bass Creek Road and drive west for 2.5 miles to Bass Creek Trailhead.
GPS: 46.5745, -114.1460 Elevation: 3,750 feet

The Hike

The wide, well-maintained trail begins on the north side of Bass Creek. You begin to follow the creek closely along tumbling cascades formed by logjams and terraces of rock. At times you can hear the echo of the stream bouncing off the canyon walls.

Some of the cliffs have overhangs under which one could find shelter in a hailstorm.

The trail climbs steadily through tall forests of Douglas fir, grand fir, and cottonwood to another view of the cascading stream. Later, you pass a scenic pond with a jagged north ridgeline as a perfect backdrop. Hike through thick forest to a sign marking entrance to the Selway-Bitterroot Wilderness.

After some gentle climbing, you reach a junction. Turn left and hike down the open-forested ravine to a ford over Bass Creek. Depending on the season, you can choose to wade or walk across big logs. After crossing, hike another tenth of a mile to an inconspicuous game trail leaving the trail on the right. Take this path through thick timber toward the sound of the waterfall. You reach an opening in the forest at the creek's bank, where the 40-foot Abha Falls displays its beauty and uniqueness.

Abha Falls. Photo by Brendan Knowles.

Whitewater slides down yellowish rock into a narrow chute and into a pool. The stream banks are upholstered with a thick carpet of green moss.

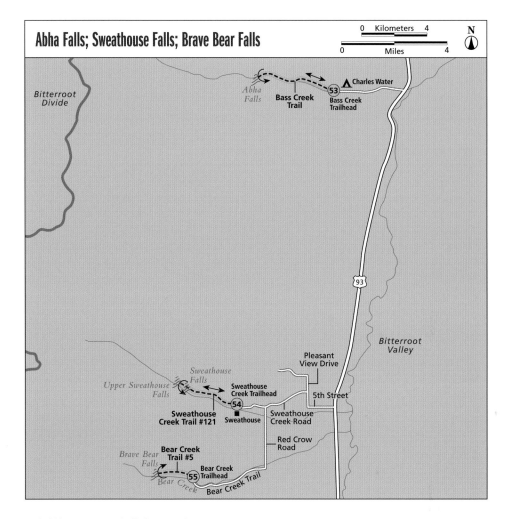

Abha Falls; Sweathouse Falls; Brave Bear Falls

Miles and Directions

0.0 Bass Creek Trailhead

1.7 Large pond

2.4 Sign marking entrance into Selway-Bitterroot Wilderness

2.6 Turn left at junction.
GPS: 46.5828, -114.1978 Elevation: 4,495 feet

2.7 Ford Bass Creek or cross over large logs.

2.8 Turn right on game trail leading to falls.
GPS: 46.5817, -114.2011 Elevation: 4,740 feet

2.9 Base of Abha Falls
GPS: 46.5814, -114.2022 Elevation: 4,695 feet

5.8 Arrive back at the trailhead.

54 Sweathouse Falls

The hike to Sweathouse Falls is a moderate 1,250-foot climb along a rushing stream through a rugged, glacially carved valley. The trail gains fabulous views of the waterfalls amid a background of Bitterroot peaks.

See map on p. 205.
Stream: Sweathouse Creek
Height: Sweathouse Falls, 75 feet; Upper Sweathouse Falls, 25 feet
Distance: 4.4 miles out and back
Elevation gain: 1,245 feet
Difficulty: Moderate
Trail surface: Dirt and rock
Hiking time: 2-3 hours
Canine compatibility: Dogs are allowed
Seasons: May to Nov

County: Ravalli
Land status: National forest
Fees and permits: No fees required
Trail contact: Bitterroot National Forest, 1801 North 1st, Hamilton, MT 59840; (406) 363-7100; fs.usda.gov/bitterroot/
Maps: *DeLorme Atlas and Gazetteer Montana* Page 68, B3; *USGS Quad* Gash Point
Camping: There is a primitive campsite at the falls.

Finding the Trailhead: From Victor, turn west on 5th Street and drive 1 mile to a T-junction. Turn right on Pleasant View Drive and drive 0.4 mile. Turn left on gravel Sweathouse Creek Road and drive 2.6 miles until you arrive at a small parking area marked "Visitor Parking Area."
GPS: 46.4158, -114.2193 Elevation: 3,790 feet

The Hike

The first half mile of the hike crosses private property. Follow the dirt road on the north side of the creek to a split. Keep right and continue to Sweathouse Quarry where a wide footpath enters the trees. You pass through cottonwood, ponderosa pine, grand fir, and western larch, with large, glacially deposited boulders strewn about the forest.

Look for evidence of avalanches and rockslides below the steep rocky slopes. Small seasonal waterfalls splash off the mossy cliffs on the south slope of the canyon that is dotted with the remnants of charred forests.

After maneuvering through a boulder field, you catch your first glimpse of Sweathouse Falls. Follow the trail to the brink, using caution in the steep cliffy area.

If you're feeling ambitious, scramble down to the base for a different view of the 75-foot waterfall. Upper Sweathouse Falls is less than a quarter mile up the trail, and you can walk right up to this curtain of falling water. There is a primitive campsite between the falls for adventurous travelers wanting to spend a night in the woods listening to the rhythm of the water.

Sweathouse Falls. Photo by Martha Gunsalam.

Miles and Directions

0.0 Parking area

0.1 Keep right at fork in road.

0.5 Sweathouse Creek Trail #121 begins.

2.0 Sweathouse Falls
GPS: 46.4245, -114.2559 Elevation: 4,995 feet

2.2 Upper Sweathouse Falls
GPS: 46.4260, -114.2597 Elevation: 5,035 feet

4.4 Arrive back at the parking area.

55 Brave Bear Falls

This canyon hike into the Bitterroot Mountains is very scenic and easy enough for the kids. The tall rock spires and massive, old-growth larch trees will keep you looking up constantly, and the wildflowers and tumbling cascades will keep you looking down. Brave Bear Falls is the first in a series of waterslides, cascades, and falls along Bear Creek.

See map on p. 205.
Stream: Bear Creek
Height: 15 feet
Distance: 2.8 miles out and back
Elevation gain: 280 feet
Difficulty: Easy
Trail surface: Dirt and rock
Hiking time: 1-2 hours
Canine compatibility: Dogs are allowed
Seasons: May to Nov

County: Ravalli
Land status: National forest
Fees and permits: No fees required
Trail contact: Bitterroot National Forest, 1801 North 1st, Hamilton, MT 59840; (406) 363-7100; fs.usda.gov/bitterroot/
Maps: *DeLorme Atlas and Gazetteer Montana* Page 68, B3; *USGS Quad* Gash Point
Camping: There is a shady campsite near the creek at the trailhead.

Finding the Trailhead: From Victor, turn west on 5th Street and drive 1 mile to a T-intersection. Turn left on Pleasant View Drive and travel south for 2.5 miles. Turn left on Red Crow Road and drive 1 mile to a T-intersection. Turn right on Bear Creek Trail and drive west for 2.9 miles to the trailhead.
GPS: 46.3797, -114.2527 Elevation: 4,140 feet

The Hike

The first mile of the trail passes along the base of talus slopes on the south side of Bear Creek. The forest opens several times, offering you glimpses of peaks and rock walls along the canyon. The trail begins to follow the creek again, passing gentle cascades and rockslides.

When a few craggy peaks appear to the north, and the forest transitions to lodgepole pine, you'll know you are close to the waterfall. Brave Bear Falls is a small double waterfall whose two channels flow down both sides of a rocky island. Grassy ledges make nice benches for a picnic. The best time to see the waterfall's biggest flow is during spring runoff in May and June. You may also see kayakers paddling the whitewater rapids when water is high. Continue exploring upstream from Brave Bear Falls to find more small waterfalls and pools that are great for swimming and fishing.

Brave Bear Falls. Photo by Martha Gunsalam.

Miles and Directions

0.0 Bear Creek Trailhead #5

1.4 Brave Bear Falls

GPS: 46.3819, -114.2785 Elevation: 4,421 feet

2.8 Arrive back at the trailhead.

56 Mill Canyon Falls

This hike takes you into a rugged canyon of high rock walls. The trail follows Mill Creek through a mix of live and burned forest to the foot of a lovely cascade. Look for wildlife on this hike—you may spot beaver and songbirds by the creek and golden eagles soaring along the cliffs. There is no camping at the trailhead, but backpackers will enjoy a good campsite just upstream from the waterfall.

Stream: Mill Creek
Height: 30 feet
Distance: 6.2 miles out and back
Elevation gain: 840 feet
Difficulty: Easy
Trail surface: Dirt and rock
Hiking time: 4–6 hours
Canine compatibility: Dogs are allowed
Seasons: Apr to Nov
County: Ravalli
Land status: Wilderness area, national forest

Fees and permits: No fees required
Trail contact: Bitterroot National Forest, 1801 North 1st, Hamilton, MT 59840; (406) 363-7100; fs.usda.gov/bitterroot/
Maps: *DeLorme Atlas and Gazetteer Montana* Page 68, C3; *USGS Quad* Printz Ridge
Camping: There is a primitive site near the creek upstream from the falls. Blodgett Campground is located next to Blodgett Canyon Trailhead and has six heavily used, no-fee sites.

Finding the Trailhead: From Hamilton, drive 4.8 miles north along US 93. From Victor, drive 7.5 miles south. Turn west on paved Dutch Hill Road and drive 2.5 miles to a T-junction. Turn left onto paved Bowman Road and drive for only 0.3 mile before taking the second right on FR 1328. Drive up this gravel road for 0.7 mile to the trailhead.
GPS: 46.3106, -114.2227 Elevation: 4,045 feet

The Hike

The trail climbs steeply to a view of open slopes on the opposite side of the canyon where fires have wiped out most of the forest. Follow the creek to a scenic pool in the woods with a small waterfall and tall trees and cliffs in the background. Amble through the shady spruce forest along cascades and pools to a wooden bridge crossing to the south side of the creek.

As you enter the burned forest, you can see the canyon walls more clearly. The southern crest is called Printz Ridge, and the north wall is unnamed yet immense and beautiful. The reddish-tan, smooth-faced cliff has a sheer 1,500-foot drop and a width of over a mile from east to west. Large dead snags line the creek bottom, and a carpet of young lodgepole pine, ponderosa pine, and aspen is starting to reforest the area. The trail passes through forest scrub and talus slopes to another cliffy area with castle-like turrets typical to many canyons in the Bitterroot Mountains. Shortly after stone-stepping over a small creek, you arrive at a sign marking entrance into the Selway-Bitterroot Wilderness. Continue to a flat part of the valley where beaver dams form

Mill Canyon Falls.

ponds and channels of slow-moving water. You might notice fresh cuttings of aspen and willow along the trail where beavers have collected branches for their lodges.

The trail passes a few large aspen, and you start to hear the faint sound of falling water up the canyon. Follow a few switchbacks up to the brink of Mill Canyon Falls.

Carefully walk a couple hundred feet down smooth rock to a pool at the base of the falls. The flow of whitewater zigzags 30 feet down a large crevice. There is a nice campsite a short distance upstream where the creek meanders through clear, deep channels that are ideal for swimming.

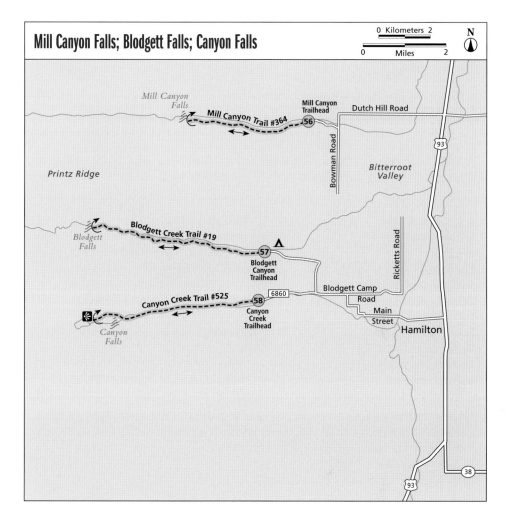

Miles and Directions

0.0 Mill Canyon Trailhead #364

0.5 First pool and small falls

0.7 Footbridge

2.1 Sign marking entrance to Selway-Bitterroot Wilderness

2.3 Beaver ponds

3.1 Base of Mill Canyon Falls

     GPS: 46.3111, -114.2810 Elevation: 4,885 feet

6.2 Arrive back at the trailhead.

57 Blodgett Falls

Situated in the Bitterroot Mountains west of Hamilton, Blodgett Canyon is a delightful place for hikers of varying skill levels. Even children with good footwear and endurance can complete this trek. With numerous primitive campsites along the way, this is an ideal destination for backpackers. The trail climbs through a unique blend of both rugged and lush terrain within constant view of the canyon walls and the meandering creek. There are three small waterfalls along the way that increase in beauty and force from one to the next.

See map on p. 213.
Stream: Blodgett Creek
Height: 50 feet
Distance: 9.2 miles out and back
Elevation gain: 1,095 feet
Difficulty: Moderate
Trail surface: Dirt and rock
Hiking time: 5–7 hours
Canine compatibility: Dogs are allowed
Seasons: May to Nov
County: Ravalli

Land status: National forest
Fees and permits: No fees required
Trail contact: Bitterroot National Forest, 1801 North 1st, Hamilton, MT 59840; (406) 363-7100; fs.usda.gov/bitterroot/
Maps: *DeLorme Atlas and Gazetteer Montana* Page 68, C3; *USGS Quad* Printz Ridge
Camping: Blodgett Campground is located next to the trailhead and has six heavily used, no-fee sites.

Finding the Trailhead: From Hamilton, drive west on Main Street for 1.2 miles. Turn right on Ricketts Road and continue for 0.5 mile. Turn left and head west on Blodgett Camp Road for 2.4 miles until the road splits. Turn right on FR 736 and follow this gravel road for 1.5 miles to the trailhead at the end of the road.
GPS: 46.2686, -114.2431 Elevation: 4,220 feet

The Hike

Climb gradually though Douglas fir and ponderosa pine to a bench on the south side of the canyon. Like most Bitterroot canyon trails, large stones and roots present frequent obstacles to step over. You soon round a bend to a view of the creek and some tall spires to the north. Blodgett Canyon is a popular rock-climbing area in the region, and you may spot a climber making a pitch up Shoshone Spire, Flathead Buttress, Blackfoot Dome, or other routes along the hike. Sweeping views of the rugged mountain terrain continue as you hike into the U-shaped valley created by receding glaciers after the ice age.

Keep hiking through patches of sunny open forest cleared by the forest fires of 2000. The semi-shaded understory creates a perfect environment for delicious huckleberries in the summer and fall. The path approaches a slow-moving section of Blodgett Creek, with a few scattered primitive campsites. You can stop and see trout

Blodgett Falls.

in these clear rocky pools. Watch for picas and marmots in the rocky habitat where the trail and stream squeeze between large talus slopes on the sides of the canyon.

As you enter an area of ponds and grassy marshes, look for moose emerging from the willows. The understory thickens and leafy vegetation hems the trail in on both sides. Shortly after, the trail approaches the creek at the first small waterfall. A white curtain of water makes a vertical plunge over a smooth ledge of bedrock, but the 5-foot cascade is no obstacle for migrating trout. If you stare long enough, you might see them jump the falls to reach higher water.

Continue walking and you'll catch a glimpse of a natural arch at the top of the southern ridge that locals call "The Horse's Head." You cross a pack bridge to the north side, passing more primitive campsites under shade trees. After skirting the base of a talus slope and reentering mixed forest, climb a boulder-laden hillside to an overlook of the second cascade. Water constricts itself through a narrow chasm in the granite and then drops vertically over a 10-foot ledge. You can easily scamper down to the water's edge below the falls.

To reach Blodgett Falls, climb up the trail through dense forest until you reach a flat bench hosting a tall stand of lodgepole pine. Soon after, you emerge from the woods to a view. Blodgett Falls is a slide waterfall that descends for 50 feet, splashing over the ledges and down the sloped bedrock. At the bottom, you can soak in a small pool in the company of curious little trout.

Miles and Directions

0.0 Blodgett Canyon Trailhead #19

2.7 First waterfall on the right
GPS: 46.2730, -114.2945 Elevation: 4,815 feet

3.0 Pack bridge

4.1 Second waterfall on the left
GPS: 46.2763, -114.3212 Elevation: 4,970 feet

4.6 Base of Blodgett Falls
GPS: 46.2769, -114.3297 Elevation: 5,315 feet

9.2 Arrive back at the trailhead.

58 Canyon Falls

The scenery along Canyon Creek Trail displays the typical ruggedness of a Bitterroot canyon, but with less fire damage than most other places. Canyon Falls is the tallest waterfall on the Montana side of the range. In addition to the falls, the views of peaks and valleys from the ridge are breathtaking and a fine recompense for the short but difficult climb. Continue hiking to Canyon Lake and make an off-trail approach to the brink of the falls for a closer look. Due to the large amount of elevation gain, this hike is most suitable for intermediate to advanced hikers.

See map on p. 213.
Stream: Canyon Creek
Height: 400 feet
Distance: 8.2 miles out and back
Elevation gain: 1,750 feet to ridge; 2,255 feet to Canyon Lake
Difficulty: Moderate to difficult
Trail surface: Dirt and rock
Hiking time: 5–7 hours
Canine compatibility: Dogs are allowed
Seasons: July to Oct
County: Ravalli

Land status: Wilderness area, national forest
Fees and permits: No fees required
Trail contact: Bitterroot National Forest, 1801 North 1st, Hamilton, MT 59840; (406) 363-7100; fs.usda.gov/bitterroot/
Maps: *DeLorme Atlas and Gazetteer Montana* Page 68, C3; *USGS Quad* Ward Mountain
Camping: In addition to primitive campsites along the trail, you can camp at nearby Blodgett Campground, located at the end of Blodgett Camp Road. This heavily used campground has eight no-fee sites.

Finding the Trailhead: From Hamilton, drive west on Main Street for 1.2 miles. Turn right on Ricketts Road and continue for 0.5 mile. Turn left and head west on Blodgett Camp Road for 2.4 miles until the road splits. Turn left on FR 735, following the signs to Canyon Creek Trail. After 2.8 miles on this bumpy yet well-maintained gravel road, you arrive at the trailhead. Camping is not allowed at the trailhead.
GPS: 46.2529, -114.2473 Elevation: 5,030 feet

The Hike

The trail immediately splits with a path to Blodgett Overlook on the right. Stay left on Canyon Creek Trail, entering the north side of the canyon. The trail advances between the stream and talus fields under steep rock walls. Dense timber of spruce, fir, and pine dominate the canyon bottom, while the north slope is rocky with scattered sun-loving ponderosa pines and aspen. Most of the route stays in the cool of the trees, but there are plenty of openings with views of the impressive rock walls.

The trail ascends a few switchbacks to a bench above the stream in open forest. As you drop back into the shade of the trees, notice the giants of old-growth Engelmann spruce. You pass a sign marking entrance into the Selway-Bitterroot Wilderness, and soon after, the trail approaches the stream, offering a pleasant place to rest. After

Canyon Falls.

passing some large glacially deposited boulders in thick woods, you enter a dense aspen grove. You reach the first primitive campsite as the forest transitions gradually into lodgepole pine. This is a good option for campers who want to lighten their load before hiking the steep final mile to the ridge and lake.

Beyond the campsite, the trail begins to climb very steeply up the rocky slope on the north side of the canyon near Romney Ridge. After a quarter mile, you gain your first view of Canyon Falls, which slides for 400 feet at a steep angle down a granite wall. Leave the trail and walk a few yards out onto the rock ledges to find a good vantage point. The water level varies from spring to fall, but anytime you come you will enjoy a spectacular panorama of peaks, canyon, forest, and the Bitterroot Valley.

You can camp along the ridge in a few flat spots with views of the falls and the 9,000-foot Downing Mountain. However, beware of fierce winds that can kick up at any time and whip through the exposed areas of the canyon.

The final three-quarter mile to Canyon Lake is well worth the extra effort. Follow rock cairns until you reach the east side of the lake and the end of the trail. Similar to other high-mountain lakes in the Bitterroots, a dam was built over a century ago to store snowmelt water for irrigation in the Bitterroot Valley. The lake cirque is surrounded by craggy peaks dominated by the high point of Canyon Peak at 9,155 feet. Backpackers will find several good campsites here, and advanced hikers can do some additional off-trail hiking to explore nearby East Lake and Wyatt Lake. The area of the brink of the falls is also interesting but be very careful scrambling around steep places if the rock is wet. Use good judgment and bring a topographical map if you plan to leave the trail.

Miles and Directions

0.0 Canyon Creek Trailhead

1.6 Enter Selway-Bitterroot Wilderness.

3.0 Small campsite

3.2 View of Canyon Falls from ridge
GPS: 46.2476, -114.3154 Elevation: 6,780 feet

4.1 Canyon Lake
GPS: 46.2454, -114.3282 Elevation: 7,285 feet

8.2 Arrive back at the trailhead.

59 Rock Creek Falls

This popular trail for families and novice hikers follows the north shore of beautiful Lake Como. You will likely observe waterfowl and songbirds and other wildlife, too. Rock Creek Falls, also known as Lake Como Falls, is located near the mouth of Rock Creek on the lake's western shore. Although not a large waterfall, it's a very scenic destination below the majestic Como Peaks of the Bitterroot Mountains. This route can be combined with Trail #580 to Little Rock Creek Falls to complete an 8-mile loop around Lake Como.

Stream: Rock Creek
Height: Top 20 feet; bottom 40 feet
Distance: 6.0 miles out and back
Elevation gain: 20 feet
Difficulty: Easy
Trail surface: Dirt, rock, and some asphalt
Hiking time: 3–5 hours
Seasons: Apr to Nov
Canine compatibility: Dogs are allowed
County: Ravalli
Land status: National forest recreation area
Fees and permits: From Memorial Day through Labor Day all vehicles parked within the recreation area must display a valid Recreation Pass. You will have to pay for Recreation Passes per day and per vehicle or per season.
Trail contact: Bitterroot National Forest, 1801 North 1st, Hamilton, MT 59840; (406) 363-7100; fs.usda.gov/bitterroot/
Maps: *DeLorme Atlas and Gazetteer Montana* Page 68, 2E; *USGS Quad* Como Peaks
Camping: Three Frogs Campground is located adjacent to the trailhead and has twenty-one sites for a fee.

Finding the Trailhead: From Hamilton, drive 12.8 miles south on US 93. Make a right turn on Lake Como Road and drive 2.9 miles until you reach a sign marked "Beach/Day Use and Lake Como Campground." Turn right and drive 0.7 mile to a road marked "To Como Lake." Turn left and drive another 0.7 mile to the trailhead parking next to Three Frogs Campground.
GPS: 46.0661, -114.2479 Elevation: 4,310 feet.

The Hike

The hike begins as a paved interpretive trail with signs describing the natural ecology.

There are benches to sit on to enjoy the views of Lake Como and the Como Peaks. The trail passes above the lakeshore through forest of tall ponderosa pine with a Douglas fir understory. If you look closely, you may see ravens, woodpeckers, chickadees, and red-breasted nuthatches moving through the trees. When you reach a rocky clearing, you begin to hear the faint sound of Little Rock Creek Falls across the lake.

Shortly after crossing a creek, you arrive at a grassy meadow area at the edge of the lake. This is a good place to rest and appreciate the unobstructed views.

After crossing another small stream, you begin to hear the sound of Rock Creek Falls to the west. Pass through brushy terrain until you arrive at a trail junction at the

Rock Creek Falls. Photo by Brendan Knowles.

west end of Lake Como near the medium-sized inlet stream, Rock Creek. Trail #502 merges with Trail #580, which heads east along the south shore and west into the Selway-Bitterroot Wilderness.

From the junction you can approach Rock Creek Falls in several ways. You can turn right, walk a couple hundred feet, and then turn left on a small footpath. This

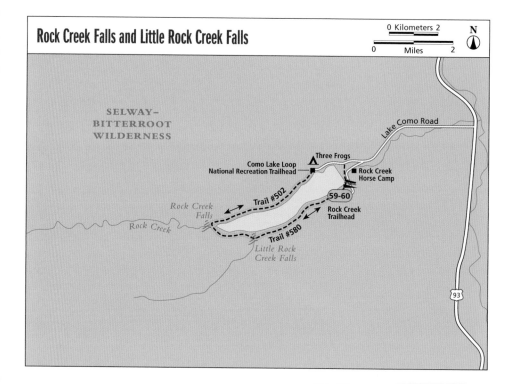

will lead you to a small campsite at the top of the falls. You can also turn left and hike down to the wooden footbridge and climb up the rocks along the cascades. A third option is to view the falls from the other side of the creek: cross the bridge and climb to the right to discover a rock platform with a straight-on view. Rock Creek Falls consists of two major drops. The upper cascade falls abruptly for about 20 feet, and the lower cascade slides for about 40 feet down angled rock into a pool. Sit and enjoy the view of the falls and the lake.

Miles and Directions

0.0 Como Lake Loop National Recreation Trailhead #502

0.4 End of paved portion of trail

1.8 Open view of mountains and lake

2.8 Junction of Trail #502 and Trail #580

3.0 Rock Creek Falls
   GPS: 46.0473, -114.2978 Elevation: 4,330 feet

6.0 Arrive back at the trailhead.

60 Little Rock Creek Falls

Situated near the south shore of Lake Como, Little Rock Creek Falls tumbles for 75 feet down a narrow, rocky canyon in multiple cascades. This lakeside hike can be combined with the Rock Creek Falls hike to complete an 8-mile loop around the entire lake, but the out-and-back jaunt is also very rewarding. On the way, backpackers will enjoy primitive campsites scattered along Lake Como's sandy beaches. Since the falls are barely visible from the trail, an off-trail approach is recommended for experienced hikers and requires scrambling up steep forest scrub, boulders, and deadfall for a quarter mile.

See map on p. 222.
Stream: Little Rock Creek
Height: Several cascades totaling 75 feet
Distance: 5.4 miles out and back
Elevation gain: 20 feet
Difficulty: Difficult
Trail surface: Dirt and rock
Hiking time: 4–6 hours
Seasons: May to Nov
Canine compatibility: Dogs are allowed
County: Ravalli

Land status: National forest
Fees and permits: No fees required
Trail contact: Bitterroot National Forest, 1801 North 1st, Hamilton, MT 59840; (406) 363-7100; fs.usda.gov/bitterroot/
Maps: *DeLorme Atlas and Gazetteer Montana* Page 68, 2E; *USGS Quad* Como Peaks
Camping: Rock Creek Horse Camp is located three-quarters of a mile before the trailhead and has eleven sites for a fee.

Finding the Trailhead: From Hamilton, drive south for 12.9 miles on US 93. Turn right on Lake Como Road and drive 4.1 miles. The trailhead is located in a large pullout on the right side of the road.
GPS: N46 03.503'/W114 14.023' Elevation: 4,410 feet

The Hike

Trail #580 descends for a few hundred feet and then merges with a horse trail originating at Rock Creek Horse Camp. Keep left and follow the rocky trail down to the lake. The trail passes scattered boulders through open forests of Douglas fir and ponderosa pine. After following the south shore of Lake Como for a couple of miles, the forest begins to thicken with additions of lodgepole pine, aspen, and larch. Look for paths that leave the main trail and lead down to sandy beaches lined with dwarf cottonwood trees. Here, you can see the whole lake from east to west as well as up into the Rock Creek drainage. Look carefully for the whitewater of Rock Creek Falls tumbling toward the lake at the west end.

You pass a couple more beach campsites before finally meeting Little Rock Creek.

From the two footbridges, look left and up the creek through the trees at the barely visible whitewater from Little Rock Creek Falls. To really appreciate the

Little Rock Creek Falls.

spectacle, you have to make a final trail-less climb up rough terrain. Immediately after crossing the second bridge, climb to the left through boulders, deadfall, shale, and small lodgepole pine regrowth for a couple hundred feet to some rock ledges near the base of the falls. Don't try to go too high, as the canyon walls get dangerously steep.

You gain outstanding panoramic views of mountains, waterfall, and lake at the end of the challenging scramble. Little Rock Creek plunges furiously down a long series of cascades in a rocky ravine, making a much quicker descent than its nearby counterpart, Rock Creek.

Miles and Directions

0.0 Rock Creek Trailhead #580

0.1 Trail merges left onto horse trail.

2.1 Sandy beaches with primitive campsites

2.5 Two footbridges over Little Rock Creek. Turn left immediately after crossing the second bridge and scramble uphill to the falls.

2.7 Little Rock Creek Falls
GPS: 46.0428, -114.2773 Elevation: 4,430 feet

5.4 Arrive back at the trailhead.

61 Trapper Creek Falls

Trapper Creek Falls is located about 2 miles north of Trapper Peak, the highest mountain in the Bitterroots. Numerous scrambles over deadfall and a ford that requires good river shoes at high water are an added challenge on this lightly used trail. Enjoy the beautiful scenery of craggy ridges and cool, healthy forests. The rugged access makes this seldom-seen waterfall a good place to find solitude in the mountains.

Stream: Trapper Creek
Height: 20 feet
Distance: 4.6 miles out and back
Elevation gain: 720 feet
Difficulty: Moderate
Trail surface: Dirt and rock
Hiking time: 2–4 hours
Canine compatibility: Dogs are allowed
Seasons: May to Nov
County: Ravalli

Land status: Wilderness area, national forest
Fees and permits: No fees required
Trail contact: Lolo National Forest, 24 Fort Missoula Road, Missoula, MT 59804; (406) 329-3750; fs.usda.gov/lolo/
Maps: *DeLorme Atlas and Gazetteer Montana* Page 68, F3; *USGS Quad* Trapper Peak
Camping: In addition to some primitive sites along Trapper Creek Road, the nearby Sam Billings Campground has twelve no-fee sites.

Finding the Trailhead: From Darby, drive south on US 93 for 4.0 miles to paved West Fork Road, County Road 473. Turn right and drive for 6.4 miles to the sign marking Trapper Creek Access. Turn right onto FR 347 and drive 0.5 mile. Head left at the sign for Trapper Creek Road #5628 and drive 2.5 miles to the trailhead at the end of the road.
GPS: 45.9223, -114.2259 Elevation: 4,585 feet

The Hike

A rocky slope dotted with pine and mountain mahogany greets you to the north as you begin your hike on Trapper Creek Trail. You start to climb a rough and rocky path through shady forests dominated by Douglas fir. The poorly maintained trail presents many obstacles, like fallen trees and large roots. After walking along an overgrown portion of the trail and crossing stands of old-growth lodgepole pine, you suddenly approach a vertical headwall below jagged spires.

While passing through talus fields lined with tall aspen, enjoy the gorgeous

Trapper Creek Falls.

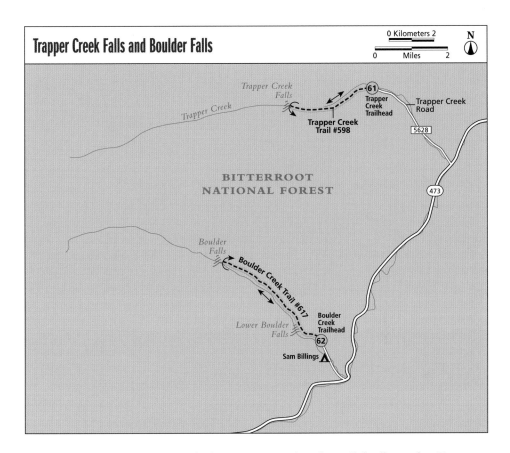

Trapper Creek Falls and Boulder Falls

0 Kilometers 2

N

0 Miles 2

Trapper Creek Falls

Trapper Creek

Trapper Creek Trail #598

Trapper Creek Trailhead

61

Trapper Creek Road

5628

BITTERROOT NATIONAL FOREST

473

Boulder Falls

Boulder Creek Trail #617

Lower Boulder Falls

Boulder Creek Trailhead

62

Sam Billings

views of crest lines leading to high Bitterroot peaks. The trail finally reaches Trapper Creek where you can ford or use stepping-stones or fallen logs to cross. Find the trail in the thick brush on the other side of the creek and continue to a sign marking entrance into the Selway-Bitterroot Wilderness.

The last half mile of the hike increases in steepness and more frequent fallen trees cover the trail. You finally reach a side view of Trapper Creek Falls at the end of a rocky switchback. Hike down to the stream edge along granite boulders to the base of the 20-foot cascade. There is a small pool deep enough for a refreshing dip on a hot day, and a fine backdrop of towering peaks completes the scene.

Miles and Directions

0.0 Trapper Creek Trailhead #598

1.8 Ford creek

1.9 Enter Selway-Bitterroot Wilderness.

2.3 Base of Trapper Creek Falls
GPS: 45.9157, -114.2708 Elevation: 5,305 feet

4.6 Arrive back at the trailhead.

62 Boulder Falls

Boulder Falls Trail combines all the fantastic features of a Bitterroot Mountains hike: interesting rock formations, steep canyon walls, massive boulders, cool and diverse forests, and lots of running water. You'll love the views along the way of the high ridges and be able to spot dozens of old-growth ponderosa pine trees. Watch for moose and pika. The numerous fallen trees and ruts in the trail make this a moderately difficult hike.

See map on p. 227.
Stream: Boulder Creek
Height: 40 feet
Distance: 8.0 miles out and back
Elevation gain: 860 feet
Difficulty: Moderate
Trail surface: Dirt and rock
Hiking time: 4–6 hours
Canine compatibility: Dogs are allowed
Seasons: May to Nov

County: Ravalli
Land status: Wilderness area, national forest
Fees and permits: No fees required
Trail contact: Bitterroot National Forest, 1801 North 1st, Hamilton, MT 59840; (406) 363-7100; fs.usda.gov/bitterroot/
Maps: *DeLorme Atlas and Gazetteer Montana* Page 68, F3; *USGS Quad* Boulder Peak
Camping: Sam Billings Campground is located near the trailhead and has twelve no-fee sites.

Finding the Trailhead: From Darby, drive south on US 93 for 4.3 miles. Make a right turn to the southwest on MT 473, West Fork Road. Drive 13.6 miles until you see signs for Boulder Creek Trailhead and Sam Billings Campground. Turn right onto Boulder Creek Road #5631 and drive 1.5 miles to the far end of the campground, where the road ends at Boulder Creek Trailhead #617.
GPS: 45.8296, -114.2526 Elevation: 4,540 feet

The Hike

The trail climbs gently through forests of ponderosa pine, Douglas fir, and lodgepole pine. Moss-covered boulders both big and small are strewn throughout the timber.

You approach the creek and follow it for a few minutes before the trail suddenly curves to the right and climbs a hill. Turn onto a small path on the left and walk to a view of Lower Boulder Falls, where a short but vigorous cascade tumbles through the mountain ravine. Back on the main trail, climb gradually through dense spruce forests until you reach a series of talus slopes on the north side of Boulder Creek.

The trail later returns to the streamside where Boulder Point rises above you at 7,750 feet. Soon, the trail arrives at a sign marking entrance into the Selway-Bitterroot Wilderness.

The trail crosses a tributary stream called Crow Creek, bordered by large mature spruce trees and moss-covered boulders. You can use a small bridge constructed with large sticks if the water is too high for stone-stepping. The trail comes to a huge boulder in a forest clearing with a gorgeous view of an unnamed peak standing 9,370

Boulder Falls.

feet tall. After you pass an area of multiple aspen groves and open shale slopes, the trail begins to steepen and you make a steady ascent along the edge of a talus slope. The mountainous country is breathtakingly beautiful in all directions.

When you reach 3.9 miles and hear the sound of rushing water, it is time to leave the trail. Find a game trail and head toward the creek for a few hundred feet until you spot the waterfall cascading gracefully down a rockslide. In the background, Boulder Peak towers proudly at 9,805 feet. Hike upstream another tenth of a mile to encounter a couple more lovely cascades. Water forms a large natural swimming pool that is perfect for cooling off on a hot day.

Miles and Directions

0.0 Boulder Creek Trailhead #617

0.5 Side trail to Lower Boulder Creek Falls

1.8 View of Boulder Point near creek

1.9 Enter Selway-Bitterroot Wilderness.

2.5 Cross Crow Creek.

3.9 Boulder Falls
GPS: 45.8595, -114.3073 Elevation: 5,440 feet

4.0 20-foot waterfall and pool
GPS: 45.8614, -114.3118 Elevation: 5,660 feet

8.0 Arrive back at the trailhead.

63 Overwhich Falls

At 200 feet tall, Overwhich Falls is one of the highest waterfalls in the region and well worth the 2-day trek. Unlike the many stream-following routes in this book, this hike has the unique characteristic of following ridgeline terrain for more than half the distance. Be sure to carry plenty of drinking water. As you wander the grassy slopes in the lower Bitterroot Mountains, there are opportunities to spot wildlife and obtain views in the distance of Trapper Peak, the Como Peaks, and the Beaverhead Mountains. From the falls, you can also visit nearby Pass Lake and Capri Lake. Alternatively, you can hike this route as a 2-day shuttle to Warm Springs Trailhead via Warm Springs Trail #103.

Stream: Overwhich Creek
Height: 200 feet
Distance: 19.0 miles out and back
Elevation change: 590 feet gain; 1,145 feet loss
Difficulty: Moderate
Trail surface: Dirt and rock
Hiking time: 9–11 hours as an overnight backpacking trip
Canine compatibility: Dogs are allowed
Seasons: June to Oct

County: Ravalli
Land status: National forest
Fees and permits: No fee required
Trail contact: Bitterroot National Forest, 1801 North 1st, Hamilton, MT 59840; (406) 363-7100; fs.usda.gov/bitterroot/
Maps: *DeLorme Atlas and Gazetteer Montana* Page 80, A4; *USGS Quad* Overwhich Falls
Camping: Indian Trees Campground is located en route to the trailhead and has sixteen sites for a fee.

Finding the Trailhead: From Darby, drive south on US 93 for 24 miles. Turn right on a road marked "Indian Trees Campground" and follow it for 0.7 mile. Just before reaching the campground, turn left on FR 729. After 0.8 mile, keep right on the gravel road that becomes FR 8112. Travel for 6.0 miles to another right turn, onto FR 73503. Drive the final 1.1 miles to the trailhead at the end of the road. Low-clearance vehicles should take it slow on these narrow, bumpy roads. **GPS:** 45.7443, -113.9790 Elevation: 7,025 feet

The Hike

Travel through a lodgepole burn for a quarter mile before entering Douglas fir forest and meadow parkland near Porcupine Saddle. At the summit, views open up of the grassy meadows bordered with sagebrush. In the morning or evening you have a good chance of spotting mule deer or elk grazing at the forest edges. Turn left when you intersect Warm Spring Ridge Trail and head downhill, passing a ridgeline campsite. The trail begins to skirt the mountainside below Saddle Mountain through alternating patches of burned and live forest. Take a right at the junction with Shields Creek Trail at a pass between two ridges. During this next mile, topographical maps show a couple of springs near the trail to access drinking water. On a clear day you

Overwhich Falls.

can scramble to the top of the 8,140-foot mountain for a panoramic view of count-less Idaho and Montana mountains from north to south.

Continue your pleasant stroll through meadows of abundant wildflowers to a grassy hilltop. When you reach a fork in the trail, keep left and begin a gradual, 800-foot descent for 2 miles into the thickly wooded Overwhich Creek drainage. After a series of steep switchbacks, you come to a T-junction. Take a right to continue on Shields Creek Trail. The path follows the winding creek through a flat valley dominated by healthy lodgepole pines. Willow and Engelmann spruce line the small stream, and grassy clearings give you a chance to spot wildlife coming to the stream. The trail steepens and you arrive at a sudden cliff area.

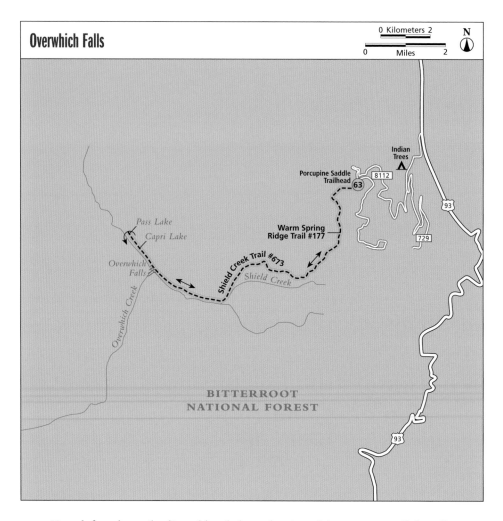

Keep left at the trail split and head along the rim of the canyon until the tall cascade comes into sight. If conditions are dry, you can access the base of the falls for the best views. From the primitive campsite at the edge of the canyon, scramble down the steep hillside, being careful to avoid rocky areas.

When you reach the creek bottom, hike up to the very foot of Overwhich Falls, stepping lightly to avoid damaging the delicate moss and flowers. At normal flow, water drops in several braided channels down the colorful cliffs and ledges to a small gentle pool. If going to the bottom isn't an option, hike up the trail to a junction of five merging trails. Take a left at the wooden sign board that reads "Overwhich Falls Vista" and walk a couple hundred feet to a view of the falls through an opening in the trees.

From the same junction, take the trail marked to Capri Lake. You soon reach Pass Lake, a shallow pond that's a good place to spot waterfowl. Continue to Capri Lake, whose deep water, healthy timber, and rugged cliffs make it a scenic final destination. There are backcountry campsites at both lakes.

Miles and Directions

0.0 Porcupine Saddle Trailhead #196

0.6 Turn left onto Warm Spring Ridge Trail #177 at junction at Porcupine Saddle.
GPS: 45.7455, -113.9868 Elevation: 7,200 feet

3.0 Turn right onto Shields Creek Trail #673 at junction at top of pass.
GPS: 45.7191, -114.0000 Elevation: 7,615 feet

6.3 Turn right to stay on Shields Creek Trail at the T-junction with Trail #650 merging on the left.
GPS: 45.7096, -114.0438 Elevation: 6,765 feet

8.2 Primitive campsite at view of Overwhich Falls
GPS: 45.7193, -114.0774 Elevation: 6,615 feet

8.3 Base of Overwhich Falls
GPS: 45.7185, -114.0775 Elevation: 6,470 feet

8.4 Junction of five trails. Take a left to falls lookout. Take a right on Trail #400 to the lakes.

8.6 Pass Lake

9.5 Capri Lake
GPS: 45.7307, -114.0907 Elevation: 6,600 feet

19.0 Arrive back at the trailhead.

Anaconda Range

The Anaconda Range is drained by the Big Hole River on the east side and the Bitterroot River on the west side. The range stretches directly along the Continental Divide and much of its area is contained within the Anaconda-Pintler Wilderness.

Anaconda Range. Photo by Martha Gunsalam.

64 Star Falls

Star Falls pours through a small canyon of granite and gneiss in the pine and fir timberlands of the East Fork Bitterroot River. The 11-mile round trip is ideal as a long day-hike or an overnight backpacking trip. The gentle trail follows the river upstream through willow flats and forests scorched during the 2000 fire season.

Stream: East Fork Bitterroot River
Height: 15 feet
Distance: 11.0 miles out and back
Elevation gain: 605 feet
Difficulty: Moderate due to length
Trail surface: Dirt and rock
Hiking time: 7-9 hours
Canine compatibility: Dogs are allowed
Seasons: June to Oct
County: Ravalli

Land status: Wilderness area, national forest
Fees and permits: No fees required
Trail contact: Bitterroot National Forest, 1801 North 1st, Hamilton, MT 59840; (406) 363-7100; fs.usda.gov/bitterroot/
Maps: DeLorme Atlas and Gazetteer Montana Page 69, F7; USGS Quad Kelly Lake
Camping: Jennings Campground is located at mile 10 of East Fork Road and has four no-fee sites near the river.

Finding the Trailhead: From Darby, drive south on US 93 for 17.6 miles. Turn left on East Fork Road #9700 and drive 15.6 miles. Turn right on FR 724 and drive 1.8 miles to the trailhead at the end of the road.
GPS: 45.9078, -113.7041 Elevation: 5,420 feet

The Hike

The flat trail is sprinkled with tiny specks of muscovite that shimmer in the sun. Along the north side of the East Fork Bitterroot River, you move upstream through lodgepole pine and Douglas fir and soon pass a sign marking entrance to the Anaconda-Pintler Wilderness. The forest opens up to a burned area throughout the wide valley and you gain a view of the river for the first time. The willow along the valley and stream are spectacularly colorful in the fall and make excellent habitat for species such as black bear, beaver, and moose.

You pass a small pond at Moss Creek where you can spot mallard ducks or other waterfowl. Later, you come to an easy crossing over Cub Creek and a scenic bend in the river where you can look south to the Carmine Creek drainage of rolling, pine forested hills. The willow-bottomed valley widens even more and blankets of young lodgepole pine repopulate the burned landscape. Some dead snags remain standing, while others pile up like matchsticks across the slopes. A gentle climb takes you to a bench with an overlook of the valley where Sun Creek joins the East Fork.

Keep right on East Fork Trail when you come to a junction with Clifford Trail below a craggy half-burned hillside. A few logs make a fairly easy crossing over this

Star Falls.

medium-sized tributary stream. Look for a bend in the river that makes a nice resting spot with some shade and a place to soak. Stay left on East Fork Bitterroot Trail when Trail #198 merges on the right at Kurtz Flats. After leaving the meadows, you begin to climb moderately through unburned forest and reach a campsite to the right of the trail in an area of large boulders.

Just before arriving at the waterfall, use stepping-stones to make an easy crossing over Star Creek. You then approach the 50-foot-tall granite walls where the East Fork passes through a wide opening in the cliff. An easy scramble over boulders and logs takes you to the edge of the waterfall. The river abruptly descends the mossy channel

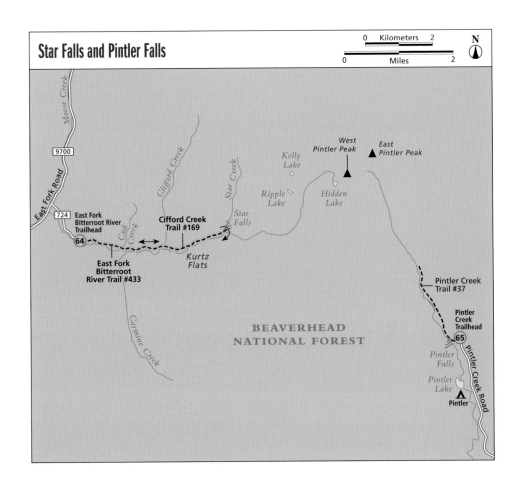

Star Falls and Pintler Falls

for 10 feet and then stair-steps down the remaining sections of whitewater. Clear pools will entice you to get wet on a hot day.

Carefully approach the brink of Star Falls along a smooth outcropping of gneiss to reach a bird's-eye view. A backcountry campsite with a view lies near the gorge just past the falls. To extend the hike, continue a few miles deeper into the Anaconda Range to access Ripple Lake, Kelly Lake, and Hidden Lake.

Miles and Directions

0.0 East Fork Bitterroot River Trailhead #433

0.1 Enter Anaconda-Pintler Wilderness.

1.1 Pond between Moss Creek and Cub Creek

3.0 Keep right on East Fork Bitterroot River Trail at junction with Clifford Trail #169.
GPS: 45.9056, -113.6479 Elevation: 5,520 feet

3.9 Keep left on East Fork Bitterroot River Trail at junction with Trail #198 at Kurtz Flats.
GPS: 45.9056, -113.6309 Elevation: 5,560 feet

5.0   Campsite at large granite boulders

5.5   Base of Star Falls
          GPS: 45.9123, -113.6014 Elevation: 6,025 feet

11.0 Arrive back at the trailhead.

65 Pintler Falls

Pintler Falls is a great destination for waterfalls enthusiasts looking for a quiet place to hike and camp. The short trail to the cascade enters the timbered valley of Pintler Creek in the Pintler Mountains. These mountains teem with wildlife, and the nearby meadows and stream banks are good places to look for deer, elk, bear, and fox. The Anaconda-Pintler Wilderness begins less than a mile to the west of the falls and offers additional hiking opportunities. Mosquito repellent is a must in the summer.

See map on p. 237.
Stream: Pintler Creek
Height: 20 feet
Distance: 0.5 mile out and back
Elevation gain: 5 feet
Difficulty: Easy
Trail surface: Dirt and rock
Hiking time: 15-20 minutes
Canine compatibility: Dogs are allowed
Seasons: May to Oct
County: Deerlodge
Land status: National forest

Fees and permits: No fees required
Trail contact: Beaverhead-Deerlodge National Forest, 420 Barrett St., Dillon, MT 59725-3572; (406) 683-3900; fs.usda.gov/bdnf
Maps: *DeLorme Atlas and Gazetteer Montana* Page 69, F8; *USGS Quad* Pintler Lake
Camping: Pintler Lake Campground is located on a side road on the left 4.2 miles up Pintler Creek Road. It has four spacious, no-fee sites near the lake. There is also a walk-in campsite near the falls.

Finding the Trailhead: From Wisdom, drive 15.0 miles north on MT 43. Turn left onto Lower North Fork Road and drive 5.1 miles. Turn right on Pintler Creek Road and drive 5.9 miles to the trailhead at the end of the road.
GPS: 45.8610, -113.4398 Elevation: 6,390 feet

The Hike

After leaving the parking area, the trail takes you to a signed T-junction. Take a left and amble on the lightly used footpath through tall lodgepole pines and Engelmann spruce. As you cross a small clearing and campsite, the trail disappears in the grass.

Look for a sign for Pintler Falls at the end of the field to locate the trail again. The forest opens and gives space to wildflower-filled clearings between the large trees. After dropping into an old-growth stand of tall timber, climb over big logs and around large boulders to make your final approach to the falls area.

The whole scene around Pintler Falls is absolutely gorgeous. Brightly colored rocks, clear pools of water, and many shades of lush green forest complement the beauty of the small but powerful waterfall. The main cascade drops about 20 feet after making a 50-foot diagonal slide down a smooth face of granite. Mist rises above the boulders, logs, and whitewater rapids.

Pintler Falls.

Downstream from the falls there are several small pools separated from the torrent by logs. Small sandy beaches give you easy access to the water, but you might have to share the swimming holes with a small spotted frog or two. To extend your hike and access some amazing backcountry, return to the junction at the trailhead and enter the Anaconda–Pintler Wilderness via the Pintler Creek Trail.

Miles and Directions

0.0   Pintler Creek Trailhead #37

0.05 Turn left at the T-junction onto side trail to falls.

0.1   Primitive campsite

0.2   Base of Pintler Falls

      GPS: 45.8589, -113.4440 Elevation: 6,395 feet

0.5   Arrive back at the trailhead.

Flint Creek Range

The Flint Creek Range creates a mountainous barrier between Philipsburg Valley on the west and Deer Lodge Valley on the east. Mount Powell crowns the range's highest point just outside the town of Deer Lodge. The lakes and cirques are all glacially formed, and evidence of moraine stretches almost to the floor of Deer Lodge Valley. These mountains take their name from the stream that separates them from the Sapphire Mountains to the west.

Quaking aspen in the Flint Creek Range.

66 Rock Creek Falls

Rock Creek Falls is located near Rock Lake in the western portion of the Flint Creek Range. Hikers of most ability levels will enjoy the short stroll through thick lodgepole pine and mossy granite boulders, but getting to the trailhead requires a long drive on bumpy backcountry roads with a high-clearance vehicle. The falls have many sections to explore where you will certainly find beauty and solitude.

Stream: Rock Creek
Height: Upper Rock Creek Falls, 30 feet; Lower Rock Creek Falls, 20 feet
Distance: 1.6 miles out and back
Elevation gain: 170 feet
Difficulty: Easy with a moderate final approach
Trail surface: Dirt and rock
Hiking time: 30-60 minutes
Canine compatibility: Dogs are allowed
Seasons: June to Oct
County: Powell

Land status: National forest
Fees and permits: No fees required
Trail contact: Beaverhead-Deerlodge National Forest, 420 Barrett St., Dillon, MT 59725-3572; (406) 683-3900; fs.usda.gov/bdnf
Maps: *DeLorme Atlas and Gazetteer Montana* Page 70, B1; *USGS Quad* Rock Creek Lake
Camping: Dispersed camping is allowed along FR 168 before reaching the private land at Rock Lake, or you can backpack to the primitive campsite near the falls.

Finding the Trailhead: From Deer Lodge, follow Milwaukee Avenue west from downtown for 1.9 miles. Turn right on Old Stage Road, a bumpy gravel road, and drive 5.6 miles until you reach an unmarked three-way split at a cattle guard. Take the leftmost road, which heads west toward the mountains along a fence line and drive 2.3 more miles until you come to another three-way split. Take the middle road, which becomes FR 168. A high-clearance vehicle is required due to the many large rocks and ruts. Keep right at mile 2.4 when you reach Rock Lake.

At 3.9 miles you reach a group of cabins. Park your vehicle at the small area marked "Parking for Upper Lakes." Do not attempt to drive on the road beyond the parking area, as it quickly becomes impassable.

GPS: 46.4172 , -112.9571 Elevation: 5,945 feet

The Hike

Hike along the road past the group of houses. The road steepens, with large rocks forming a natural staircase. Looking back, Rock Lake reflects through the pines like a mirror. The forest is strewn with boulders and granite outcroppings, and the sound of the cascades along Rock Creek combines with the frequent calls of pine squirrels.

Continue along the rocky path to the "Keep a Clean Camp" sign. Turn left on the inconspicuous side trail and walk a few hundred feet to the creek. As you approach the edge of the canyon, you pass a primitive campsite on the left and a small pool and cascade on the right.

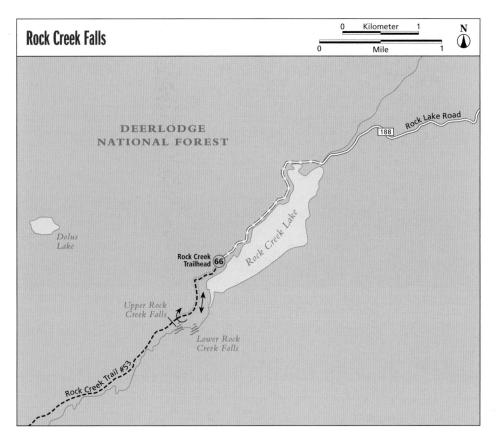

Rock Creek Falls

Follow the paths to the left downstream through the trees. After a couple of minutes you reach the base of Upper Rock Creek Falls. This gorgeous 30-foot curtain-style waterfall is the tallest portion of Rock Creek Falls. Although the hike increases in difficultly after this point, you can continue downstream a few more minutes to reach the base of 20-foot Lower Rock Creek Falls. These are the main two waterfalls, but you can explore the creek for hours and find many secluded cascades with clean and clear pools.

Miles and Directions

0.0 Rock Creek Trailhead #53. Walk past residences.

0.1 End of Rock Creek Road. Keep walking forward up the old roadbed.

0.6 Turn left on faint side trail.
  GPS: 46.4109, -112.9637 Elevation: 6,115 feet

0.7 Head downstream from primitive campsite.

0.7 Base of Upper Rock Creek Falls
  GPS: 46.4101, -112.9628 Elevation: 6,050 feet

Rock Creek Falls.

0.8 Base of Lower Rock Creek Falls

GPS: 46.4102, -112.9616 Elevation: 6,030 feet

1.6 Arrive back at the trailhead.

67 Lost Creek Falls

Lost Creek Falls is located in Lost Creek State Park in the Flint Creek Mountains near Anaconda. A short, paved trail leads to the base of the falls and is accessible by wheelchair. The 50-foot waterfall cascades diagonally over a ledge in a gorgeous natural setting of mixed forest, smooth granite boulders, and limestone cliff walls. To fully appreciate the beauty of this canyon, extend your hike along Lost Creek Trail into beautiful country with abundant wildlife and fantastic views.

Stream: Lost Creek
Height: 50 feet
Distance: 0.1 mile out and back
Elevation gain: 50 feet
Difficulty: Wheelchair accessible
Trail surface: Asphalt
Hiking time: 5–10 minutes
Canine compatibility: Dogs are allowed
Seasons: May to Nov
County: Deer Lodge County
Land status: State park

Fees and permits: Entrance to state parks is free for Montana resident vehicles, but nonresident vehicles have to pay a fee.
Trail contact: Lost Creek State Park, Montana Fish, Wildlife and Parks, PO Box 489, Whitehall, MT 59759; (406) 287-3541; stateparks.mt.gov/lost-creek/
Maps: *DeLorme Atlas and Gazetteer Montana* Page 69, C10; *USGS Quad* West Valley
Camping: Lost Creek Campground has twenty-five sites dispersed along the road and throughout the loop at the end the road. Check for current prices at stateparks.mt.gov/fees/.

Finding the Trailhead: From Anaconda, drive east on MT 1 for 2.8 miles until you reach the junction with MT 48 on the left. Take MT 48 for only 0.2 mile, then merge left onto MT 273, Galen Road. Drive north on MT 273 for 1.9 miles. Turn left on Lost Creek Road and drive 7.3 miles to the trailhead at the end of the campground loop.
GPS: 46.2096, -113.0043 Elevation: 6,120 feet

The Hike

The very short, paved path takes you into lush forest of aspen, lodgepole pine, Douglas fir, Engelmann spruce, and willow to a lookout of the cascade. Lost Creek Falls begins as a vertical drop and then pours at an angle over the rocks of the snake-grass-lined creek. The medium-sized stream swells during spring runoff to offer a more intense display of force. Skilled hikers can scramble around the undeveloped paths winding through the willows and up to the top of the falls. If you come during the weekend at peak season, be prepared to share the small viewing area with a steady flow of visitors.

To take a more significant hike while visiting the area, follow an old abandoned mining road that leaves the campground at its north end and becomes Lost Creek Trail. It takes you along Lost Creek and into some spectacular country with great views of the 3,000-foot-deep canyon. You might encounter a moose along the marshy

Lost Creek Falls.

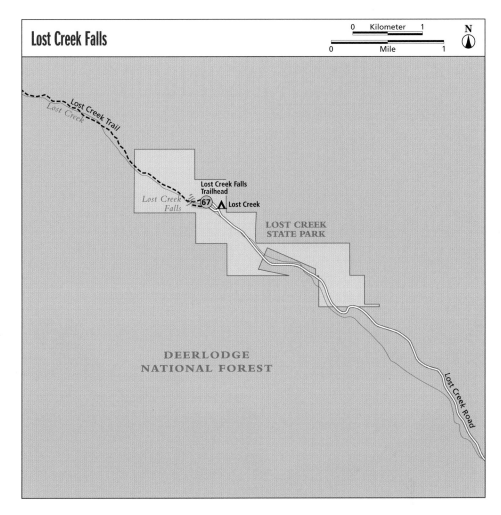

creek bottom or spot bighorn sheep or mountain goats where the steep rocky terrain meets the grassy slopes.

Miles and Directions

0.0 Lost Creek Falls Trailhead

0.05 Base of Lost Creek Falls

GPS: 46.2096, -113.0050 Elevation: 6,170 feet

0.1 Arrive back at the trailhead.

Elkhorn Mountains

The Elkhorn Mountains are a relatively small mountain range that lies immediately south of the state capital, Helena. They contain a large roadless portion and support a sizable herd of elk. The Elkhorns are of medium height and are characterized by open parks and coniferous forests. Crow Peak is the highest in the range, topping out at 9,415 feet.

Meadows in the Elkhorn Mountains.

68 Crow Creek Falls

The rewarding drive to the trailhead takes you from open prairie to deep forests of fir and juniper in the Elkhorn Mountains. Crow Creek Trail is mostly level and leads you through forests and meadows to the foot of Crow Creek Falls. The waterfall plummets for 40 feet over a steep rugged cliff. Wading is certainly possible, but the vigorous whirlpool may be too dangerous for swimming. Both backpackers and day-hikers will enjoy this satisfying trek.

Stream: Crow Creek
Height: 40 feet
Distance: 5.0 miles out and back
Elevation gain: 235 feet
Difficulty: Easy except for a few steep climbs
Trail surface: Dirt and rock
Hiking time: 3-4 hours
Canine compatibility: Dogs are allowed
Seasons: May 15 to Nov
County: Jefferson

Land status: National forest
Fees and permits: No fees required
Trail contact: Helena National Forest, 2880 Skyway Drive, Helena, MT 59602; (406) 449-5201; fs.usda.gov/helena/
Maps: *DeLorme Atlas and Gazetteer Montana* Page 71, B7; *USGS Quad* Crow Creek Falls
Camping: Primitive campsites are located at the trailhead and downstream from the falls area.

Finding the Trailhead: From Townsend, take US 287 south from Broadway and drive 10.9 miles. After crossing the bridge over the Missouri River, turn right (west) on MT 285. Drive 9.5 miles to Radersburg and keep driving straight on what becomes Crow Creek Road. At 15.1 miles from Radersburg, you reach a sign for Trailhead #109. Turn right here and drive a few hundred feet to the start of the trail.
GPS: 46.3215, -111.7627 Elevation: 5,515 feet

The Hike

The hike begins by dropping 200 feet along switchbacks. Before reaching the creek, you pass a junction with Hall Creek Trail on the left. Keep right and cross a bridge over Hall Creek at its confluence with Crow Creek. The trail follows the stream until crossing a bridge to the north side, where the terrain becomes rocky. You proceed to pass through forests of juniper and Douglas fir and climb to a view above the winding creek. The trail suddenly curves north and makes a steep climb to the top of a ridge.

A large meadow with tall grass and sagebrush makes a good midway resting spot in the shade of the firs. Songbirds echo throughout the area and you might see a mule deer or an elk emerge at the forest edges at dawn or dusk.

Keep left on Crow Creek Trail at the junction with Long Park Trail. Follow the creek for a while and then head up a slope through thick forests with periodic meadows abounding with geraniums and lupines in early summer. When Falls Creek Trail merges on the right, keep left and hike up over a hill and into a wooded ravine. After

Crow Creek Falls.

crossing a small stream, you reach the edge of a gorge where the trail splits. Head left on the trail that winds and zigzags down the steep slope toward the sound of rushing water. You pass a couple of primitive campsites along the stream just below the falls.

At the base of the impressive cascade, cross a big log in the creek to obtain the best view from the other side. Crow Creek Falls tumbles over a curved precipice rounded by water over time. The cascade pours down an almost vertical slide until splashing forcefully into a dark-green, bubbling pool.

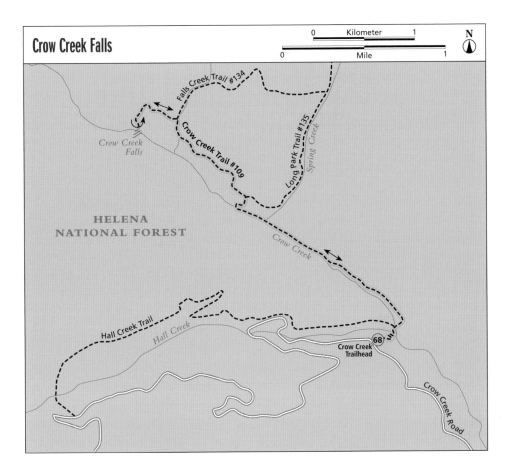

Crow Creek Falls

Falls Creek Trail #134

Crow Creek Trail #109

Long Park Trail #135

Spring Creek

Crow Creek Falls

HELENA
NATIONAL FOREST

Crow Creek

Hall Creek Trail

Hall Creek

Crow Creek
Trailhead

68

Crow Creek Road

Miles and Directions

0.0 Crow Creek Trailhead #109

0.2 Keep right on Crow Creek Trail at the junction with Hall Creek Trail.

0.4 Cross footbridge over Hall Creek where it enters Crow Creek.

1.2 Keep left on Crow Creek Trail at the junction with Long Park Trail #135.

2.0 Keep left on Crow Creek Trail at the junction with Falls Creek Trail #134.

2.4 Turn left onto side trail to falls.

2.5 Primitive campsites

2.5 Base of Crow Creek Falls
GPS: 46.3386, -111.7921 Elevation: 5,750 feet

5.0 Arrive back at the trailhead.

Rocky Mountain Front

The Rocky Mountain Front is one of the wilderness ranges in Montana, best known for its great relief. From the prairies to the east to the pointed summits and towering limestone walls to the west, the range ascends more than 4,500 feet. It supports a wealth of wildlife including a large herd of native bighorn sheep and a good population of grizzly bears that occasionally still venture east into the willow swamps and rolling grasslands as they once did. Subranges in the Rocky Mountain Front include the Sawtooth Range and the Teton Range.

Rocky Mountain Front viewed from the prairie. Photo by Martha Gunsalam.

69 Dearborn River Cascades

Dearborn River Cascades is a unique water formation that's certainly worth a visit. After tumbling rapidly over rock terraces, a large amount of water compacts and flows between slabs of rock. The river enters a gorge that's almost narrow enough to jump across. The Dearborn River Trail offers diverse terrain and splendid views. You have the option of a short hike to the falls or a longer trek into the Scapegoat Wilderness.

Stream: Dearborn River
Height: 20 feet
Distance: 4.6 miles out and back
Elevation gain: 155 feet
Difficulty: Easy to moderate
Trail surface: Dirt and rock
Hiking time: 3–5 hours
Canine compatibility: Dogs are allowed
Seasons: Apr to Nov
County: Lewis and Clark

Land status: National forest
Fees and permits: No fees required
Trail contact: Lewis and Clark National Forest, 101 15th St. N., Great Falls, MT 59401; (406) 791-7700; fs.usda.gov/lcnf/
Maps: *DeLorme Atlas and Gazetteer Montana* Page 40, B3; *USGS Quad* Steamboat Mountain
Camping: There is a backcountry campsite 0.3 mile up the trail from Dearborn River Cascades.

Finding the Trailhead: From Augusta, drive southwest on County Road 435 for 15.8 miles. Turn right (west) on Dearborn Canyon Road and drive 6.2 miles to the trailhead. The drive takes you from grassy prairie to a forested canyon below the massive peaks of the Rocky Mountain Front. **GPS:** 47.2702, -112.5162 Elevation: 5,120 feet

The Hike

The first mile of the hike goes through a stretch of cabins on private land. The path parallels the left side of a dirt road until it reaches a bridge at the last cabin. At this point you leave the signs of civilization behind and follow an abandoned road across the river. Climb steadily up the north slope through a scrub forest of juniper, whitebark pine, aspen, and fir. After a long switchback, you reach the top for a spectacular view. Twin Buttes stand at over 7,000 feet, and giant bands of rock emerge from the forested slopes.

The trail then takes you downhill to the edge of a cliff overlooking the Dearborn River. Follow the precipice for a half mile until you hear the sound of raging water. Find an inconspicuous path and descend to the bottom of the gorge. Below the forceful cascade there is a beautiful backdrop of Skull Gulch up the canyon. The deep pool below the 20-foot falls is excellent for swimming. If you want to continue up the trail, there are more water formations in Devil's Glen, as well as campsites for backpackers.

Dearborn River Cascades.

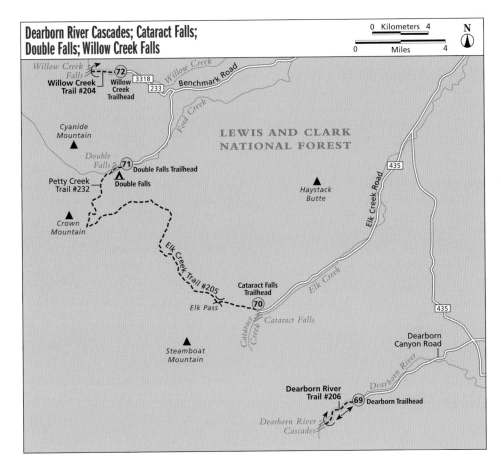

Miles and Directions

0.0   Dearborn Trailhead #206

1.0   Bridge across Dearborn River at end of private land

1.6   Trail reaches high point with marvelous view.

2.3   Turn left on small path and climb down for 200 feet to the falls.
     GPS: 47.2570, -112.5441 Elevation: 4,975 feet

2.3   Dearborn River Cascades
     GPS: 47.2567, -112.5442 Elevation: 4,965 feet

4.6   Arrive back at the trailhead.

70 Cataract Falls

Cataract Falls is an excellent camping and hiking destination in a remote area of the Rocky Mountain Front. At the beginning of the short stroll, be prepared for a challenging creek crossing. The elegant cascade tumbles 90 feet down a cliff, feathering into multiple channels. The area is especially beautiful in the fall when the aspen and cottonwood leaves turn yellow and orange.

See map on p. 255.
Stream: Cataract Creek
Height: 90 feet
Distance: 0.4 mile out and back
Elevation gain: 25 feet
Difficulty: Easy
Trail surface: Dirt and rock
Hiking time: 20 minutes
Canine compatibility: Dogs are allowed
Seasons: May to Oct

County: Lewis and Clark
Land status: National forest
Fees and permits: No fees required
Trail contact: Lewis and Clark National Forest, 101 15th St. N., Great Falls, MT 59401; (406) 791-7700; fs.usda.gov/lcnf/
Maps: *DeLorme Atlas and Gazetteer Montana* Page 56, A3; *USGS Quad* Steamboat Mountain
Camping: There is a no-fee campsite at the trailhead.

Finding the Trailhead: From Augusta, drive southwest for 6.9 miles on paved County Road 435. Turn right on Elk Creek Road and drive 10.2 miles to the trailhead at the end of the road. **GPS:** 47.3242, -112.6030 Elevation: 5,110 feet

The Hike

The trailhead is located where Horse Creek and Cataract Creek both enter Elk Creek. What would normally be an easy hike does have one significant obstacle: crossing medium-sized Elk Creek. Depending on the height of the water, you may choose to wade, find a log to cross upstream, or step across the large stones. Once you get across, the wide trail leads you around a curve to the left through tall Douglas fir.

Cross Cataract Creek over some logs and climb around a corner to the sound of the falls. Some planks take you back across the stream to a viewpoint at the end of the trail. Cataract Creek plunges for 90 feet over a cliff outcropping made of layered folds of sedimentary rock. A small, sparkling pool at the base invites you to take a cool dip on a hot day. If you're interested in a longer hike, Elk Creek Trail #205 also starts at the trailhead and climbs to Elk Pass and beyond.

Cataract Falls.

Miles and Directions

0.0 Cataract Falls Trailhead

0.2 Base of Cataract Falls

      GPS: 47.3220, -112.6037 Elevation: 5,135 feet

0.4 Arrive back at the trailhead.

71 Double Falls

Double Falls is a fabulous destination for hiking and camping in a cool, mossy forest of the southern Sawtooth Range. The easy hike to the falls reveals two dramatic descents of whitewater making a 30-foot total drop. It's a long haul on good gravel roads to reach the trailhead, but the transitioning landscapes in the Rocky Mountain Front are outstanding, and you have a chance of seeing a diversity of wildlife. A trip to Double Falls also puts you at the doorstep of the Bob Marshall Wilderness Complex, with its numerous hiking opportunities.

See map on p. 255.
Stream: Ford Creek
Height: 30 feet
Distance: 0.2 mile out and back
Elevation gain: 30 feet
Difficulty: Easy
Trail surface: Dirt and rock
Hiking time: 10 minutes
Canine compatibility: Dogs are allowed
Seasons: May to Oct

County: Lewis and Clark
Land status: National forest
Fees and permits: No fees required
Trail contact: Lewis and Clark National Forest, 101 15th St. N., Great Falls, MT 59401; (406) 791-7700; fs.usda.gov/lcnf/
Maps: *DeLorme Atlas and Gazetteer Montana* Page 40, F2; *USGS Quad* Double Falls
Camping: Double Falls Campground has three no-fee campsites.

Finding the Trailhead: From Augusta, drive south on County Road 435 and turn right at the sign for Benchmark. Follow Benchmark Road for 14.6 miles until you arrive at a junction. Turn left onto FR 235 following the signs to Benchmark and Wood Lake Campgrounds and drive 4.8 miles. Turn left on FR 236 following the signs to Double Falls Campground. The short but steep road down to the campground is in bad condition and a high-clearance vehicle is recommended. **GPS:** 47.40717, -112.7223 Elevation: 5,265 feet

The Hike

Even though the hike to the foot of the waterfall is very short, grab your bear spray just in case. You are in prime grizzly bear country and need to take precautions. There were huge tracks on the hill above the falls on a visit in late March.

Find the rugged path at the west end of the campground leading upstream. After a short stroll through the trees, you approach the base of Double Falls. A tall stand of spruce and fir surrounds the cascade and green moss brightens the logs and boulders strewn across the forest floor. Use a log to cross the creek for an even better view. If you want to extend your hike up the nearby Crown Mountain, Petty Creek Trail #232 leaves the campground across the stream to the south.

Double Falls. Photo by Martha Gunsalam.

Miles and Directions

0.0   Double Falls Trailhead

0.1   Base of Double Falls
GPS: 47.4070, -112.7237 Elevation: 5,295 feet

0.2   Arrive back at the trailhead.

72 Willow Creek Falls

The diversity of landscape and habitat on this short hike is matched only by the diversity of wildlife. You could encounter everything from pronghorn to mountain goats, to moose and grizzly bears. Only the American bison is sadly missing from this magical place where peak meets prairie. Willow Creek Falls is a seldom-visited beauty accessible by way of a lightly used trail that's sometimes hard to follow. There are several different cascades of varying style and size that cut through a rocky ravine below the imposing peaks of the Sawtooth Range.

See map on p. 255.
Stream: Willow Creek
Height: Lower falls, 80 feet; middle falls, 40 feet; upper falls, 15 feet
Distance: 3.2 miles out and back
Elevation gain: 650 feet
Difficulty: Moderate
Trail surface: Dirt and rock
Hiking time: 2-3 hours
Canine compatibility: Dogs are allowed
Seasons: May to Oct
County: Lewis and Clark

Land status: National forest
Fees and permits: No fees required
Trail contact: Lewis and Clark National Forest, 101 15th St. N., Great Falls, MT 59401; (406) 791-7700; fs.usda.gov/lcnf/
Maps: *DeLorme Atlas and Gazetteer Montana* Page 40, F2; *USGS Quad* Double Falls
Camping: There is dispersed camping on road #3318 to the trailhead, and the nearby Double Falls Campground, located a few miles farther up Benchmark Road, has three no-fee campsites.

Finding the Trailhead: From Augusta, drive south on County Road 435 and turn right at the sign for Benchmark. Follow good gravel Benchmark Road for 14.6 miles to a junction at the foot of the Rockies. Turn right on Beaver-Willow Road #233 and drive 1.2 miles. Take a left on FR 3318, marked "Willow Creek Administrative Site," and drive 1.7 miles. A high-clearance vehicle is recommended on this final road. Park your vehicle at the gate at the end of the road.
GPS: 47.4625, -112.7247 Elevation: 5,340 feet

The Hike

Tall, jagged peaks of the Sawtooth Range welcome you as you begin the hike in lush, green grassland at the foot of the Rocky Mountain Front. After two gates and an easy creek crossing, you pass a few Forest Service cabins and climb to a grassy bluff above the aspen- and cottonwood-forested drainage. Follow an open extension of the prairie through fields of lupine, wild iris, arrowleaf balsamroot, wild rose, and other colorful wildflowers until you are enveloped in a small but thick grove of young aspen.

You approach the limestone headwall that wraps around Willow Creek on the lower flanks of the 8,345-foot Fairview Mountain. Douglas fir and whitebark pine begin to close around you, and you finally leave the grasslands behind. A short distance later, the trail climbs onto the north headwall and curves up the rugged canyon,

Willow Creek Falls.

clinging to the sheer cliffs. Watch for bighorn sheep and mountain goats in this area, but especially watch your footing as you scamper along the harrowing path high up on the wall.

Thankfully, you soon begin to skirt a much less inclined slope and are rewarded with the first glimpse of Willow Creek Falls in the canyon ahead of you. As you come around the bend you realize you were only seeing the much smaller upper portion of the waterfall. Willow Creek plummets about 80 feet in a lower section and about 40 feet in a middle section. The gorgeous landscape of the Sawtooths creates an amazing backdrop to the scene. Continue walking to a closer view of the middle falls as it splashes into a large pool. If you're willing to scramble down the boulders to the bottom of the ravine, you could potentially enjoy a refreshing dip here.

Just a short distance farther you come to a third waterfall. This one is only 15 feet tall, but it is remarkably beautiful. A rough side trail takes you right up to the curtain of gently falling water that pours into a little pool. More awesome country lies ahead of you if you wish to journey deeper into the mountains toward the Fairview Plateau. On the way back to the trailhead, you'll certainly admire cone-shaped Haystack Butte, which rises abruptly to the east.

Upper Willow Creek Falls.

Miles and Directions

0.0 Willow Creek Trailhead #204

0.1 Cross the second gate.

0.2 Ford Willow Creek.

1.3 View of Lower and Middle Willow Creek Falls
GPS: 47.4639, -112.7477 Elevation: 5,960 feet

1.6 Base of Upper Willow Creek Falls
GPS: 47.4638, -112.7518 Elevation: 5,990 feet

3.2 Arrive back at the trailhead.

73 Mill Falls

Mill Falls is a great place for families looking for a shady place to camp adjacent to a lovely waterfall. The drive into South Fork Teton Canyon shows you a diverse display of changing vegetation and geological features. You leave the treeless prairie and pass below huge cliffs of the Sawtooth Range rising on both sides. Use binoculars to try to spot mountain goats clinging to these sheer faces. When you reach Mill Falls Campground, you're at the doorstep of the Bob Marshall Wilderness, with splendid peaks looming before you. The short walk to Mill Falls passes through dense timber to a hidden cliff outcropping where the small creek makes a vertical drop into shimmering pools.

Stream: Mill Creek
Height: 70 feet
Distance: 0.2 mile out and back
Elevation gain: 30 feet
Difficulty: Very easy
Trail surface: Dirt and rock
Hiking time: 10–15 minutes
Seasons: May to Oct
Canine compatibility: Dogs are allowed
County: Teton

Land status: National forest
Fees and permits: No fees required
Trail contact: Lewis and Clark National Forest, 101 15th St. N., Great Falls, MT 59401; (406)-791-7700; fs.usda.gov/lcnf/
Maps: *DeLorme Atlas and Gazetteer Montana* Page 40, F2; *USGS Quad* Our Lake
Camping: Mill Falls Campground is a no-fee camping area with four sites.

Finding the Trailhead: From Choteau, drive north along US 89 for 5.5 miles. Turn left toward the mountains on Teton Canyon Road, which is marked with signs for Teton Pass Ski Area. Drive 12 miles on this good, paved road. Turn left at the turnoff for Bellview Cutacross Rd. Drive south on this gravel road for 0.4 mile, crossing a bridge over the Teton River. Turn right on South Fork Teton Road #109, marked with a sign for Ear Mountain Outstanding Natural Area. Drive along South Fork Teton Road for 8.7 miles. Turn right up a narrow road when you reach a sign for Mill Falls Campground. Find the trail at the end of the road.
GPS: 47.8589, -112.7736 Elevation: 5,680 feet

The Hike

It's a quick jaunt of only a few hundred feet to the falls. The thick, tall spruce and fir make it hard to get good glimpses of surrounding peaks to the west. The trail follows the stream to a steep cliff in the middle of the dense forest where Mill Creek makes a sudden, free-fall drop for 70 feet in the shape of a horsetail. Wooden planks lead to the other side, where you approach pools at the base of a mossy wall of rock.

To extend the hike, there are numerous trails nearby leading into the Bob Marshall Wilderness, including Trail #164 to Headquarter Pass.

Mill Falls.

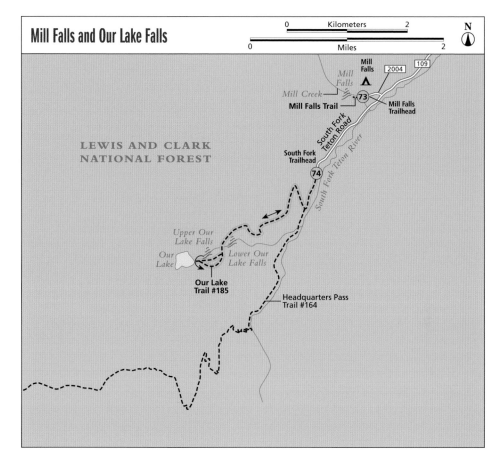

Mill Falls and Our Lake Falls

0   Kilometers   2

0   Miles   2

N

Mill Falls

Mill Falls

2004

109

Mill Creek

Mill Falls Trail

73

Mill Falls Trailhead

LEWIS AND CLARK
NATIONAL FOREST

South Fork Trailhead

South Fork Teton Road

South Fork Teton River

74

Upper Our Lake Falls

Our Lake

Lower Our Lake Falls

Our Lake Trail #185

Headquarters Pass Trail #164

Miles and Directions

0.0   Mill Falls Trailhead

0.1   Base of Mill Falls

      GPS: 47.8587, -112.7749 Elevation: 5,715 feet

0.2   Arrive back at the trailhead.

74 Our Lake Falls

Located in the Sawtooth Mountains of the Rocky Mountain Front, Our Lake is a popular destination for families, day-hikers, and backpackers. On the way to the lake, you pass two tall waterfalls that pour gracefully out of the mountains.

The steady climb to the lake basin is a good workout with excellent views. Wildlife like deer, songbirds, and mountain goats is abundant, and a vast array of wildflowers decorates the pristine landscape in the summer.

See map on p. 265.
Stream: Our Lake Creek
Height: Lower falls, about 200 feet; upper falls, about 100 feet
Distance: 5.5 miles out and back
Elevation gain: 1,435 feet
Difficulty: Moderate to difficult
Trail surface: Dirt and rock
Hiking time: 3–5 hours
Seasons: June to Oct
Canine compatibility: Dogs are allowed

County: Teton
Land status: National forest
Fees and permits: No fees required
Trail contact: Lewis and Clark National Forest, 101 15th St. N., Great Falls, MT 59401; (406) 791-7700; fs.usda.gov/lcnf/
Maps: *DeLorme Atlas and Gazetteer Montana* Page 40, F2; *USGS Quad* Our Lake
Camping: Mill Falls Campground, located a mile before the trailhead, is a no-fee camping area with four sites.

Finding the Trailhead: From Choteau, drive north along US 89 for 5.5 miles. Turn left toward the mountains on Teton Canyon Road, which is marked with signs for Teton Pass Ski Area. Drive 12 miles on this good, paved road. Turn left at the turnoff for Bellview Cutacross Road. Drive south on this gravel road for 0.4 mile, crossing a bridge over the Teton River. Turn right on South Fork Teton Road #109, marked with a sign for Ear Mountain Outstanding Natural Area. Drive along South Fork Teton Road for 9.8 miles to the trailhead at the end of the road.
GPS: 47.8475 , -112.7825 Elevation: 5,830 feet

The Hike

Follow Headquarters Pass Trail #164 until you reach a trail junction after a third of a mile. Turn right onto Our Lake Trail #185 and begin to ascend moderately along switchbacks through cool forests of fir and pine. After about a mile of hiking, you gain views to the south of the 9,390-foot Rocky Mountain, the tallest peak in the Bob Marshall Wilderness.

You enter a windswept talus area favored by whitebark pines. Looking up toward the lake basin, you soon come to the first views of two prominent waterfalls. The lower falls plunges vertically out of a glade of alpine spruce and then slides another 100 feet to the base of the ravine. The upper falls cascades steeply out of the outlet area of the lake. You can scramble down a steep wooded area for a better view of the lower waterfall from deeper in the gorge. In its entirety, it falls for about 200 feet

Our Lake Falls.

down a colorful cliff face. A dangerous spur trail leads to the top, but it's best avoided since it doesn't offer a view.

Keep walking a short distance up the trail to a campsite in a sunny location within view of the upper waterfall. Cross the small stream and enter some shady woods. The trail soon leads to a spectacular view from the base of Upper Our Lake Falls. Shimmering whitewater feathers its way down a rock face formed by stacks of exposed sediment. Climb the final switchbacks to alpine heaven at Our Lake, where you'll gaze at the gorgeous, sparkling waters and immense peaks. Watch for mountain goats scaling the rocky crags and ridges.

Our Lake.

Miles and Directions

0.0 South Fork Teton Trailhead

0.3 Turn right at junction with Our Lake Trail #185.
    GPS: 47.8434, -112.7854 Elevation: 5,845 feet

1.7 First view of both Upper and Lower Our Lake Falls
    GPS: 47.8404, -112.7985 Elevation: 6,685 feet

1.9 Campsite and pit toilet

2.1 Base of Upper Our Lake Falls
    GPS: 47.8363, -112.8064 Elevation: 6,860 feet

2.7 Our Lake
    GPS: 47.8357, -112.8084 Elevation: 7,265 feet

5.5 Arrive back at the trailhead.

75 Muddy Creek Falls

The hike to Muddy Creek Falls offers dramatic mountain scenery, the chance to see wildlife, and the rare opportunity to explore a slot canyon in Montana. The graceful waterfall inside the cool gorge is a great place to beat the heat on a summer day. Bring sturdy hiking shoes for this scramble along the dry, rocky riverbed of Muddy Creek. Most of the stream flows underground except at the end where you meet the falls.

Stream: Muddy Creek
Height: 40 feet
Distance: 5.0 miles out and back
Elevation gain: 490 feet
Difficulty: Moderate
Trail surface: Mostly rock
Hiking time: 3-4 hours
Canine compatibility: Dogs are allowed
Seasons: May 15 to Dec 15
County: Teton

Land status: Wildlife management area and national forest
Fees and permits: No permits required
Trail contact: Lewis and Clark National Forest, 101 15th St. N., Great Falls, MT 59401; (406) 791-7700; fs.usda.gov/lcnf/
Maps: *DeLorme Atlas and Gazetteer Montana* Page 40, B2; *USGS Quad* Cave Mountain
Camping: There are a few dispersed camping sites before reaching the trailhead, but there is no water.

Finding the Trailhead: Drive to Bynum, which is 12 miles north of Choteau on US 89. Just south of the old grocery store, turn west onto Central Ave. Drive two blocks and turn right onto 3rd Street N, passing in front of the historic schoolhouse. The gravel road becomes Blackleaf Road, #145. After 13.5 miles, turn left at the junction to stay on Blackleaf Road. After one more mile, turn left onto Knowlton Road. Drive 1.3 miles and then turn right onto Blackleaf Cutacross Road. After less than a half mile, take a right onto a narrow unmarked road, entering Blackleaf Wildlife Management Area. Continue ahead through a gate and then for a final 2.8 miles to the trailhead at the end of the road.
GPS: 47.9911, -112.6639, Elevation: 4,990 feet

The Hike

Near the signs at the trailhead, follow the scant trail that curves toward the steep cliffs of Muddy Creek canyon. It becomes a gravel two-track and follows the dry braided stream channels. You walk across a flat alluvial fan covered with stunted whitebark pine, cottonwood, and aspen forest. The wind plays a role in causing the dwarfed trees along the foothills of the Front Range. The views west toward Mt. Wright display forested slopes and tall walls of rock. The dramatic scenery is easy to appreciate while walking through the semi-open scrub forest.

The path disappears and you find yourself following the dry bed of the subsurface stream. Occasionally you can pick up a faint path to follow on the north side of the creek bed. After almost 2 miles you reach the flowing water of the small creek, and

Muddy Creek Falls. Photo by Martha Gunsalam.

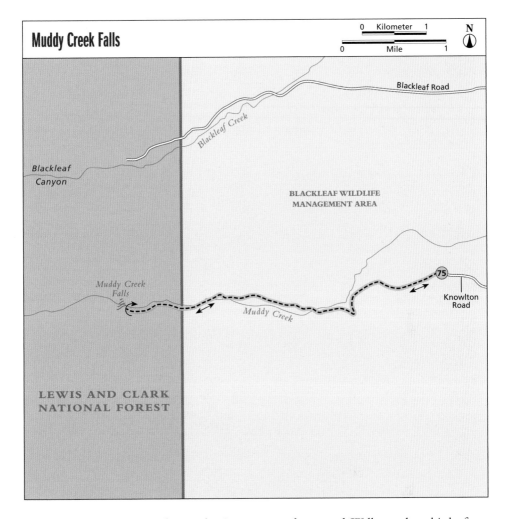

it is interesting to see where it begins to go underground. Walk another third of a mile to reach the end of the trees and the entrance to the slot canyon. The bottom of the canyon sees little sunlight and there is often thick icepack to walk on in the early season.

Stroll a quarter mile through the gorge to the base of Muddy Creek Falls where the cliff walls converge. There is a large boulder wedged in between the rocks that at some point had fallen from the ridge above. The water comes down a steep chute and lands in a large pool. Please note that the trail was closed in 2020 because of a grizzly bear that charged at visitors as it defended a moose carcass inside the canyon. Carry bear spray and obey closures to give grizzlies and other wildlife the protection they need.

Miles and Directions

0.0 Muddy Creek Falls Trailhead

1.9 Creek starts

2.2 Enter slot canyon

2.5 Base of Muddy Creek Falls

      GPS: 47.9907, -112.7094 Elevation: 5,480 feet

5.0 Return to trailhead.

Upper Missouri River Basin

The Missouri River passes through a land of scattered buttes and rolling hills of prairie. East of the city of Great Falls, the river enters a ravine and spills over a series of large waterfalls within a 10-mile area. Four out of five of the falls have been dammed for power production, giving Great Falls its nickname the Electric City. The River's Edge trail system offers access to scenic river gorge terrain.

Prairie and ravines along the Missouri River.

76 Rainbow Falls and Crooked Falls

A leisurely walk on a paved section of the River's Edge Trail takes you along the top of the gorge on the south shore of the Missouri River. Rainbow Dam diverts water away from both Rainbow Falls and Crooked Falls, so they no longer possess their original volume of water. Even though the powerhouse and power lines take away from the pristine nature of the gorge, the waterfalls and canyon are a worthwhile destination just outside Great Falls.

Stream: Missouri River
Height: Rainbow Falls, 45 feet; Crooked Falls, 20 feet
Distance: 1.4 miles out and back
Elevation loss: 85 feet
Difficulty: Easy
Trail surface: Paved trail
Hiking time: 30-60 minutes
Canine compatibility: Dogs are allowed
Seasons: Year-round
County: Cascade

Land status: State park
Fees and permits: No fees required
Trail contact: Giant Springs State Park, 4803 Giant Springs Rd., Great Falls, MT 59405; (406) 727-1212; stateparks.mt.gov/giant-springs/
Maps: *DeLorme Atlas and Gazetteer Montana* Page 58, D4; *USGS Quad* Neihart
Camping: Freezeout Lake Wildlife Management Area is located on US 89 north of Fairfield and has a no-fee camping area.

Finding the Trailhead: From Great Falls and from the 15th Street Bridge, drive east on River Drive North for 1.3 miles. Stop at the overlook to view Black Eagle Falls and its accompanying dam above. After continuing another 0.5 mile on River Drive North, turn left on Giant Springs Road, which enters Giant Springs State Park. Drive 2.5 miles to the trailhead at the Lewis and Clark Overlook.
GPS: 47.5315 , -111.2043 Elevation: 3,370 feet

The Hike

Rainbow Falls is visible as you begin the hike along the top of the gorge. Two trails head east from the Lewis and Clark Overlook. You can choose to take either the single-track trail on the left or the wide paved path on the right. As you walk along the cliff edge, you pass a variety of views of the 45-foot Rainbow Falls. Water spills over the 1,320-foot-wide Rainbow Dam and then down different sections of a brightly colored wall in the riverbed.

At the end of the paved trail you come to another overlook, perched atop the cliffs. Crooked Falls drops in multiple sections over an irregular shelf about 20 feet high. It is the only undammed waterfall in the area. Because of the curved shape of the ledge, the cascade has also been given the name Horseshoe Falls. Enjoy the wildflowers and abundant wildlife where the prairie and river gorge habitats meet.

Rainbow Falls; Crooked Falls; and Big Falls

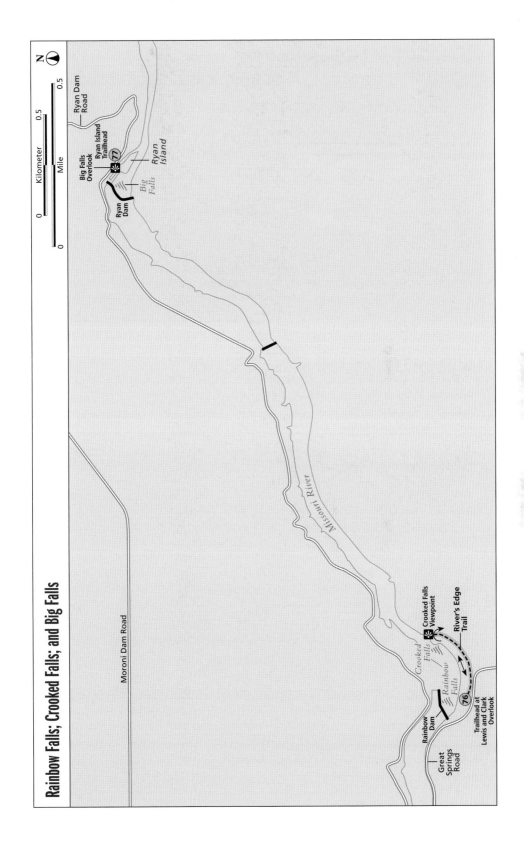

Crooked Falls.

Miles and Directions

0.0   Lewis and Clark Overlook Trailhead

0.4   Midway bench and overlook

0.7   Overlook of Crooked Falls
GPS: 47.5343 , -111.1941 Elevation: 3,285 feet

1.4   Arrive back at the trailhead.

77 Big Falls

At 90 feet high, Big Falls is the tallest of the five waterfalls known as the Great Falls of the Missouri River. Before the dam was built in 1915, it was undoubtedly one of the most dynamic waterfalls in Montana. Although the Ryan Dam and powerhouse now detract from the wildness of the location, these noble falls are still worth a visit. It's a very short stroll to the overlook on Ryan Island.

See map on p. 275.
Stream: Missouri River
Height: 90 feet
Distance: 0.3 mile out and back
Elevation loss: 5 feet
Difficulty: Easy
Trail surface: Asphalt
Hiking time: 10–20 minutes
Canine compatibility: Dogs are allowed
Seasons: May to Sep
County: Cascade

Land status: State park
Fees and permits: No fees required
Trail contact: Giant Springs State Park, 4803 Giant Springs Rd., Great Falls, MT 59405; (406) 727-1212; stateparks.mt.gov/giant-springs/
Maps: *DeLorme Atlas and Gazetteer Montana* Page 58, D4; *USGS Quad* Neihart
Camping: Freezeout Lake Wildlife Management Area is located on US 89 north of Fairfield and has a no-fee camping area.

Finding the Trailhead: From Great Falls, take US 87 north from the 15th Street Bridge and drive 3.6 miles. Turn right on Morony Dam Road and drive east for 6.9 miles. Take a right on Ryan Dam Road and drive 1.7 miles down into the gorge and to Ryan Island Trailhead at the end of the road.
GPS: 47.5688 , -111.1189 Elevation: 2,925 feet

The Hike

A wooden swinging bridge takes you across a swift channel of the Missouri River to Ryan Island. From here you follow the paved path through a shady park with tall cottonwoods and picnic tables. On both sides of the gorge, steep ravines of juniper and scrub brush provide habitat for mule deer, rabbits, and eagles. You ascend a walkway to the overlook area with spectacular vistas of the roaring waterfall. The 900-foot-wide river channel descends from the dam in multiple sections. Large numbers of birds congregate below the falls, especially seagulls, Canada geese, and swallows. This was the first of the waterfalls the Lewis and Clark Expedition found in 1805 that forced them to begin an 18-mile portage upriver.

The Great Falls Portage was one of the greatest challenges Lewis and Clark faced during their expedition in 1805. All supplies had to be hand-carried or moved in makeshift wagons for more than 18 miles in order to complete the portage around the series of large waterfalls on the Missouri River. The portage began at the confluence of the Belt River.

Big Falls.

Miles and Directions

0.0 Ryan Island Trailhead
0.1 Overlook of Big Falls
      GPS: 47.5681 , -111.1206 Elevation: 2,920 feet
0.3 Arrive back at the trailhead.

Little Belt Mountains

The Little Belt Mountains are situated to the west of the Big Belts and to the south of the city of Great Falls. The coniferous forests are home to good populations of elk, deer, and black bear. Showdown Ski Area holds the state record for snowfall in one year at 33 feet.

Belt Creek flowing in the Little Belt Mountains.

78 Memorial Falls

Memorial Falls is located only a quarter mile from US 89 in the Little Belt Mountains. A hidden canyon of quartzite cliffs rises abruptly in the coniferous forest. The trail climbs up a ravine along Memorial Creek to the base of the falls. The perfectly formed waterfall drops vertically over a ledge. This popular trail is often crowded, but the second cascade upstream receives less visitors.

Stream: Memorial Creek
Height: 20 feet
Distance: 0.6 mile out and back
Elevation gain: 125 feet to Memorial Falls;
325 feet to the second cascade
Difficulty: Easy
Trail surface: Dirt and rock
Hiking time: 20–30 minutes
Canine compatibility: Dogs are allowed
Seasons: May to Nov
County: Cascade

Land status: National forest
Fees and permits: No fees required
Trail contact: Lewis and Clark National Forest, 101 15th St. N., Great Falls, MT 59401; (406) 791-7700; fs.usda.gov/lcnf/
Maps: *DeLorme Atlas and Gazetteer Montana* Page 58, D4; *USGS Quad* Neihart
Camping: Many Pines Campground is located a few miles south on US 89 and has twenty-two sites for a fee.

Finding the Trailhead: From Great Falls, take US 89 south and drive 54.5 miles to Neihart. Drive another 1.5 miles south on US 89 and turn left at the sign for the trailhead to Memorial Falls.
GPS: 46.9132, -110.6978 Elevation: 5,870 feet

The Hike

Towering rock formations and talus slopes emerge from the thick lodgepole pine and Douglas fir forests. The trail crosses a bridge over Belt Creek and then curves left to follow Memorial Creek. High walls of Neihart quartzite welcome you into an interesting gorge. The small canyon narrows and curves left again as you make the final approach to the falls. The waterfall makes a splendid horsetail dive over a 20-foot-tall cliff. Three walls of the ravine form a box around the creek. A steep climb past the brink of Memorial Falls will lead you to another pretty cascade.

Miles and Directions

0.0 Memorial Falls Trailhead
0.2 Base of Memorial Falls
   GPS: 46.9131 , -110.6938 Elevation: 5,990 feet

Memorial Falls.

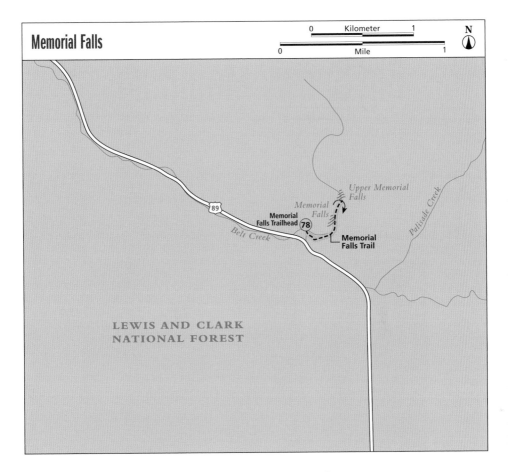

Memorial Falls

LEWIS AND CLARK
NATIONAL FOREST

0.3 Upper Memorial Falls
GPS: 46.9135, -110.6938 Elevation: 6,195 feet

0.6 Arrive back at the trailhead.

Big Snowy Mountains

The Big Snowy Mountains lie to the south of Lewistown and are considered to be one of Montana's island mountain ranges. There are numerous caves in the range, including the intriguing Ice Cave, to the south of Crystal Lake.

Dense forest along a stream in the Big Snowy Mountains.

79 Crystal Cascades

The Crystal Cascades Trail is a fun challenge, with rewarding scenery along densely forested East Fork Big Rock Creek. Be prepared with a good walking stick and sturdy footwear for crossing the stream. Sixteen thigh-deep fords each way will keep your feet wet the entire hike. However, the beauty and uniqueness of the falls magically flowing out of a cave in the mountainside make up for the obstacles along the way. Connect with a network of nearby trails to extend your hiking in the Big Snowy Mountains.

Stream: East Fork Big Rock Creek
Height: 100 feet
Distance: 5.0 miles out and back
Elevation gain: 965 feet
Difficulty: Difficult due to numerous fords
Trail surface: Dirt, rock, and streambed
Hiking time: 3-4 hours
Canine compatibility: Dogs are allowed
Seasons: Late June to Sep
County: Fergus
Land status: National forest

Fees and permits: No fees required
Trail contact: Lewis and Clark National Forest, 101 15th St. N., Great Falls, MT 59401; (406) 791-7700; fs.usda.gov/lcnf/
Maps: *DeLorme Atlas and Gazetteer Montana* Page 60, E2; *USGS Quad* Jump Off Peak
Camping: Crystal Lake Campground is located a few miles farther up Crystal Lake Road and has twenty-eight sites for a fee. There are primitive campsites along the creek near the trailhead.

Finding the Trailhead: From Lewistown, drive west on US 200 for about 10 miles. Turn left on Crystal Lake Road and drive south for 18.7 miles, following the signs for Crystal Lake Recreational Area. Turn left into the Crystal Cascades trailhead parking area.
GPS: 46.8125, -109.4957 Elevation: 5,500 feet

The Hike

The overgrown trail begins to follow East Fork Big Rock Creek closely, and in the first mile and a half, makes fifteen creek crossings. You repeatedly move from one side of the drainage to the other, passing pretty rapids and pools. Healthy forests of Douglas fir and scattered ponderosa and lodgepole pines carpet the mountains and the understory is adorned with maple, wildflowers, and lichens. After a mile, you reach a more rugged section of the gorge where the gentle stream flows down rockslides and below overhangs and mossy cliffs.

Continue following the cascading water to a fork in the stream where a tributary trickles down an adjoining rocky ravine. Cross the creek again to the south side and enjoy a pleasant climb along a wooded bench. After dropping back to the stream and making a final ford to the northeast, you arrive at a junction. To reach the falls, turn left onto Trail #445A. (You could alternatively convert this into a shuttle hike by returning to this junction after visiting the falls, heading east, and later connecting

Crystal Cascades.

with Uhlhorn Trail #493 that leads to the Ice Caves Trailhead at Crystal Lake. Leave a bike at the lake and enjoy a downhill ride back to your vehicle at Crystal Cascades Trailhead.)

After the junction, you climb a moderate slope for a half mile and then meet the creek at a breathtaking viewpoint from the base of Crystal Cascades. In multiple drops and stair-steps, water descends over 100 feet along mossy green banks. A difficult, rugged spur trail on the left takes you a short distance up the mountainside to the source of the waterfall—the creek mysteriously emerges from a spring deep inside a dark cave in the forest. Be very cautious if you choose to make the precarious climb to the top of the falls.

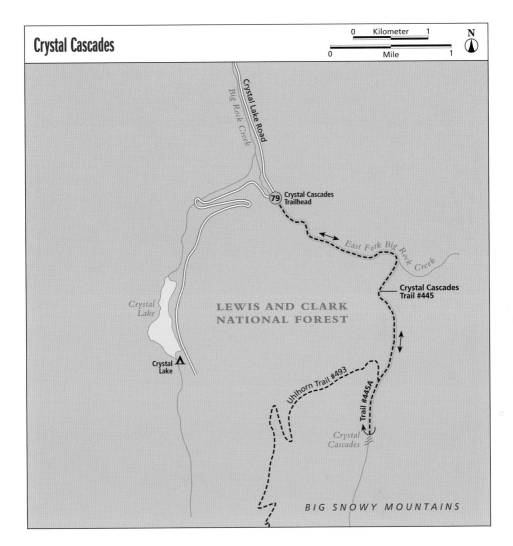

Crystal Cascades

0   Kilometer   1

0   Mile   1

N

Big Rock Creek

Crystal Lake Road

79   **Crystal Cascades Trailhead**

East Fork Big Rock Creek

Crystal Cascades Trail #445

Crystal Lake

LEWIS AND CLARK NATIONAL FOREST

Crystal Lake

Uhlhorn Trail #493

Trail #445A

Crystal Cascades

BIG SNOWY MOUNTAINS

Miles and Directions

0.0   Crystal Cascades Trailhead #445

1.8   Final creek crossing to northeast side

2.0   Turn left on Crystal Cascades Trail #445A at the junction with Trail #445 to Uhlhorn Trail #493.
GPS: 46.7934, -109.4789 Elevation: 6,185 feet

2.4   Base of Crystal Cascades
GPS: 46.7871, -109.4813 Elevation: 6,465 feet

2.5   Cave at the top of Crystal Cascades

5.0   Arrive back at the trailhead.

Spanish Peaks

The Spanish Peaks are a northern subrange of the Madison Range and are the most popular hiking destination in the range due to their closeness to Bozeman. The Lee Metcalf Wilderness offers miles of hiking trails. This group of peaks is made up of very old gneiss, and Gallatin Peak leads in height at 11,015 feet.

Spanish Peaks viewed from a mountain meadow.

80 Pioneer Falls

Pioneer Falls is located in the forested foothills of the Spanish Peaks in the Lee Metcalf Wilderness. Water crashes down for over 40 feet, putting on an impressive display. Views of Blaze Mountain and other 10,000-foot peaks will lure you along the gentle trail through scenic meadows and woods, and the visibility and pristine habitat will give you a good chance of seeing wildlife. This is a great family hike, and backpackers will love this stop on the way to lakes and summits in the area.

Stream: Falls Creek
Height: 40 feet
Distance: 6.0 miles out and back
Elevation gain: 710 feet
Difficulty: Easy
Trail surface: Dirt and rock
Hiking time: 2-3 hours
Canine compatibility: Dogs are allowed
Seasons: May to Oct
County: Madison

Land status: Wilderness area, national forest
Fees and permits: No fees are required
Trail contact: Custer Gallatin National Forest, PO Box 130, 10 East Babcock Ave., Bozeman, MT 59771; (406) 587-6701; fs.usda.gov/main/custergallatin
Maps: *DeLorme Atlas and Gazetteer Montana* Page 83, C10; *USGS Quad* Willow Swamp
Camping: There are four no-fee campsites at the trailhead.

Finding the Trailhead: From Belgrade, take Jackrabbit Lane, MT Highway 85, south from exit 298, on I-90 and drive 6.5 miles to a junction with US 191. Take US 191 south for 13.3 miles to Spanish Creek Road. Turn right and drive another 9.3 miles. There are two trailheads in the area, Little Roaring Trailhead and Spanish Creek Trailhead. Spanish Creek Trail #407 begins on the west side.
GPS: 45.4483, -111.3776 Elevation: 6,080 feet

The Hike

The trail promptly leaves the meadow area and enters open fir, spruce, and pine forest. You cross a bridge over South Fork Spanish Creek and pass a junction with Cherry Creek Trail on the right. Take a left to continue on South Fork Spanish Creek Trail. Amble gently along the willow bottoms on a wide, well-maintained trail until you arrive at a sign marking entrance to the Lee Metcalf Wilderness. The trail then passes through a meadow of tall grass and fragrant wildflowers with open views of the winding creek. As you head south through gorgeous country, rocky crags appear on the right, and ahead of you, 10,300-foot Blaze Mountain beckons in the distance. After venturing through fields of wild bergamot flowers, you enter a glade of tall, conical spruce like you might imagine in an enchanted forest.

Pass through more patches of field and forest until you come to a signed junction and a small primitive camping area. To the left, South Fork Spanish Creek Trail continues toward Mirror Lake. Take a right onto Falls Creek Trail and begin climbing

Pioneer Falls.

gradually while enjoying the aroma of sage and spruce. The trail curves west and begins climbing more steeply up a series of switchbacks along the north side of Falls Creek, a tributary to South Fork Spanish Creek. When you begin to hear the rhythm of a splashing waterfall, look for a side trail on the left of the falls. Pioneer Falls drops for 40 feet over exposed granite and colorfully polished logs. If you're a skilled hiker, it is possible to reach the base of the falls via a crack in the boulders. Use the roots and trees to help you lower yourself down. The benefits of making it to the bottom include the refreshing feeling of steady mist on your face.

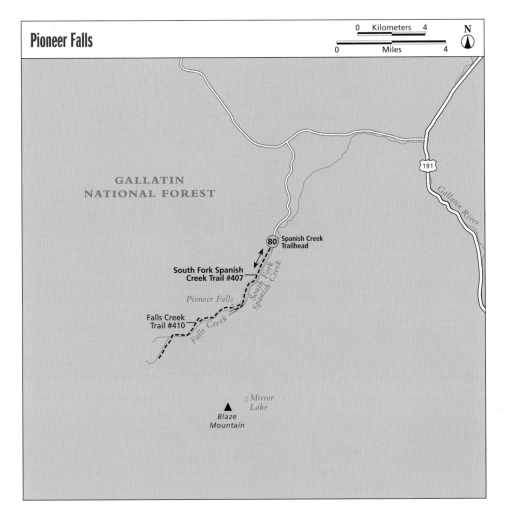

Pioneer Falls

GALLATIN
NATIONAL FOREST

Spanish Creek
Trailhead

South Fork Spanish
Creek Trail #407

Pioneer Falls

Falls Creek
Trail #410

Mirror
Lake

Blaze
Mountain

Miles and Directions

0.0   Spanish Creek Trailhead #407

0.1   Cross a bridge and turn left to stay on South Fork Spanish Creek Trail at the T-junction with Cherry Creek Trail #401.

0.5   Sign marking entrance to Lee Metcalf Wilderness

2.4   Turn right onto Falls Creek Trail #410 at Y-junction.

2.9   Turn left onto side trail to falls.

3.0   Base of Pioneer Falls
       GPS: 45.4154, -111.4074 Elevation: 6,790 feet

6.0   Arrive back at the trailhead.

Madison Range

The Madison Range's eastern flank drains into the Gallatin River, while its western streams pour into the Madison River. Ranking second in high elevation summits in the state, the range has 120 peaks that are 10,000 feet and higher. Hilgard Peak is the tallest at 11,315 feet.

Subalpine scenery in the Madison Range.

81 Ousel Falls

This relaxed walk descends into a wooded ravine and passes several smaller waterfalls en route to the 50-foot Ousel Falls. It is a good trail for families because of its easy access and scattered picnic tables along the stream. Ousel Falls, named after a common water-loving bird, is especially attractive due to its year-round accessibility. During colder months, much of the falls freezes and creates amazing spectacles to explore. The trail is located adjacent to Big Sky residential areas, making it busy most of the year.

Stream: South Fork West Fork Gallatin River
Height: 50 feet
Distance: 1.8 miles out and back
Elevation gain: 105 feet
Difficulty: Easy
Trail surface: Dirt and rock
Hiking time: 30-60 minutes
Canine compatibility: Dogs are allowed
Seasons: Year-round
County: Gallatin
Land status: National forest
Fees and permits: No fees required

Trail contact: Custer Gallatin National Forest, PO Box 130, 10 East Babcock Ave., Bozeman, MT 59771; (406) 587-6701; fs.usda.gov/main/custergallatin
Maps: *DeLorme Atlas and Gazetteer Montana* Page 83, E10; *USGS Quad* Ousel Falls
Camping: Three nearby campgrounds in Gallatin River Canyon include Swan Creek Campground, Moose Creek Flat Campground, and Greek Creek Campground. They each have about thirteen sites for a fee.

Finding the Trailhead: From Big Sky, drive to Big Sky Town Center, which is located 2.8 miles west of US 191 on MT 64. Take Ousel Falls Road south for 1.7 miles until you reach the well-marked trailhead on the left.
GPS: 45.2441, -111.3323 Elevation: 6,585 feet

The Hike

You are not far from civilization at the trailhead, and you can even see a few houses from the trail. However, it is surprising how quickly you escape the bustle of the resort town once you enter the ravine. The South Fork West Fork Gallatin River is a small river that originates near Cedar Mountain in the Madison Range. The trail drops to the bottom of the ravine and begins to follow the river upstream. After crossing the first bridge, you begin to see inviting resting spots at picnic tables along the banks. The trail comes to several small falls that pour into the river along feeder streams and form spectacular ice formations in winter.

Be sure to stay right when you pass the junction with Yellow Mule Trail. Continue past the South Fork Cascades, a series of vigorous drops on your right. After crossing the second bridge, you soon arrive at Ousel Falls. Several trails diverge to give access to different overlooks, including the base and top of the falls. The force of

Ousel Falls during spring runoff.

The American dipper, or water ouzel, is a common sight along fast-moving streams where the birds nest and feed on aquatic insects. Photo by Martha Gunsalam.

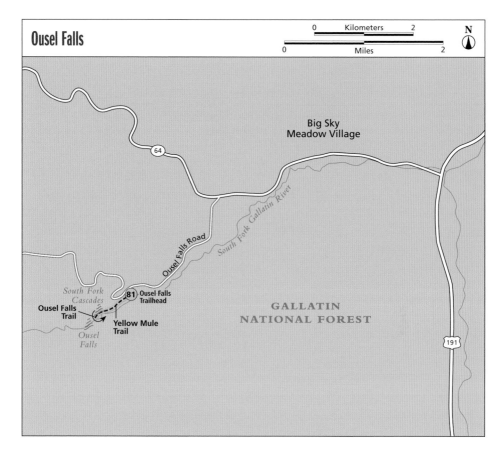

the water thunders and creates blankets of mist. Because of the wetness of the place, the surrounding rocks are covered with green moss, and the paths can be slippery. Be careful when approaching the steep drop-offs.

Miles and Directions

0.0 Ousel Falls Trailhead

0.3 First bridge

0.7 South Fork Cascades
  GPS: 45.2410, -111.3378 Elevation: 6,480 feet

0.8 Second bridge

0.9 Ousel Falls
  GPS: 45.2401, -111.3395 Elevation: 6,565 feet

1.8 Arrive back at the trailhead.

82 Cedar Falls

The hike to Cedar Falls, this guidebook's highest-elevation waterfall, is a multiday backpacking adventure into the remote alpine wilderness of Cedar Mountain. The route is well used by equestrians and hikers, so the junctions and trails are easy to follow. The trek takes you through changing landscape: forested canyons, wildflower-filled meadows, subalpine parkland, and an alpine lake basin above the tree line. Enjoy a couple of smaller waterfalls on the way up to Cedar Falls and culminate the trip at glacial Cedar Lake. Watch for an array of Rocky Mountain wildlife and be sure to practice bear-safe backcountry camping. Both black bears and grizzly bears are commonly found throughout the Madison Range.

Stream: Cedar Creek
Height: 480 feet
Distance: 23 miles out and back
Elevation gain: 3,625 feet
Difficulty: Difficult
Trail surface: Dirt and rock
Hiking time: 15-20 hours in two or three nights of backcountry camping
Canine compatibility: Dogs are allowed
Seasons: July to Oct
County: Madison

Land status: National forest, wilderness area
Fees and permits: No fees required
Trail contact: Beaverhead-Deerlodge National Forest, 420 Barrett St., Dillon, MT 59725-3572; (406) 683-3900; fs.usda.gov/bdnf/
Maps: *DeLorme Atlas and Gazetteer Montana* Page 83, E9; *USGS Quad* Fan Mountain, Lone Mountain, Lake Cameron
Camping: Valley Garden Fishing Access Site is located just north of Ennis on Jeffers Road and has several campsites for a fee.

Finding the Trailhead: From Ennis, drive south on US 287 for 0.6 mile. Turn left on Jeffers Road and drive 4.0 miles to a T-junction. Take a right on Jack Creek Road and continue on this good gravel road for 8.7 miles to the trailhead at the end of the road. Camping is not allowed at the trailhead.
GPS: 45.3472, -111.5299 Elevation: 5,885 feet

The Hike

Jack Creek Trail begins at a bridge, enters an easement of private land, and starts heading east while closely following the medium-sized stream. The well-maintained path soon crosses another bridge back to the north side of Jack Creek and then advances between the stream and steep talus slopes on the left. You consistently stay within sight of the pools and rapids of the creek as you hike the first couple of miles through forests of fir, juniper, cottonwood, spruce, and pine. At the base of some large exposed cliffs, you arrive at a junction with Jack Creek Preserve Low Pass Interpretive Trail.

Keep right to stay on Jack Creek Trail and continue below the talus to a large pack bridge and campsite near the confluence of South Fork Jack Creek.

Cedar Falls.

After climbing out of the trees, you begin a gentle ridge walk through fields of bluebell, sage, and native grasses. Lone Mountain, Cedar Mountain, and Fan Mountain stand majestically before you as you start heading south. Continue along a bench above South Fork Jack Creek, passing through more wildflower-laden meadows with fabulous panoramic views. You then ascend the mountain along a tract of previously logged forest, and after crisscrossing a couple of old logging roads, you come to a T-junction with a third logging road in an old burn area. Make a right turn and walk along the roadbed for a half mile until you merge back onto a footpath at a trail sign. A short distance later, you arrive at a ford over a medium-sized tributary and South

Fork Jack Creek. At normal water level, both streams are easy to cross over stones. Walk through a willow flat with iconic views of Lone Mountain to the east. The trail slowly reenters the pines and later approaches a scenic lookout of the creek at the rim of a wooded canyon.

After 6 miles of hiking, you pass a sign marking entrance to the Lee Metcalf Wilderness. Bear scratches on trees along the trail also announce the wildness of the area. Keep right to merge onto Cedar Meadows Trail #344 and make a steep descent to a scenic meadow with a good campsite. Just ahead, you arrive at a final junction.

Veer to the left onto Cedar Creek Trail #321 and drop down to a ford over Cedar Creek. After a few more miles of forest hiking, you reach a second ford. Downstream from this location, check out two 20-foot falls that spill into a ravine along separate forks of Cedar Creek. By way of a challenging scramble, you can reach the base area and cool off with a mountain shower under the lower falls. After exploring the twin waterfalls, continue climbing steadily through open forest, enjoying the occasional views of the approaching headwalls of Cedar Mountain.

You suddenly come to a large alpine meadow, with your first glimpse of Cedar Falls in the distance. After passing a campsite, follow the trail toward the falls through fields of lupine and aster. The 480-foot cataract flows from the outlet of Cedar Lake and gushes down the cliff face in several dramatic drops. Plumes of mist lift into the air. You can scramble through the talus to the base area, where large blocks of melting ice and snow remain until late summer. After exploring the falls, use cairns to locate the trail to the lake that winds up over the headwall just west of the waterfall. After a series of switchbacks along steep rocky terrain, you slowly enter a glacially sculpted amphitheater. Teal-colored Cedar Lake sits in a flat, treeless hanging valley covered in alpine grasses and flowers and surrounded by the impressive ring of ridges and peaks of Cedar Mountain.

Miles and Directions

0.0 Jack Creek Trailhead #317

0.3 Footbridge over Jack Creek

2.0 Keep right on Jack Creek Trail #317 at junction with Jack Creek Preserve Low Pass Interpretive Trail.
GPS: 45.3347, -111.4950 Elevation: 6,185 feet

2.4 Footbridge and campsite at confluence of South Fork Jack Creek

4.2 Turn right at the T-junction and walk south on old logging road.
GPS: 45.3110, -111.4847 Elevation: 7,040 feet

4.8 Turn right onto foot trail at trail sign.
GPS: 45.3023, -111.4880 Elevation: 7,105 feet

4.9 Cross medium-sized tributary and South Fork Jack Creek.

6.2 Pass sign marking entrance to Lee Metcalf Wilderness.

6.6 Keep right to merge onto Cedar Meadows Trail #344.
GPS: 45.2810, -111.4966 Elevation: 7,565 feet

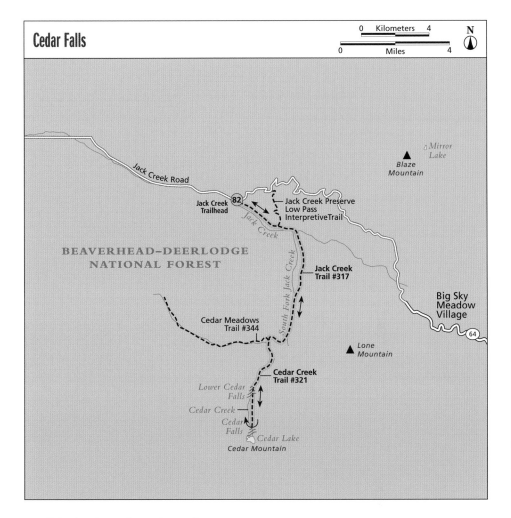

Cedar Falls

7.1 Scenic meadow and campsite

7.2 Merge to the left onto Cedar Creek Trail #321.
GPS: 45.2829, -111.5073 Elevation: 7,350 feet

9.1 Ford Cedar Creek

9.4 Base of Lower Cedar Creek Falls and ford over Cedar Creek
GPS: 45.2564, -111.5186 Elevation: 8,305 feet

9.9 First view of Cedar Creek Falls in large meadow

10.3 Campsite near falls

10.7 Base of Cedar Falls
GPS: 45.2396, -111.5174 Elevation: 8,835 feet

11.5 Cedar Lake
GPS: 45.2378, -111.5212 Elevation: 9,510 feet

23.0 Arrive back at the trailhead.

Gallatin Range

The Gallatin Range stretches from Bozeman southward into Yellowstone National Park. The Gallatin River borders its western flank and the Yellowstone River flows through Paradise Valley on its eastern edge. The range has ten volcanically carved peaks over 10,000 feet, the tallest being Yellowstone Park's Electric Peak at 10,970 feet.

Hyalite Lake in the Gallatin Range.

83 Waterfalls of Hyalite Creek

There are few hikes that offer so much to a waterfall lover. On the Hyalite Creek Trail, you visit ten waterfalls up close and finish at Hyalite Lake on a tour that feels much shorter than a 12-mile round trip. Surprises await around every corner in this rugged, forested canyon, and each cascade you pass has a distinct character. The first waterfall is accessible by wheelchair, and beyond that, the trail becomes rocky and steep in places. The portion below Champagne Falls is reachable in the late spring or even during the winter by ski or snowshoe. Some of the cascades create a popular destination for ice climbing in the frozen months. The area above Champagne Falls often remains snowbound until late June and early July. Bozeman residents love this trail, so you'll find it less crowded on a weekday or during the off-season. Backpackers can spend a night at Hyalite Lake.

Stream: Hyalite Creek and tributaries
Height: Ranging from 15 to 80 feet
Distance: 11.9 miles out and back
Elevation gain: 2,000 feet
Difficulty: Easy to Champagne Falls, moderate beyond Champagne Falls
Trail surface: Dirt and rock
Hiking time: 8–10 hours
Canine compatibility: Dogs are allowed
Seasons: Winter access up to Champagne Falls, June to Nov to Hyalite Lake
County: Gallatin

Land status: National forest
Fees and permits: No fees required
Trail contact: Custer Gallatin National Forest, PO Box 130, 10 East Babcock Ave., Bozeman, MT 59771; (406) 587-6701; fs.usda.gov/main/custergallatin
Maps: *DeLorme Atlas and Gazetteer Montana* Page 84, C3 and D3; *USGS Quad* Fridley Peak
Camping: Hood Creek Campground and Chisholm Campground are located on the reservoir about 11 miles up Hyalite Canyon Road and have thirty-eight sites for a fee.

Finding the Trailhead: From Bozeman, take 19th Ave. south from exit 305 on I-90 and drive 9.5 miles. Turn left onto Hyalite Canyon Road and drive 11.7 miles to a split in the road. Turn right, following the signs to Upper Hyalite Trailhead. Drive 2.0 miles to the trailhead at the end of the road.
GPS: 45.4474, -110.9625 Elevation: 6,875 feet

The Hike

A wide path heads south through lush forests of spruce, fir, and pine. Rugged peaks rise on both sides of Hyalite Canyon. The trail soon meets Hyalite Creek and follows it to the junction with Grotto Falls Trail #432 on the left. Follow this detour, which crosses Hyalite Creek Trail several times before ending at the base of Grotto Falls. The creek tumbles down a 30-foot-tall white staircase to a foamy pool surrounded by mossy walls. This is the only waterfall on this hike where swimming is a possibility at its base.

You can take a shortcut back to Hyalite Creek Trail by turning right at the picnic table and ascending the path to the south. After a tenth of a mile of steep climbing, Grotto Creek Trail rejoins the main trail. Turn right and continue to the second waterfall of the hike. Arch Falls cascades through a mossy orange arch of stone in a small area of exposed granite. There is a steep path that takes you down with a bit of difficulty to the base for a better view of the small but wondrous falls.

Just after a tributary crossing, you reach a sign marking the spur trail to Silken Skein Falls on the left. Take this half-mile side trip to another pretty cascade. The trail is steep, rooted, and rocky, but well worth it. You not only get to see the 40-foot cascade that pours down slick rock, but the elevation you gain on the trail also reveals two other waterfalls across the canyon in the distance: Maid of the Mist Creek Falls and Swim Falls.

Maid of the Mist Mountain rises majestically between the two ravines. In addition, the path leads to some interesting rock formations with overhangs and small caves to explore.

Return to the main trail and continue left. The trail climbs gently along the cascading creek, passing some small grassy meadows. The mountain backdrop and the sound of songbirds accompany you as you venture up the canyon. When you reach a spur trail that leads to the fourth waterfall, Champagne Falls, turn right for a short side trip. It's a spectacular, 80-foot-tall splash of whitewater that makes its way through a narrow gorge in the canyon. The adjacent grassy slope and bright moss on the rocks give abundant color to the picturesque scene.

Travel back to the main trail and continue south. Go left at a large side trail that leads to a canyon overlook, and climb steadily to some more open meadows and views of the slope to the west. These are good places to watch for wild animals that emerge from the woods to feed.

During the next stretch of trail, you cross numerous tributary streams. In June, it feels like water is flowing everywhere. You soon pass Chasm Falls, next to the trail where the stream splashes through a 15-foot-tall gorge covered by crisscrossing logs. There is a tiny footbridge over a section of the creek that makes a nice viewing platform at the top of the cascade. The path then winds up to a view of Shower Falls, where water creates a wide curtain as it descends about 15 feet. Although there is a path leading right up to the edge of the falling water, enjoy a mountain shower here only when the water is low and gentle.

You soon arrive at a footbridge over Hyalite Creek at Apex Falls, one of the highest waterfalls of the hike. Looking up from the bridge gives you an unobstructed view, but a path also leads up to explore the base. The waterfall cascades over 75 feet along mossy banks and down a wooded slope. Healthy groves of Engelmann spruce thrive with so much water irrigating the earth. You might have to get your feet wet when crossing stepping-stones over Shower Creek a short distance ahead. After a scenic opening in the trees looking north down Hyalite Canyon, you cross a footbridge over the creek at some small cascades. S'il Vous Plait Falls appears on your right and

Shower Falls.

provides a perfect resting spot after the steep switchbacks you just climbed. This waterfall makes a small drop and then cascades diagonally along a rocky outcropping.

Whitebark pines begin to appear along the ridge, and the alpine views are spectacular as you approach 9,000 feet. The trail continues to climb up to the base of Alpine Falls. This waterfall forms in a cliffy area just below the outlet of Hyalite Lake. The trail crosses the lower cascades, so be prepared to possibly get your feet wet again. You soon pass the top of Hyalite Basin Falls, the final waterfall of the journey, as you climb onto the basin. A signed junction offers two options to complete your hike: a 2-mile ascent to the summit of Hyalite Peak or a short walk to the shores of Hyalite Lake. If you're backpacking, Hyalite Lake is an excellent place to camp. This small mountain lake is surrounded by patches of subalpine forest, meadows full of wildflowers, and reddish-colored willows. A ring of peaks over 10,000 feet tall, including Fridley Peak and Hyalite Peak, encircles the basin. Scan the ridges for mountain goats and other animals that inhabit alpine zones.

Miles and Directions

0.0 Hyalite Creek Trailhead #427

0.4 Turn left at junction with Grotto Falls Trail #432.

1.1 Base of Grotto Falls
GPS: 45.4357, -110.9638 Elevation: 7,105 feet

1.3 Return to Hyalite Creek Trail via cutoff trail from Grotto Falls. Continue right.

2.0 Arch Falls
GPS: 45.4275, -110.9613 Elevation: 7,435 feet

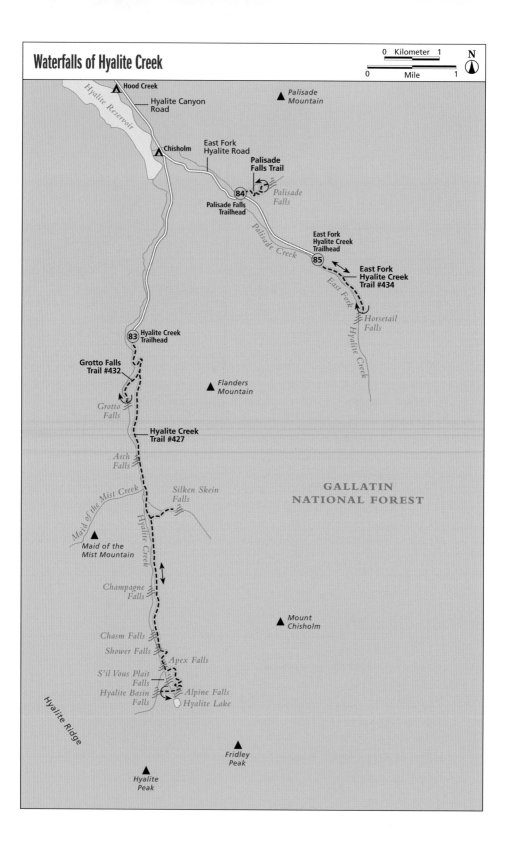

Waterfalls of Hyalite Creek

0   Kilometer   1

0   Mile   1

N

Hood Creek

Hyalite Reservoir

Hyalite Canyon Road

Chisholm

East Fork Hyalite Road

Palisade Falls Trail

Palisade Mountain

84

Palisade Falls Trailhead

Palisade Falls

Palisade Creek

East Fork Hyalite Creek Trailhead

85

East Fork Hyalite Creek Trail #434

East Fork Hyalite Creek

Horsetail Falls

83

Hyalite Creek Trailhead

Grotto Falls Trail #432

Flanders Mountain

Grotto Falls

Hyalite Creek Trail #427

Arch Falls

Maid of the Mist Creek

Silken Skein Falls

GALLATIN NATIONAL FOREST

Hyalite Creek

Maid of the Mist Mountain

Champagne Falls

Mount Chisholm

Chasm Falls

Shower Falls

Apex Falls

S'il Vous Plait Falls

Hyalite Basin Falls

Alpine Falls

Hyalite Lake

Hyalite Ridge

Fridley Peak

Hyalite Peak

Alpine Falls.

2.8 Turn left on a side trail to Silken Skein Falls.

2.9 Base of Silken Skein Falls
GPS: 45.4200, -110.9544 Elevation: 7,830 feet

3.1 Return to Hyalite Creek Trail. Turn left.

3.7 Turn right on side trail to Champagne Falls.

3.8 Base of Champagne Falls
GPS: 45.4083, -110.9582 Elevation: 7,680 feet

3.9 Return to Hyalite Creek Trail. Turn right.

4.4 Top of Chasm Falls

GPS: 45.3998, -110.9563 Elevation: 7,960 feet

4.5 Base of Shower Falls

GPS: 45.3985, -110.9563 Elevation: 8,065 feet

4.8 Base of Apex Falls at footbridge

GPS: 45.3974, -110.9579 Elevation: 8,195 feet

5.4 Base of S'il Vous Plait Falls

GPS: 45.3940, -110.9532 Elevation: 8,555 feet

5.7 Base of Alpine Falls

GPS: 45.3928, -110.9528 Elevation: 8,745 feet

5.9 Base of Hyalite Basin Falls

GPS: 45.3927, -110.9566 Elevation: 8,855 feet

6.1 Hyalite Lake

GPS: 45.3912, -110.9534 Elevation: 8,875 feet

11.9 Arrive back at the trailhead.

84 Palisade Falls

Palisade Creek is a small stream in the Gallatin Mountains that drops spectacularly over a volcanic cliff on its way to join East Fork Hyalite Creek. You enter an old-growth forest and meet the creek at a glorious, open lookout point of 100-foot Palisade Falls. This short hike is ideal for children and beginner hikers. Advanced hikers can find plenty of scrambling opportunities in the vicinity of the falls to obtain diverse vantage points. Ice climbers can often be seen clambering up the falls in winter.

See map on p. 304.
Stream: Palisade Creek
Height: 100 feet
Distance: 1.0 mile out and back
Elevation gain: 485 feet
Difficulty: Easy
Trail surface: Asphalt
Hiking time: 20–30 minutes
Canine compatibility: Dogs on leash
Seasons: May to Oct, winter access dependent on road conditions
County: Gallatin

Land status: National forest
Fees and permits: No fees required
Trail contact: Custer Gallatin National Forest, PO Box 130, 10 East Babcock Ave., Bozeman, MT 59771; (406) 587-6701; fs.usda.gov/main/custergallatin
Maps: *DeLorme Atlas and Gazetteer Montana* Page 84, C3 and D3; *USGS Quad* Fridley Peak
Camping: Hood Creek Campground and Chisholm Campground are located on the reservoir about 11 miles up Hyalite Canyon Road and have thirty-eight sites for a fee.

Finding the Trailhead: From Bozeman, take 19th Ave. south from exit 305 on I-90 and drive 9.5 miles. Turn left onto Hyalite Canyon Road and drive 11.7 miles to a split in the road. Turn left on East Fork Hyalite Road and drive 1.0 mile to Palisade Falls Trailhead.
GPS: 45.4691, -110.9388 Elevation: 6,900 feet

The Hike

Tall, mature Engelmann spruce and lodgepole pines line the paved path as you travel toward an interesting cliff of exposed volcanic rock. You climb steadily and soon reach a talus field and the first open view of high-reaching Palisade Falls. Follow the creek until the trail ends at an impressive viewpoint from below the cataract. Water splashes for 100 feet down the yellow- and orange-colored columns of rock.

The waterfall begins as a vertical drop and then cascades steeply until it terminates in a gentle, winding creek bed at the bottom. There is no pool for swimming, but the stream is usually shallow and safe for wading. Palisade Falls can be viewed from many different angles. With good footwear, you can explore many areas around the base and up into the craggy slope to the south.

Since this is a very popular day-hike for Bozeman locals, expect to see a steady flow of visitors at the falls in the summer season. The most impressive time to view this tall and graceful waterfall is in late spring and early summer when the water level

Palisade Falls in winter.

Palisade Falls.

is highest. Depending on road conditions, Palisade Falls is sometimes accessible by ski or snowshoe during the winter.

Miles and Directions

0.0 Palisade Falls Trailhead

0.4 Viewing area at end of paved trail

0.5 Base of Palisade Falls
GPS: 45.4694, -110.9315 Elevation: 7,385 feet

1.0 Arrive back at the trailhead.

85 Horsetail Falls

Horsetail Falls is a scenic destination in a thick-timbered canyon for ambitious hikers who enjoy making a trail-less final approach to a lesser-known cascade. At normal water level, you can ford the stream and scramble to the base of the falls without too much difficulty.

See map on p. 304.
Stream: Unnamed tributary to East Fork Hyalite Creek
Height: 30 feet
Distance: 3.0 miles out and back
Elevation gain: 655 feet
Difficulty: Moderate
Trail surface: Dirt and rock
Hiking time: 2-3 hours
Canine compatibility: Dogs are allowed
Seasons: May to Oct
County: Park

Land status: National forest
Fees and permits: No fees required
Trail contact: Custer Gallatin National Forest, PO Box 130, 10 East Babcock Ave., Bozeman, MT 59771; (406) 587-6701; fs.usda.gov/main/custergallatin
Maps: *DeLorme Atlas and Gazetteer Montana* Page 84, C3; *USGS Quad* Fridley Peak
Camping: Hood Creek Campground and Chisholm Campground are located on the reservoir about 11 miles up Hyalite Canyon Road and have thirty-eight sites for a fee.

Finding the Trailhead: From Bozeman, take 19th Ave. south from exit 305 on I-90 and drive 9.5 miles. Turn left onto Hyalite Canyon Road and drive 11.7 miles to a split in the road. Turn left on East Fork Hyalite Road and drive 2.2 miles to the trailhead at the end of the road.
GPS: 45.4580, -110.9208 Elevation: 7,095 feet

The Hike

The hike starts with a steady climb through Engelmann spruce and Douglas fir following East Fork Hyalite Creek on its east side. On the southwest side of the canyon there is a tall cliff that is a prime habitat for mountain goats. Bring your binoculars and stop to scan the high rocky terrain while you hike.

After over a mile, you reach a view through the trees of the upper portion of Horsetail Falls several hundred yards up the cliff face. It makes a fast plunge down the rock wall. A short scramble to the base isn't too difficult as long as the stream level isn't too high. Find the inconspicuous path on the right that leads you to a good fording spot. Once across the creek, you're on your own for the final scramble. The forest is open enough for you to find passage along the rocks of the small creek, but watch for stinging nettle along the way. Soon enough you arrive at an excellent view from the base of the cascade. The lower portion of Horsetail Falls zigzags almost vertically down the face of the cliff between bright green lichen that clings to the rock wall.

Horsetail Falls.

Miles and Directions

0.0 East Fork Hyalite Creek Trailhead #434

1.3 First view of Horsetail Falls appears in the distance to the west.

1.4 Turn right onto the inconspicuous path to ford over East Fork Hyalite Creek.
GPS: 45.4417, -110.9097 Elevation: 7,545 feet

1.5 Base of Horsetail Falls
GPS: 45.4417, -110.9129 Elevation: 7,750 feet

3.0 Arrive back at the trailhead.

Absaroka Range

The Absaroka Range is the largest single range in the Rockies, and it extends from the Wind River Range of Wyoming, across the northwestern portion of Yellowstone National Park, and northward to Livingston.

It is often referred to as the core of the Greater Yellowstone Ecosystem and has vast expanses of remote territory. The highest peak in the Montana region of the range is Mount Cowan, which rises to 11,210 feet.

Jewel Lake Falls cascades into a small lake.

86 Pine Creek Falls, Jewel Lake Falls, and Pine Creek Lake Falls

Located in the Absaroka Mountains east of Paradise Valley, the trail to Pine Creek Falls and beyond is very popular for its high scenic value and closeness to Livingston. It is an easy 2.2-mile round trip to Pine Creek Falls, which comprises three separate waterfalls. There are more rewards for those willing to hike another 7 miles and gain over 3,000 feet in an arduous ascent. Attractions include high-mountain gems like Jewel Lake and Pine Creek Lake as well as the 200-foot Jewel Lake Falls and other pretty waterfalls. There is so much beauty to appreciate along the way that you'll most likely forget to notice the length and steepness of the climb. There are also backcountry campsites at all the lakes.

Stream: Pine Creek
Height: Pine Creek Falls, 80 feet; Jewel Lake Falls, 200 feet; Pine Creek Lake Falls, 30 feet
Distance: 2.2 miles out and back to Pine Creek Falls, 9.2 miles out and back to Pine Creek Lake
Elevation gain: 375 feet to Pine Creek Falls, 3,415 feet to Pine Creek Lake
Difficulty: Easy to Pine Creek Falls, difficult to Pine Creek Lake
Trail surface: Dirt and rock
Hiking time: 1-3 hours to Pine Creek Falls, 8-10 hours to Pine Creek Lake
Canine compatibility: Dogs are allowed

Seasons: May to Oct to Pine Creek Falls, July to Sep to Pine Creek Lake
County: Park
Land status: Wilderness area, national forest
Fees and permits: No fees required
Trail contact: Custer Gallatin National Forest, PO Box 130, 10 East Babcock Ave., Bozeman, MT 59771; (406) 587-6701; fs.usda.gov/main/custergallatin
Maps: DeLorme Atlas and Gazetteer Montana Page 85, C6; USGS Quad Mount Cowen
Camping: Pine Creek Campground is located just before the trailhead and has twenty-five sites for a fee.

Finding the Trailhead: From Livingston and from exit 333 on I-90, head south on US 89 for 3.3 miles. Turn left on East River Road and drive south for 7.7 miles. Turn left on Luccock Park Road and drive 3.0 miles past the campground and picnic area to the trailhead at the end of the road.
GPS: 45.4975, -110.5188 Elevation: 5,645 feet

The Hike

The wide, rocky path enters a forest of Douglas fir, lodgepole pine, aspen, and mountain maple. Immediately after climbing to a junction on the right with George Lake Trail, keep going straight on Pine Creek Trail. Cross a tributary and then a bridge over Pine Creek, a medium-sized, braided stream lined with a few tall cottonwood

Jewel Lake Falls at nameless alpine lake.

trees. Shortly after the bridge, you pass a sign marking entrance into the Absaroka-Beartooth Wilderness.

The trail steepens for the final push up to the base of Pine Creek Falls. From a footbridge or from the banks of the cascading stream, you can view this gorgeous waterfall that stands over 80 feet tall and bounces down dark-colored rocks into a shallow pool. Pine Creek Falls is actually a triple waterfall. Walk just past the bridge to find the sibling falls to the right that zigzags down the steep ravine. Return to the trail, cross the other portion of the creek over logs, and climb a few switchbacks. A side trail on the left takes you to a view of the upper portion of Pine Creek Falls, which is likely the most impressive of the three.

Pine Creek Falls is an ideal destination for a short family hike, but more great hiking lies beyond if you're looking for a more challenging adventure. Keep ascending steep switchbacks past the falls area, gaining elevation very quickly. Be careful near the edge of the brink of the upper falls if you decide to stop for a closer look.

The next stretch of the trail remains steep and passes through a mix of live and burned forest. Recent damage from the Pine Creek Fire of 2012 is intermittent throughout the trek. Except for an occasional live evergreen or large boulder, shade is not present in the burned sections. After crossing a tall slide cascade where the creek drops over a boulder-covered hillside, you cross Pine Creek at a logjam. This is easy to do in the summer but could prove too dangerous at high water. Fabulous views appear of forests and slopes leading to rocky peaks.

Pine Creek Falls.

A short climb later, you encounter another lovely cascade of whitewater, with a beautiful backdrop of a high unnamed Absaroka peak. You reencounter the stream and follow it closely past some grassy meadows full of wildflowers in late July. The trail climbs the open hillside to the foot of some tall, craggy rocks and then cuts across a forest of subalpine spruce. Looking back down at Paradise Valley to the west, you can see the winding Yellowstone River. The trail grade finally gets gentler as you enter a lake basin, and the spectacular sight of Jewel Lake Falls appears ahead of you at the end of the cirque. Look for a side trail on the left that takes you past a few campsites. From the shore of the unnamed lake, you obtain a

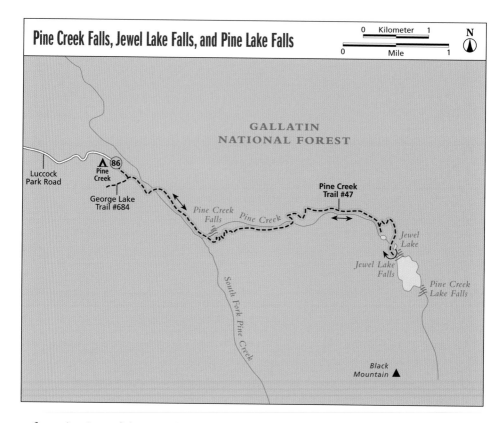

fantastic view of the 200-foot-tall waterfall plummeting down on the other side. Relaxing beside this small lake and admiring the lofty cascade is subalpine heaven. Whitebark pines and Engelmann spruce offer some shade, and the tiny lake is ideal for swimming.

Take the trail farther up the steep slope to high views of the lake and falls. Black Mountain, standing at 10,940 feet, beckons you into the next lake basin a mile ahead. Snowfields last well into August on this peak that encompasses the large cirque whose long ridges stretch from west to east. At shimmering Jewel Lake, there is a small waterfall and more campsites. Deeper water makes for even better swimming. Cross Pine Creek over stones and logs between the outlet of Jewel Lake and the high brink of Jewel Lake Falls. Stop here to enjoy the wildflowers and spot cutthroat trout circling near the grassy banks.

Make the last push up the quartzite boulders along a faint trail that leads to the edge of Pine Creek Lake and the end of the route. It's a round, deep lake that has a few scattered primitive campsites. Pine Creek Lake Falls, a 30-foot slide waterfall on the other side of the lake, concludes the spectacular show of falls on this hike.

Miles and Directions

0.0 Pine Creek Trailhead #47

0.2 Keep going straight on Pine Creek Trail at the junction with George Lake Trail #684.

0.4 Bridge over Pine Creek

0.5 Enter Absaroka-Beartooth Wilderness.

1.1 Base of Pine Creek Falls
GPS: 45.4887, -110.5008 Elevation: 6,020 feet

1.2 View of Upper Pine Creek Falls

2.0 Slide cascade and stream crossing over logjam

2.4 Unnamed waterfall

3.8 Jewel Lake Falls at small, unnamed lake
GPS: 45.4890, -110.4696 Elevation: 9,060 feet

4.4 Unnamed waterfall at Jewel Lake

4.6 View of Pine Lake Falls across Pine Creek Lake
GPS: 45.4859, -110.4666 Elevation: 9,055 feet

9.2 Arrive back at the trailhead.

87 Passage Falls

Passage Creek is located in the Mill Creek drainage of the Absaroka Range northeast of Gardiner. Popular on summer weekends, the hike to the falls is a lovely walk through a unique landscape. The practically flat trail takes you through the remains of the Wicked Fire of 2007. The blaze took out the old growth, and new trees are beginning to make a comeback. Due to lack of shade, this hike is most enjoyable on cool or cloudy days. At the falls you finally enter the cover of green forest. Passage Falls forms a gorgeous curtain over a cliff and comes down 50 feet into a gentle stream.

Stream: Passage Creek
Height: 50 feet
Distance: 5.1 miles out and back
Elevation gain: 285 feet
Difficulty: Easy
Trail surface: Dirt and rock
Hiking time: 2–4 hours
Canine compatibility: Dogs are allowed
Seasons: June to Oct
County: Park
Land status: National forest

Fees and permits: No fees required
Trail contact: Custer Gallatin National Forest, PO Box 130, 10 East Babcock Ave., Bozeman, MT 59771; (406) 587-6701; fs.usda.gov/main/custergallatin
Maps: *DeLorme Atlas and Gazetteer Montana* Page 85, E6; *USGS Quad* Mount Wallace
Camping: Snow Bank Campground is located 11 miles up Mill Creek Road and has eleven sites for a fee.

Finding the Trailhead: From Livingston, take US 89 south from exit 333 on I-90 and drive 16.1 miles. Turn left onto Mill Creek Road and drive southeast for 14.0 miles. Pull into the trailhead parking area on the right.
GPS: 45.2739, -110.5012 Elevation: 6,120 feet

The Hike

You cross a bridge over Mill Creek and start to follow Passage Creek along the east side through a burned landscape. Not a single live tree is left standing, so it can be very hot during the day in summer. Nonetheless, the hilly terrain, with lush grass and green vegetation, is quite beautiful. After a quarter mile of gentle hiking, you cross a bridge to the west side of Passage Creek. Tall fields of fireweed and bushes of ripe red raspberry grow along the sides of the trail in late July. Distant Mount Wallace comes into view to the south after the first mile. After crossing a small tributary, you come to a junction with Wallace Pass Trail. Take a right onto Passage Falls Trail and climb steeply to a small ridge. A large meadow spotted with willows lies to the east beyond a cabin, but it is private and off-limits for exploration.

A winding path takes you down a few switchbacks in the remaining quarter mile to the falls. Take your time descending into the canyon because of the loose gravel and unstable trail. Once you get to the bottom, hike upstream a few minutes to

Passage Falls.

encounter Passage Falls making its gorgeous display. The waterfall drops down a wide rocky cliff and culminates in a flat and shallow pool. Deep in this ravine, temperatures are much cooler, and there is plenty of shade. The cool misty air is especially enjoyable after a hot walk through the dry and desolate landscape of Passage Creek.

Miles and Directions

0.0 Passage Creek Trailhead #558

0.2 Second bridge

1.0 View of Mount Wallace

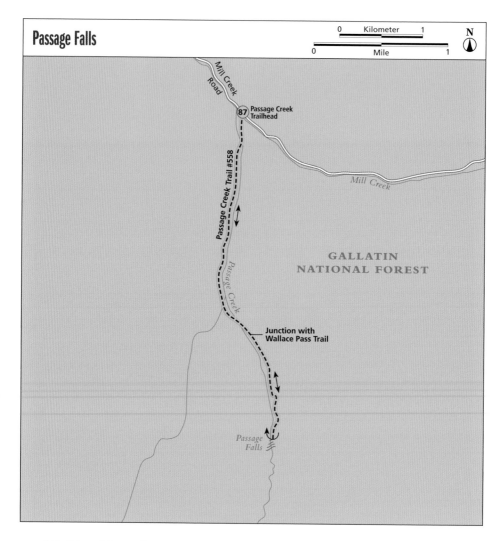

Passage Falls

GALLATIN
NATIONAL FOREST

Passage Creek
Trailhead

Passage Creek Trail #558

Mill Creek Road

Mill Creek

Passage Creek

Junction with
Wallace Pass Trail

Passage
Falls

1.7 Take a right onto Passage Falls Trail #588 at junction with Wallace Pass Trail.
GPS: 45.2522, -110.4997 Elevation: 6,255 feet

2.4 Pass private ranch on the right.

2.5 Base of Passage Falls
GPS: 45.2420, -110.4974 Elevation: 6,405 feet

5.1 Arrive back at the trailhead.

88 Knowles Falls

The best way to beat the crowds at Yellowstone National Park is to get on the trails. The lightly used Yellowstone River Trail into Black Canyon enters the lowest elevation area of the park, so the landscape and wildlife diversity is very high. This is also the most arid of all waterfall hikes in Montana, so be prepared for very little shade and desert-like conditions in the summer. The trail drops almost 800 feet to follow the river into the wild, scenic canyon. The 13-mile round trip can be done as a long day-hike, or you can camp at one of the two backcountry sites along the route. Be sure to secure your permit in advance from the backcountry office at Mammoth Visitor Center. Knowles Falls is not a giant in stature, but its powerful volume is an impressive sight to experience. Alternatively, you can explore the Black Canyon of the Yellowstone via a shuttle-hike to Hellroaring Creek Trailhead. Be sure to carry adequate topographical maps and bear spray when venturing into the Yellowstone backcountry.

Stream: Yellowstone River
Height: 15 feet
Distance: 13.4 miles out and back
Elevation loss: 555 feet
Difficulty: Moderate
Trail surface: Dirt and rock
Hiking time: 6–8 hours
Canine compatibility: Dogs are not allowed
Seasons: May to Oct
County: Park
Land status: Yellowstone National Park

Fees and permits: National Park Pass is required to enter Yellowstone National Park, nps.gov/yell/planyourvisit/fees.htm
Trail contact: Park Headquarters, PO Box 168, Yellowstone National Park, WY 82190-0168; (307) 344-7381; nps.gov/yell/
Maps: *DeLorme Atlas and Gazetteer Montana* Page 84, F5; *USGS Quad* Ash Mountain
Camping: Eagle Creek Campground is located near the trailhead and is open year-round. It has sixteen campsites for a fee.

Finding the Trailhead: From Gardiner just north of the bridge over the Yellowstone River, turn east on Fourth Street North, which becomes Jardine Road. Follow this road for 2.2 miles to Eagle Creek Campground. Turn left into the campground and drive 0.3 mile to the trailhead at the end of the road near the horse corrals.
GPS: 45.0454, -110.6780 Elevation: 6,135 feet

The Hike

The Yellowstone River Trail begins in an open prairie of sagebrush with a few scattered junipers. After crossing Jardine Road, you immediately come to a bluff with distant views to the south of Mammoth Hot Springs and Electric Peak. Farther to the left, you can see the forested Black Canyon, which you will soon enter to follow the Yellowstone River upstream. The first few miles of the hike are especially hot in the summer, so wear sunscreen and bring plenty of water. The trail passes through dry habitat that offers the unique possibility of seeing prickly pear cactus, sagebrush

Knowles Falls.

lizards, and grizzly bears in the same environment. It is also home to rattlesnakes, so be alert.

After the bluff, you start descending long switchbacks into Bear Creek Canyon. Be sure to stay left after the first mile to ignore a merging side trail. You reach the creek and follow it downstream to its confluence with the Yellowstone River. Here you can find shade under occasional cottonwoods, whitebark pine, and Douglas fir. Next, the trail curves west, climbing a ridge over a beautiful rock formation, and from the top, it drops to the east to the banks of the mighty river.

You pass Old Yellowstone River Trail on the right, which is no longer in use due to private development in Gardiner that blocks its access. Stay left along the river and notice the increased sootiness of the trail and a few seemingly dormant geyser cones on the left. These geothermal features add an interesting element to the landscape that is uniquely Yellowstone. At the beach near the wooden bridge that crosses the mouth of Bear Creek, consider taking a refreshing dip in the creek if the water level isn't hazardous.

As you travel along the benches of the Yellowstone River, you are in prime wildlife habitat. Pronghorn, bighorn sheep, elk, mule deer, grizzly bear, black bear, coyote, wolf, bison, eagle, and osprey can all be found here. Since the canyon is critical low-elevation wintering ground for big game, you will see a greater concentration of animals in the early season. If you decide to hike in the spring, be especially alert

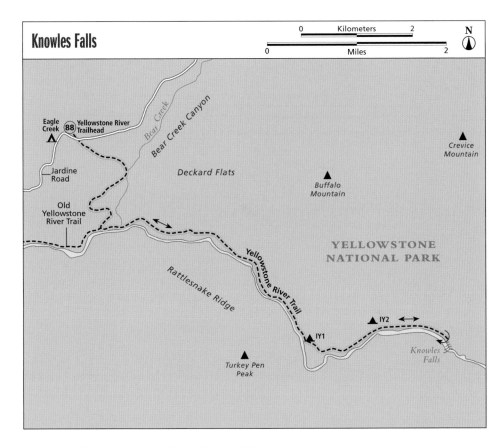

Knowles Falls

for grizzlies taking possession of winterkill carcasses. A grizzly bear on a carcass is as dangerous, if not more dangerous, than a sow protecting her cubs.

The level trail reaches a sign marking entrance into Yellowstone National Park. No bikes, dogs, or dispersed camping are allowed beyond this point. A half mile later, the canyon narrows and 100-foot walls of rock rise up along both sides of the river. Here, you enter the west end of Black Canyon. The canyon meanders through the mountains for over a dozen miles and crosses a less-visited region of the park.

You soon reach the first designated backcountry campsite (IY1). It is situated next to a nice sandy beach at a calm section of the river. At normal water level, there are shallow pools that are ideal for swimming.

As you go deeper into the canyon, there are more numerous junipers and firs under which to find relief from the scorching sun. You come to a view of some thunderous rapids and skirt the base of a slope of massive boulders. The trail climbs steeply through the talus until you are several hundred feet above a narrow, rocky gorge. After dropping to another calm and wide stretch of river, a side trail leads to the second designated backcountry campsite (IY2). You cross a bridge over a seasonal tributary creek and start to glimpse Knowles Falls upstream. Continue another quarter mile to a shady spot in the firs and take a short spur trail on the right to a lookout of the falls.

Knowles Falls is not tall like its upstream cousins Upper and Lower Falls that dazzle thousands of park visitors each year. However, the Yellowstone River's large volume of water spills over the 15-foot drop with awesome force and terminates in a large foamy pool. The deep and torrential channel below the falls is too dangerous for swimming. Given the remoteness and light use of this trail, you're likely to have the falls to yourself. Stay a while and contemplate the flowing river that brings abundant life to the arid landscape of the Northern Range of Yellowstone Park. If you wish to hike farther, Crevice Lake lies about a mile ahead.

Miles and Directions

0.0 Yellowstone River Trailhead

0.1 Cross Jardine Road.

1.1 Stay left, ignoring the false trail on the right.

1.4 Trail meets Bear Creek.

2.0 Keep left when passing Old Yellowstone River Trail.

2.1 Dry geyser area

2.2 Bridge over mouth of Bear Creek

3.3 Enter Yellowstone National Park.

4.8 Black Canyon Campsite IY1

5.1 Rapids and gorge

5.8 Back Canyon Campsite IY2

6.3 View of Knowles Falls

6.7 Lookout of Knowles Falls

      GPS: 45.0133, -110.5957 Elevation: 5,580 feet

13.4 Arrive back at the trailhead.

89 Natural Bridge Falls

Natural Bridge Falls is a mandatory stop if you're recreating in the Boulder River area south of Big Timber. Over time, water has carved underground channels in the limestone bedrock. The falls varies greatly with the seasons. At high water, water flows forcefully through the aboveground and belowground channels and you see a spectacular 100-foot waterfall in the canyon. At low water, the aboveground channel is dry, but a 20-foot waterfall gushes out of an opening in the rock. Previous to its collapse in 1988, a natural bridge was located at the falls. There are two separate trails to access the falls, and both are short and worthwhile. A wheelchair-accessible path takes you along the west side of the river to several overlooks. However, you can reach better views of Natural Bridge Falls along East Rim Trail. There is a moderately difficult side trail to reach the base area.

Stream: Boulder River
Height: 20 feet at low water, 100 feet at high water
Distance: Two short routes total 1.2 mile, 0.4-mile lollipop loop on west rim, and 0.8-mile out and back on east rim
Elevation loss: 60 feet
Difficulty: Easy
Trail surface: West rim is paved; east rim is dirt and rock
Hiking time: 30-60 minutes
Canine compatibility: Dogs are allowed
Seasons: May to Nov
County: Sweet Grass

Land status: National forest
Fees and permits: No fees required
Trail contact: Custer Gallatin National Forest, PO Box 130, 10 East Babcock Ave., Bozeman, MT 59771; (406) 587-6701; fs.usda.gov/main/custergallatin
Maps: *DeLorme Atlas and Gazetteer Montana* Page 85, B8; *USGS Quad* McLeod Basin
Camping: There are several campgrounds along Main Boulder Road several miles south of the trailhead. Falls Creek Campground is a no-fee, tent-only campground with eight sites and Big Beaver Campground is a no-fee campground with five sites.

Finding the Trailhead: From Big Timber, take McLeod Street south, which becomes Main Boulder Road, County Highway 298. Drive 25.8 miles on this paved road until you reach a sign for Natural Bridge Falls. Turn left into the trailhead parking area.
GPS: 45.5498, -110.2082 Elevation: 5,160 feet

The Hike

The terrain of the river valley consists of open scrub forest with grassy clearings full of wildflowers. The area is great for watching a variety of neo-tropical, migratory birds such as the mountain bluebird, violet-green swallow, and chipping sparrow. The asphalt path splits right after the trailhead, with two options to explore the falls:

Natural Bridge Falls. Photo by Martha Gunsalam.

West Rim: On the left is a 0.4-mile, lollipop-shaped trail with several lookouts of the waterfall and gorge. The paved path is lined with neatly placed stones, and there are benches and natural railings at the overlooks. A view of Lion's Head Peak to the west is prominent as you hike along the canyon. After 0.2 mile, the paved route loops back to the start.

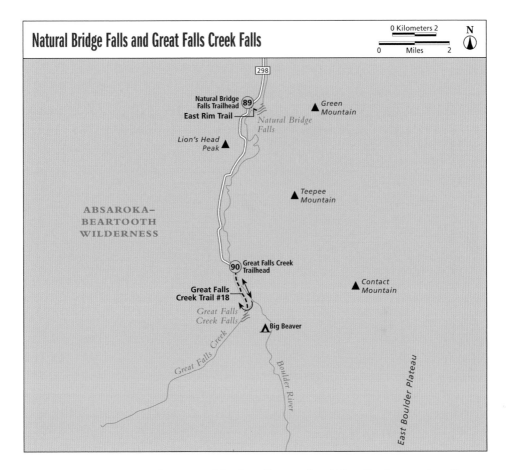

Natural Bridge Falls and Great Falls Creek Falls

0 Kilometers 2

0 Miles 2

N

298

Natural Bridge Falls Trailhead 89

East Rim Trail

Natural Bridge Falls

Green Mountain

Lion's Head Peak

Teepee Mountain

ABSAROKA–BEARTOOTH WILDERNESS

Great Falls Creek Trailhead 90

Contact Mountain

Great Falls Creek Trail #18

Great Falls Creek Falls

Big Beaver

Great Falls Creek

Boulder River

East Boulder Plateau

East Rim: This 0.8-mile, out-and-back walk on a dirt path offers better vistas from the south and east sides of the canyon as well as access to the base. Take a right at the fork onto Green Mountain Trail. After crossing a large footbridge over the Boulder River, walk over the wooded hill with views of the canyon. Merge onto East Rim Trail, which has a few mild climbs and some close encounters with the canyon edge. The well-marked Lower Access Trail appears on your left to descend to the base. Enjoy the lush vegetation of harebells, wild rose, and wild bergamot watered by the mist of the falls. But also watch out for the plentiful stinging nettle on the way down. Down in the canyon, there are large boulders to explore and excellent swimming spots in the large pools below the falls. The slot canyon area downstream attracts rock climbers. Return to the top to reach the end of the trail with amazing views of the waterfall.

Natural Bridge Falls is a marvelous sight that tells a story of the river's role in the erosion of the canyon. Both mechanical and chemical erosion have caused solution holes to slowly form in the limestone, thus altering the course of the river.

Miles and Directions

0.0 Natural Bridge Falls Trailhead. Turn left at Y-junction.

0.2 End of paved trail with partial view of Natural Bridge Falls
GPS: 45.5492, -110.2052 Elevation: 5,100 feet

0.4 Return to trailhead and take the trail to the south over the bridge.

0.6 Marked side trail on left leading to base

0.7 Base of falls area

0.8 Return to East Rim Trail.

0.9 View of Natural Bridge Falls from terminus of East Rim Trail
GPS: 45.5487, -110.2052 Elevation: 5,115 feet

1.2 Arrive back at the trailhead.

90 Great Falls Creek Falls

This trail is located in the Absaroka Mountains between the West and East Boulder Plateaus on a steep slope to the west of the Boulder River. The route takes you from Falls Creek drainage to Great Falls Creek drainage in a mile-long traverse across the mountainside. It's a gradual climb in which you gain 500 feet in elevation and can appreciate nice views toward the mountains and the valley to the east. The final approach to Great Falls Creek Falls takes you down a short but very steep path that not all hikers will be able to manage. You can also incorporate the short hike to the falls into a longer hiking adventure to explore the network of trails on the West Boulder Plateau.

See map on p. 327.
Stream: Great Falls Creek
Height: 15 feet
Distance: 2.4 miles out and back
Elevation gain: 500 feet
Difficulty: Easy, except for the challenging final approach
Trail surface: Dirt and rock
Hiking time: 1–2 hours
Canine compatibility: Dogs are allowed
Seasons: June to Oct
County: Sweet Grass
Land status: Wilderness area, national forest

Fees and permits: No fees required
Trail contact: Custer Gallatin National Forest, PO Box 130, 10 East Babcock Ave., Bozeman, MT 59771; (406) 587-6701; fs.usda.gov/main/custergallatin
Maps: *DeLorme Atlas and Gazetteer Montana* Page 85, C8; *USGS Quad* Chrome Mountain
Camping: There are several campgrounds along Main Boulder Road near the trailhead. Falls Creek Campground is a no-fee, tent-only campground with eight sites and Big Beaver Campground is a no-fee campground with five sites.

Finding the Trailhead: From Big Timber, take McLeod St. south, which becomes Main Boulder Road, County Highway 298. Drive 30.7 miles. Turn right and drive a final 0.1 mile to Great Falls Creek Trailhead.
GPS: 45.4870, -110.2177 Elevation: 5,330 feet

The Hike

After following the Boulder River for a few minutes in open forest, you reach two splits in the trail. First, turn right on Great Falls Creek Trail and then take a left at a second split. Both junctions are well marked. Begin to traverse the mountainside, making your way south toward the next creek drainage. The trail climbs steadily along the steep slope through alternating patches of Douglas fir forest and shale slides. The woods offer shade while the talus terrain offers open views to the east of Contact Mountain and Chrome Mountain and the meadows of the Boulder River Valley. After three-quarters of a mile of hiking, you enter the Absaroka-Beartooth Wilderness.

Great Falls Creek Falls. Photo by Martha Gunsalam.

An obvious side trail appears on the left at the same time that you begin to hear the sound of Great Falls Creek. You can faintly see part of the falls through the trees, but a difficult descent to the base gives a much more rewarding view. The steep path requires you use the scattered fir trees along the way to guide yourself down.

After less than a tenth of a mile, you reach the rocky banks of the creek at the sight of Great Falls Creek Falls. Water gushes over a stack of boulders in the streambed, making several cascades and a 15-foot vertical drop. In this moist environment, lichens hang from the tree trunks and branches and thick blankets of green and orange moss drape over boulders. Large fallen trees at the base of the cascade provide places to sit and relax. It's a small and simple waterfall that offers beauty and seclusion.

Miles and Directions

0.0 Great Falls Creek Trailhead #18

0.2 Turn right and then left; stay on #18.
GPS: 45.4845, -110.2171 Elevation: 5,350 feet

0.7 Enter Absaroka-Beartooth Wilderness Area.

1.1 Side trail on the left to Great Falls Creek Falls
GPS: 45.4721, -110.2118 Elevation: 5,880 feet

1.2 Base of Great Falls Creek Falls
GPS: 45.4718, -110.2113 Elevation: 5,830 feet

2.4 Arrive back at the trailhead.

91 Bridal Falls

If you're passing between Yellowstone Park and the Beartooth Highway and are looking for a short hike, Bridal Falls is a beautiful and secluded destination at the foot of the 10,090-foot Republic Mountain. In spite of its closeness to the town of Silver Gate, the setting at the falls is pristine. Private development currently threatens to block access, so hopefully landowners will continue to allow hikers to access the waterfall.

Stream: Wyoming Creek
Height: 60 feet
Distance: 0.2 mile out and back
Elevation gain: 110 feet
Difficulty: Easy
Trail surface: Dirt and rock
Hiking time: 20-30 minutes
Canine compatibility: Dogs are allowed
Seasons: July to Sep
County: Park
Land status: National forest
Fees and permits: No fees are required

Trail contact: Custer Gallatin National Forest, PO Box 130, 10 East Babcock Ave., Bozeman, MT 59771; (406) 587-6701; fs.usda.gov/main/custergallatin
Maps: *DeLorme Atlas and Gazetteer Montana* Page 85, F9; *USGS Quad* Cooke City
Camping: Pebble Creek Campground is located in Yellowstone National Park, 9 miles west of the Northeast Entrance. It has twenty-seven sites for a fee. Be sure to arrive early in the morning to secure a campsite at this popular campground.

Finding the Trailhead: From Silver Gate, turn south on Monument Avenue and cross Soda Butte Creek. Drive 0.2 mile to a T-junction. Turn left on Bannock Trail and drive 0.8 mile to the Wyoming Creek Bridge. There is a small pullout for parking on the east side of the stream. **GPS:** 45.0085, -109.9728 Elevation: 7,505 feet

The Hike

Begin hiking south from the pullout along the east side of the stream. After passing the private development across the creek, cross the stream to the west side of Wyoming Creek and find the easily recognizable trail on public land.

Once you locate the path, continue south and enjoy the quiet of the woods and the hum of the creek. Lush forests of lodgepole pine and Engelmann spruce dominate at this elevation. Wyoming Creek is small but flows down a wide, winding stream bed of small stones. After a few hundred feet, you approach the granite cliff that hosts the fabulous waterfall. Bridal Falls pours forcefully out of a 10-foot-wide slot canyon halfway up the face of the cliff. Then, water showers down for 60 feet into a small, flat pool at the base. While the main trail ends at the falls, there are plenty of opportunities to scramble around the area to get different glimpses of the beautiful spectacle.

This is one of the few waterfalls in Montana that you can view from behind. Just be careful to not get too close to the edge. Once you reach the end of the ledge, you

Bridal Falls; Silver Falls; Sheep Creek Falls; Woody Falls

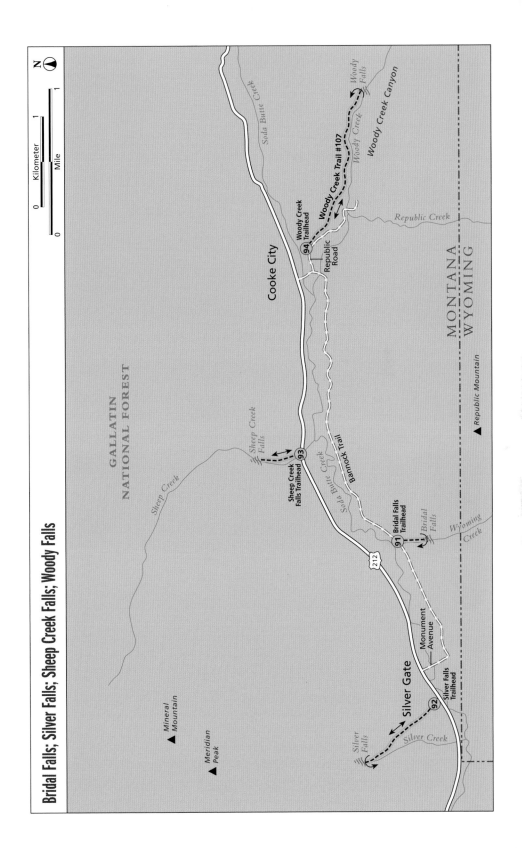

Bridal Falls. Photo by Martha Gunsalam.

obtain a remarkable view to the east through the bridal veil of falling water. From here you can also enjoy great vistas of Mineral Mountain and Meridian Peak to the north.

Miles and Directions

0.0 Bridal Falls Trailhead

0.1 Base of Bridal Falls
     GPS: 45.0061, -109.9722 Elevation: 7,615 feet

0.2 Arrive back at the trailhead.

92 Silver Falls

Silver Falls is a great destination at the end of a short trail. Since there are no trail markings, this is a fairly unknown location. Chances are you won't see any other hikers during your visit, but you have a good chance of seeing wildlife.

The falls are located west of the town of Silver Gate and just outside the boundary of Yellowstone National Park. There are great views of several Absaroka Peaks during the brief jaunt to the tall and elegant waterfall.

See map on p. 333.
Stream: Silver Creek
Height: 100 feet
Distance: 1.2 miles out and back
Elevation gain: 495 feet
Difficulty: Easy to moderate
Trail surface: Dirt and rock
Hiking time: 30-60 minutes
Canine compatibility: Dogs are allowed
Seasons: July to Sep
County: Park
Land status: National forest
Fees and permits: No fees required

Trail contact: Custer Gallatin National Forest, PO Box 130, 10 East Babcock Ave., Bozeman, MT 59771; (406) 587-6701; fs.usda.gov/main/custergallatin
Maps: *DeLorme Atlas and Gazetteer Montana* Page 85, F9; *USGS Quad* Cooke City and Cutoff Mountain
Camping: Pebble Creek Campground is located in Yellowstone National Park, 9 miles west of the Northeast Entrance. It has twenty-seven sites for a fee. Be sure to arrive early in the morning to secure a campsite at this popular campground.

Finding the Trailhead: From Silver Gate, park your vehicle in one of the public parking spaces in town and walk west along US 212 toward Yellowstone National Park. At 0.2 mile, turn up the last gravel road on the right as you leave town. Walk to the end of the road and turn left and up the path following the power lines and avoiding the private land to the east. After only a few dozen feet, turn right into the forest on the marked path.
GPS: 45.0058, -109.9939 Elevation: 7,375 feet

The Hike

After a few hundred feet of climbing through a forest of lodgepole pine and Engelmann spruce, you encounter a T-junction. Turn left and walk on this old roadbed. Although the grassy trail becomes faint at times, just keep walking straight, ignoring the side trails. You soon enter a landscape burned by the fires of 1988, with open views to the north of Meridian Peak and Mineral Mountain, both standing over 10,000 feet tall.

The trail becomes a single-track path that follows the scenic ravine of Silver Creek. It is seldom maintained, so you have to climb over a few fallen trees. Look for violets and other wildflowers along the stream and fireweed in the open burn areas.

Silver Falls.

As you climb toward the rocky outcropping of limestone to the north, watch for wildlife. Bears and moose can occasionally be seen on the slopes and mountain goats and bighorn sheep are often spotted moving along the high cliffs. Astonishing views of Republic Mountain and Amphitheater Mountain appear to the south as you gain elevation. Clamber over a talus slope of shale to the base of a belt of limestone cliffs, and the trail peters out as you reach views of the waterfall. There are some steep side paths that take you closer and to some shady resting spots on the slopes below the cliff. What Silver Creek lacks in its small volume of water is made up for by the grace and height of its waterfall. Silver Falls makes a sudden, 100-foot drop down the wall of a diamond-shaped amphitheater. You can walk right up to the foot of the cascade, and if you stand very close to the rock wall, you can enjoy a gentle and refreshing shower of cold mountain water.

Miles and Directions

0.0 Park in Silver City. Walk west along US 212.

0.2 Turn up last gravel road on the right.

0.2 Walk to the end of the road and follow the power lines to the left to start of trail.

0.3 Turn right onto trail.

0.3 Turn left at the T-junction.

0.6 Base of Silver Falls

      GPS: 45.0122, -110.0016 Elevation: 7,870 feet

1.2 Arrive back at the trailhead.

93 Sheep Creek Falls

Located between the towns of Cooke City and Silver Gate, Sheep Creek Falls is a great stop to beat the summer crowds of Yellowstone Park and the Beartooth Highway. It's a short, trail-less scramble for skilled hikers along a creek to a seldom-visited yet spectacular waterfall. Water comes down a nearly vertical 100-foot slide into a cliffy ravine.

See map on p. 333.
Stream: Sheep Creek
Height: 100 feet
Distance: 0.6 mile out and back
Elevation gain: 320 feet
Difficulty: Moderately difficult bushwhack
Trail surface: No established trail
Hiking time: 1–2 hours
Canine compatibility: Dogs are allowed
Seasons: July to Sep
County: Park
Land status: National forest
Fees and permits: No fees required

Trail contact: Custer Gallatin National Forest, PO Box 130, 10 East Babcock Ave., Bozeman, MT 59771; (406) 587-6701; fs.usda.gov/main/custergallatin
Maps: *DeLorme Atlas and Gazetteer Montana* Page 85, F9; *USGS Quad* Cooke City
Camping: Pebble Creek Campground is located in Yellowstone National Park, 9 miles west of the Northeast Entrance. It has twenty-seven sites for a fee. Be sure to arrive early in the morning to secure a campsite at this popular campground.

Finding the Trailhead: From Silver Gate, drive east on US 212 for 1.6 miles to a large, paved pullout on the north side of the road.
GPS: 45.0185, -109.9612 Elevation: 7,525 feet

The Hike

The forest from the parking area to the falls was affected by the fires of 1988. Therefore, the landscape is open and full of fallen timber. There are also sections of large boulders and shale to maneuver through. At times there is a faint foot trail along the creek, but it is difficult to follow and easy to lose. Nonetheless, plan on bushwhacking most of the time along the wide Sheep Creek ravine. The best route is probably to begin on the east side of the creek and then cross to the west side at about the halfway point. After only a tenth of a mile, the canyon curves to the east, offering you a splendid view of the waterfall. If you're not up for the challenge of getting to the base, this is a descent destination in itself.

Adventurous hikers should continue the full distance to the pool beneath the tall curtain of water. With a 20-foot width and 100-foot fall, Sheep Creek Falls makes an awesome display. Looking up the tall limestone cliff, it's clear the solid top layer is much younger than the more eroded layers at the bottom. While most of the cliff face is rough and rugged, the portion where the waterfall descends is polished and smooth.

Sheep Creek Falls.

You will certainly find solitude at the foot of the falls where a quick dip in the small pool will cool you off quickly on a hot day. Wading in this pool is a unique experience because you can reach out and touch the whitewater that slides gently along the cliff wall. From the falls, you can also admire the view of Republic Mountain standing proudly to the south.

Miles and Directions

0.0 Parking area along US 212

0.1 First view of Sheep Creek Falls

0.3 Base of Sheep Creek Falls
GPS: 45.0220, -109.9621 Elevation: 7,845 feet

0.6 Arrive back at the parking area.

94 Woody Falls

If you're passing through Cooke City, don't miss a hike to this secluded waterfall. The whole family can manage the mile-long uphill trek that gains a quick 820 feet in elevation. Woody Falls puts on a great show that's viewable from the lookout point at the edge of a steep gorge. Be careful around the dangerous canyon area. This hike also features fantastic views of the 10,000-foot-tall peaks in the Absaroka Mountains of Wyoming and Montana.

See map on p. 333.
Stream: Woody Creek
Height: 120 feet
Distance: 2.4 miles out and back
Elevation gain: 820 feet
Difficulty: Moderate
Trail surface: Dirt and rock
Hiking time: 1-2 hours
Canine compatibility: Dogs are allowed
Seasons: July to Sep
County: Park
Land status: National forest
Fees and permits: No fees required

Trail contact: Custer Gallatin National Forest, PO Box 130, 10 East Babcock Ave., Bozeman, MT 59771 (406) 587-6701, fs.usda.gov/main/custergallatin
Maps: *DeLorme Atlas and Gazetteer Montana* Page 85, F9; *USGS Quad* Cooke City
Camping: Pebble Creek Campground is located in Yellowstone National Park, 9 miles west of the Northeast Entrance. It has twenty-seven sites for a fee. Be sure to arrive early in the morning to secure a campsite at this popular campground.

Finding the Trailhead: From Cooke City, drive along US 212 to the west end of town. Take Republic Road south for 0.2 mile past a bridge over Soda Butte Creek. At the first fork in the road, take a left onto a small dirt road that leads for 0.2 mile to a grassy parking area.
GPS: 45.0176, -109.9336 Elevation: 7,545 feet

The Hike

After a short steady uphill climb on a jeep trail, an established trail marked with a rock cairn and an arrow sign appears on the left. Turn onto Woody Creek Trail and continue climbing through thick montane forest. There is plenty of shade thanks to the mature lodgepole pines and Engelmann spruce. In this verdant sanctuary, underbrush covers every inch of the forest floor except for the path in front of you.

Make an intense ascent up the wooded slope for almost a mile before finally reaching a plateau at the edge of Woody Creek Canyon. There is a side trail on the right to the canyon edge where you catch your first glimpse of the falls. Water comes out at the bottom of a vertical crevice in a mass of exposed granite. Then it pours in a triangular shape over multiple tiers of rock for over 120 feet. There is a pool of shallow water at the bottom of the gorge where the sun rarely shines.

Woody Falls. Photo by Martha Gunsalam.

Keep walking up the trail that wraps around the eastern rim of the canyon lined with occasional whitebark pines. After a few minutes, a side trail on the right leads you to a scenic area near the brink of Woody Falls. The loose dirt around the canyon edge makes it easy to slip, so be extremely careful. To the south there are magnificent vistas of two prominent mountains: the rocky head of Ram Pasture stands like a giant on the left and the north point of densely forested Woody Ridge rises to the right.

Miles and Directions

0.0 Woody Creek Trailhead

0.1 Turn left onto Woody Creek Trail #107.

1.0 Short side trail on the right leads to a lookout of Woody Falls.

1.2 Top of Woody Falls
GPS: 45.0114, -109.9133 Elevation: 8,365 feet

2.4 Arrive back at the trailhead.

Crazy Mountains

Located to the north of the Absaroka Range between the Yellowstone and Musselshell Rivers, the Crazy Mountains are volcanic in origin and are the state's largest island range. Prairie surrounds the mountains on all sides. The mountains rank third in the state in elevation, having over thirty peaks between 10,000 and 11,000 feet and a high point of 11,210 feet on top of Crazy Peak. The typical array of Rocky Mountain big game thrives in these mountains, including the largest population of wolverine in the continental United States.

Crazy Mountains viewed from the prairie.

95 Upper Big Timber Falls

Upper Big Timber Falls, the only significant trail-accessible waterfall in the Crazy Mountains, drops through a rugged gorge with scenic views of 10,000-foot peaks behind it. This is a superb destination as a short family day-hike or as a stopover for backpackers heading up to explore Granite Lake, Blue Lake, or other attractions in the Crazies. In the spring, Big Timber Creek is popular with kayakers, who brave the rapids and cascades when the water level is at its highest.

Stream: Big Timber Creek
Height: 160 feet
Distance: 0.9 mile out and back
Elevation gain: 235 feet
Difficulty: Easy
Trail surface: Dirt and rock
Hiking time: 30-60 minutes
Canine compatibility: Dogs are allowed
Seasons: May to Oct
County: Sweet Grass
Land status: National forest

Fees and permits: No fees required
Trail contact: Custer Gallatin National Forest, PO Box 130, 10 East Babcock Ave., Bozeman, MT 59771; (406) 587-6701; fs.usda.gov/main/custergallatin
Maps: *DeLorme Atlas and Gazetteer Montana* Page 73, E7; *USGS Quad* Amelong Creek
Camping: Half Moon Campground is located just beyond the trailhead at the end of Big Timber Canyon Road. It has twelve spacious sites for a fee.

Finding the Trailhead: From Big Timber, take US 191 north for 11.2 miles. Turn left onto Big Timber Canyon Road and drive 2 miles. Make a right at a three-way junction to stay on Big Timber Canyon Road. Travel another 13.2 miles to the trailhead parking area on the right. At 6.4 miles, the road gets rough, so slow down to avoid tire damage. A high-clearance vehicle is strongly recommended. **GPS:** 46.0427, -110.2396 Elevation: 6,435 feet

The Hike

Big Timber Creek Trail begins on an old roadbed that makes walking easy. Even though it is not yet a designated wilderness area, motorized vehicles and bicycles are not allowed on this trail to preserve the wilderness experience. The road climbs gradually and then drops to a wide dry creek bed that holds water only during spring runoff. You continue along the north side of the drainage a few hundred feet above Big Timber Creek. The forests of pine, spruce, and fir are healthy and lush, and tall peaks rise on both sides of the canyon. Long, rocky lower ridges of Big Timber Peak are a sentinel to the south, and other unnamed peaks over 10,000 feet high guard the northern horizon. Look for bluebells and other wildflowers that color the forest floor and meadows.

After a quarter mile, you reach a side trail to Big Timber Falls on the left, indicated by a wooden sign on a tree. Turn left onto a rocky path and drop for a tenth of a mile toward the stream. The magnificent waterfall appears as you arrive at the edge of a

Upper Big Timber Falls.

deep gorge. You can scramble around the ledges to obtain different viewpoints of the falls, but be extremely careful when the rock is wet.

Upper Big Timber Falls is a unique and beautiful waterfall that has multiple sections to view along an almost quarter-mile-long gorge. Water descends a total of 160 feet, first tumbling down various cascades, then sliding smoothly down a wide chute, and finally spilling vertically for 50 feet into a pool. At the bottom, walls of granite surround the stream on three sides, forcing it to curve abruptly to the south. You can walk right up to the ledge that offers you a perfect frontal view. The lower region of Big Timber Peak makes a lovely background to the falls.

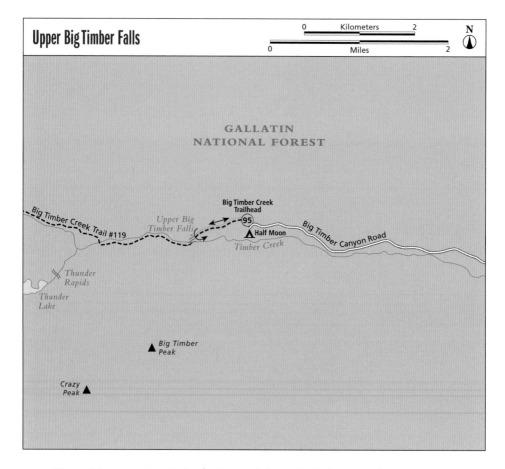

Upper Big Timber Falls

GALLATIN
NATIONAL FOREST

Big Timber Creek Trailhead

Big Timber Creek Trail #119

Upper Big
Timber Falls

95

Half Moon

Big Timber Canyon Road

Timber Creek

Thunder
Rapids

Thunder
Lake

Big Timber
Peak

Crazy
Peak

If conditions are dry, find another trail from the ledge area that goes around a boulder and up the hill on the right side of the stream. This path takes you along the rim of the ravine to views of the upper sections of the falls. When it returns you to the main trail, find another small path on the left that follows the canyon for the last tenth of a mile. You reach the end of the hike at the highest portion of the waterfall. This final view is especially beautiful because it includes an amazing backdrop of the lower ridges of the 11,200-foot Crazy Peak, the highest mountain in the range.

To extend the hike, continue up Big Timber Creek Trail through gorgeous mountain terrain. After a mile and a half, you come to a switchback in the trail. Look closely to the southwest to catch a glimpse of Thunder Rapids, a tall and scenic waterfall in the distance. Beyond this point, you can use your topographical maps to reach backcountry campsites at several high-mountain lakes nestled below Granite Peak and Crazy Peak.

Miles and Directions

0.0   Big Timber Creek Trailhead #119

0.2   Turn left on a side trail to Upper Big Timber Falls.

0.3   Base of Upper Big Timber Falls
GPS: 46.0407, -110.2460 Elevation: 6,540 feet

0.4   Return to main trail. Take a left immediately on the second side trail.

0.5   Top of gorge and last waterfall
GPS: 46.0402, -110.2489 Elevation: 6,670 feet

0.9   Arrive back at the trailhead.

Beartooth Mountains

The Beartooth Mountains lie to the northeast of Yellowstone National Park and to the west of Red Lodge. They host the tallest peaks in Montana, led by high-reaching Granite Peak at 12,800 feet. The Beartooth Highway traverses the range and reaches a high point of 10,945 feet at Beartooth Pass. The allure of high peaks, glaciers, waterfalls, and alpine lakes in the Absaroka–Beartooth Wilderness makes these mountains a popular backpacking destination. The name of the mountain range comes from the shape attributed to Beartooth Peak.

Gorgeous high-mountain scenery at Rimrock Lake.

96 Woodbine Falls

Woodbine Falls is one of the few waterfalls in Montana that you can glimpse from the road before you ever start hiking. The sneak preview of the majestic, 280-foot-tall cascade will surely get you excited for the walk. People of most hiking ability levels can manage the 345-foot climb to the overlook to enjoy a little taste of the Absaroka-Beartooth Wilderness. The trail passes through boulders and forested landscape along the rapids of Woodbine Creek. During the winter months, ice climbers test their skills scaling the waterfall.

Stream: Woodbine Creek
Height: 280 foot
Distance: 1.5 mile out and back
Elevation gain: 345 foot
Difficulty: Easy
Trail surface: Dirt and rock
Hiking time: 1-2 hours
Canine compatibility: Dogs are allowed
Seasons: May to Oct
County: Stillwater
Land status: Wilderness area, national forest

Fees and permits: No fees required
Trail contact: Custer Gallatin National Forest, PO Box 130, 10 East Babcock Ave., Bozeman, MT 59771; (406) 587-6701; fs.usda.gov/main/custergallatin
Maps: *DeLorme Atlas and Gazetteer Montana* Page 85, D9; *USGS Quad* Cathedral Point
Camping: Woodbine Campground is located near the trailhead and has forty-four sites for a fee.

Finding the Trailhead: From Columbus, take MT 78 from exit 408 on I-90. Drive through town and then southwest for 17.7 miles. Turn right on County Highway 419, Nye Road. (You can also reach this junction by driving northwest for 30 miles on the same MT 78 from Red Lodge.) Drive west for 20.4 miles on County Highway 419 past the towns of Fishtail and Dean. Keep going straight at a three-way junction on what becomes Woodbine Road. Drive 7.8 miles on this paved road to a split in the road and then turn left. Drive 0.3 mile through Woodbine Campground to the marked trailhead.
GPS: 45.3527, -109.8946 Elevation: 5,260 feet

The Hike

A well-maintained path leaves the meadow area of the campground and climbs gently through an open forest of Douglas fir and lodgepole pine. You soon reach cottonwood-lined Woodbine Creek, a medium-sized tributary to the Stillwater River. Cross a footbridge to the north side and climb switchbacks up the hillside along the stream.

Ponderosa pine, whitebark pine, and Rocky Mountain juniper soon join in the diverse blend of trees. The clearings host meadows of grasses and sage, and arrowleaf balsamroot blooms beautifully in June. After a half mile, the forest thickens in tight

Woodbine Falls.

stands of lodgepole pine and you pass a sign marking entrance to the Absaroka-Beartooth Wilderness. At this point, the loud roar of the falls becomes audible.

Just before reaching the overlook to the falls, you pass a tiny tributary creek that makes a lovely 8-foot mini waterfall on your right. You arrive at a small viewing area with a stone railing that marks the end of the trail. From here you can enjoy

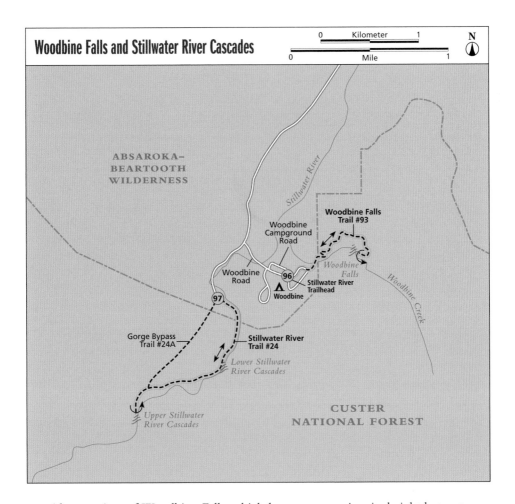

Woodbine Falls and Stillwater River Cascades

0   Kilometer   1

0   Mile   1

N

ABSAROKA–
BEARTOOTH
WILDERNESS

Stillwater River

Woodbine Falls
Trail #93

Woodbine
Campground
Road

Woodbine Falls

Woodbine
Road

96

Stillwater River
Trailhead

97

Woodbine

Woodbine Creek

Gorge Bypass
Trail #24A

Stillwater River
Trail #24

Lower Stillwater
River Cascades

CUSTER
NATIONAL FOREST

Upper Stillwater
River Cascades

a sideways view of Woodbine Falls, which lets you appreciate its height but not so much its width. The creek pours down the mountains in several sections for a total of 280 feet. If you scramble up steep paths along the ridge, you'll find different angles to admire the tall and gorgeous waterfall. From this high vantage point, you can also see the rugged canyon up the Stillwater River and the 8,240-foot unnamed mountain that lifts its pointed peak to the sky.

Miles and Directions

0.0 Woodbine Falls Trailhead #93

0.2 Footbridge over Woodbine Creek

0.5 Enter Absaroka-Beartooth Wilderness Area.

0.7 Overlook of Woodbine Falls
GPS: 45.3545, -109.8861 Elevation: 5,605 feet

1.5 Arrive back at the trailhead.

97 Stillwater River Cascades

Located just inside the border of the Absaroka-Beartooth Wilderness, Stillwater River Cascades is a beautiful destination for day-hikers looking for a short walk or a pleasant stopover for backpackers en route to the wilderness backcountry. There are numerous cascades and pools along a half-mile-long stretch of the gorge. The spot is ideal for picnicking or fishing with the family.

See map on p. 351.
Stream: Stillwater River
Height: Ranging from 5 to 15 feet
Distance: 1.2 miles out and back
Elevation gain: 290 feet
Difficulty: Easy
Trail surface: Dirt and rock
Hiking time: 30–60 minutes
Canine compatibility: Dogs are allowed
Seasons: Apr to Nov
County: Stillwater

Land status: Wilderness area, national forest
Fees and permits: No fees required
Trail contact: Custer Gallatin National Forest, PO Box 130, 10 East Babcock Ave., Bozeman, MT 59771; (406) 587-6701; fs.usda.gov/main/custergallatin
Maps: *DeLorme Atlas and Gazetteer Montana* Page 85, D9; *USGS Quad* Cathedral Point
Camping: Woodbine Campground is located a half mile before reaching Stillwater River Trailhead and has forty-four sites for a fee.

Finding the Trailhead: From Columbus, take MT 78 from exit 408 on I-90. Drive through town and then southwest for 17.7 miles. Turn right on County Highway 419, Nye Road. (You can also reach this junction by driving northwest for 30 miles on the same MT 78 from Red Lodge.) Drive west for 20.4 miles on County Highway 419 past the towns of Fishtail and Dean. Keep going straight at a three-way junction on what becomes Woodbine Road. Drive 7.8 miles on this paved road to a split in the road and then turn right. Drive 0.3 mile to Stillwater River Trailhead at the end of the road.
GPS: 45.3506, -109.9030 Elevation: 5,210 feet

The Hike

Stillwater River Trail meets up with the river on its west bank and passes a nice swimming hole after only a tenth of a mile. The trail heads south and enters a canyon of impressive tan and gray-colored rock walls. The river immediately starts displaying its force and elegance as you wind up the trail along a series of white cascades pouring into bubbling emerald pools. Massive overhanging cliffs on your right provide cool shade until late in the afternoon and the falls generate breezes through the canyon as well.

After passing a sign marking entrance into the Absaroka-Beartooth Wilderness, the trail continues to follow the flat ledge between tumbling whitewater and the rock walls. Most of the cascades are only about 5 feet tall, although a few stand over 10 feet. It's a short and exhilarating hike through the canyon. After a half mile the first series

Stillwater River Cascades.

of cascades ends and the river returns to a more gentle flow. Ignore the Gorge Bypass Trail that merges sharply on the right, which is designated for stock users. Upon reaching another rocky section of the valley a short distance ahead, you encounter a second set of large cascades. The grand finale is a sunny, 15-foot-tall waterfall that squeezes through a gorge over large boulders of granite.

A great option to extend the hike is to visit the marshy Sioux Charley Lake a few miles up the trail. These first miles can be just the beginning of a multiday backpacking adventure through the Beartooth Mountains along the 25-mile-long Stillwater River Trail.

Miles and Directions

0.0 Stillwater River Trailhead #24

0.3 Enter Absaroka-Beartooth Wilderness.

0.4 View of first series of Stillwater River Cascades
GPS: 45.3451, -109.9032 Elevation: 5,405 feet

0.5 Pass Gorge Bypass Trail #24A on the right.

0.6 View of second series of Stillwater River Cascades
GPS: 45.3411, -109.9131 Elevation: 5,500 feet

1.2 Arrive back at the trailhead.

98 Impasse Falls, via East Rosebud Cascades and Martin Falls

East Rosebud Creek Trail is a popular backpacking route that heads into the heart of the Beartooth Mountains, the tallest peaks in the state. It's a long but worthwhile trek to Impasse Falls, one of Montana's finest waterfalls. There are so many interesting features along the way that it's easy to overlook the considerable climbing and distance. From start to finish, a new wonder lies around each bend of the trail.

While the first few miles cross open terrain scorched by the Shepard Mountain Fire of 1996, you encounter more and more live timber and lush vegetation with each mile you hike. This trek is ideal for three or more days of backpacking, and there are many campsites to choose from at the numerous lakes and waterfalls along the way. Check the special regulations for camping near waterways in the Absaroka-Beartooth Wilderness.

Stream: East Rosebud Creek
Height: 190 feet
Distance: 23.6 miles out and back
Elevation gain: 2,545 feet
Difficulty: Moderate to difficult
Trail surface: Dirt and rock
Hiking time: 12–16 hours
Canine compatibility: Dogs are allowed
Seasons: July to Sep
County: Carbon
Land status: Wilderness area, national forest

Fees and permits: No fees required
Trail contact: Custer Gallatin National Forest, PO Box 130, 10 East Babcock Ave., Bozeman, MT 59771; (406) 587-6701; fs.usda.gov/main/custergallatin
Maps: *DeLorme Atlas and Gazetteer Montana* Page 85, F10; *USGS Quad* Alpine and Castle Mountain
Camping: East Rosebud Campground is located near the trailhead and has fourteen heavily used campsites for a fee.

Finding the Trailhead: From Columbus and from exit 408 on I-90, take MT 78 south for 26.8 miles to the town of Roscoe. Turn right on East Rosebud Road and drive 3.8 miles. Turn right at a fork in the road to stay on East Rosebud Road and drive another 10.6 miles to East Rosebud Trailhead.
GPS: 45.1971, -109.6354 Elevation: 6,260 feet

The Hike

East Rosebud Trail begins on the developed eastern side of East Rosebud Lake. Tall cathedral-looking peaks on both sides of the canyon loom above you from the outset of the hike. You pass a few cabins during the first half mile and then climb a short rise to an overlook of the scenic lake. Here, you enter the Absaroka-Beartooth Wilderness and turn away from civilization and toward new and exciting views. As you hike

Impasse Falls.

around the hillside where East Rosebud Creek flows into the lake, you have a brief chance of seeing a couple of large waterfalls high up on the headwall in front of you.

At a tributary crossing, a perfect view of Lower East Rosebud Cascade comes into view. It's a whitewater cascade of extreme force that makes a couple of 15-foot drops into a pool of swirling whitewater. The trail passes beneath some interesting overhanging boulders of smooth granite and a small spur trail on the right that takes you to some rocks at the base of the falls. It's worth it to take your pack off and stop here for a while. The trail gets steeper and climbs a few switchbacks to a view of some more large cascades. You cross a couple of wooden footbridges over Snow Creek, and looking east see another waterfall gushing down the walls and boulders of the mountain.

The first grove of green forest finally appears as you reach Elk Lake. This is a beautiful location that's a good option for the first night of camping in a more relaxed backpacking trip. The stream rages on both ends of the lake. Continuing up the trail, you pass through old and new forests along the boulders and gravel bars of twisting East Rosebud Creek. This is prime mountain goat habitat, so keep an eye out for the cliff-loving ungulates. A small waterfall tumbles down a boulder in a talus slope on the left as the trail crosses several sections of Five-Mile Creek. A quarter mile ahead, you encounter a row of cottonwoods lining the stream. Look up here to the northeast to spot another amazing waterfall, Arch Creek Falls, which descends over 100 feet along slides, drops, and rock stairs.

You leave the burned terrain of the hike completely as the canyon narrows and you enter cool forests of spruce and fir. After some steep switchbacks, you pass through a boulder scree field. Granite walls close in and the stream becomes a continual white chain of cascades in the narrow canyon. You pass beneath slick walls of granite painted with colorful streaks of fluorescent green and orange. The trail makes an exhilarating ledge traverse and then crosses another boulder field to a small hidden pond. Middle East Rosebud Cascade tumbles down a series of 5- to 10-foot drops until making its arrival in a calm pool. This location is perfect for a mid-hike swim in a fantastic setting.

During the next half mile, the trail climbs a few long switchbacks and levels out to a view of the turquoise waters of Rimrock Lake. The trail descends to a wooden footbridge over East Rosebud Creek at the lake's outlet. After bordering the lake surrounded by conifers, large boulders, and cliffs, you pass a couple of campsites in the trees. From the forested southern end of Rimrock Lake, you can see Upper East Rosebud Cascade, one of the most beautiful waterfalls you'll ever see. Thirty feet of whitewater tumbles over granite blocks and enters the lake. Montane forest and some of the tallest peaks in Montana encircle the lake and falls.

Leaving the shade of the woods, the trail goes back out into open talus terrain, requiring some more strenuous climbing. While making the next ascent, enjoy the view of fabulous several-hundred-foot-high waterfalls streaming down the mountainside in numerous slides and drops. The trail fortunately reenters the cool shade of spruce forest for the final push to Rainbow Lake. After passing a sunny pond and a small meadow, the path begins to follow the lake toward its densely forested southeast shore. Notice the waterfalls high above the lake looking south. You enter tall stands of pines and then reach a meadow of thick wildflowers and side trails accessing the lakeshore. The backcountry sites at the meadow are an ideal place to spend the first or second night so you can hike the remaining miles to Impasse Falls without a heavy pack.

From Rainbow Lake, the trail winds up a forested hillside and meets East Rosebud Creek again at a long series of cascades. Just after reaching 8,000 feet, you come to a postcard view of Rainbow Lake to the northeast. Shortly after, you encounter Lake at Falls and Martin Falls, where you can find more campsites. At the inlet area, there is an even better view of the two 75-foot waterfalls that plunge into the lake. The next section of the trail traverses a flat basin, passes Big Park Lake, and comes to a wooden bridge over Granite Creek. This sizable tributary to East Rosebud Creek originates near 12,800-foot Granite Peak, the highest mountain in Montana.

After the bridge, the trail climbs around a steep mountain toward Duggan Lake. This ascent is shaded and offers abundant huckleberry picking in July and August. A short side trail leads to a view to the south of another unnamed waterfall, whose 30-foot width is about equal to its height. This gorgeous cascade descends a smooth slab of bedrock and curves into a pool.

After climbing out of the trees and onto some rock ledges, you reach views of Duggan Lake, whose cirque is surrounded by rock to the east and forest to the west. Here, you get your first glimpse of the 190-foot Impasse Falls, an elegant waterfall that pours over a smooth cliff face and into the west end of the lake. The thunderous

Impasse Falls, East Rosebud Cascades, Martin Falls; Sentinel Falls and Calamity Falls

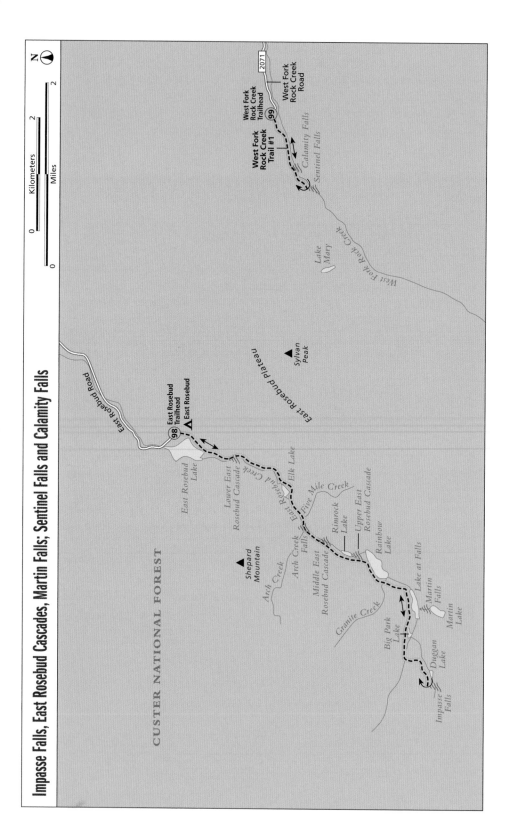

sound across the lake lures you along the shoreline. There is no obvious path, but a fairly challenging scramble over rocks gets you to the base of the stately falls.

Sit close and feel the mist produced by the cataract's roaring splash. Follow the trail another steep quarter mile to a ridgeline view of Impasse Falls and the lake. The towering peaks, rugged canyon, and shimmering emerald water of the lake add to the experience of one of Montana's most beautiful waterfalls.

Miles and Directions

0.0 East Rosebud Trailhead #15

0.7 Enter Absaroka-Beartooth Wilderness.

1.6 Base of Lower East Rosebud Cascade
GPS: 45.1798, -109.6457 Elevation: 6,325 feet

2.4 Two bridges over Snow Creek at unnamed falls

3.3 Elk Lake
GPS: 45.1650, -109.6584 Elevation: 6,805 feet

4.0 Footbridge over Five-Mile Creek

4.4 View of Arch Creek Falls to the northwest
GPS: 45.1575, -109.6772 Elevation: 6,935 feet

5.4 Pond at base of cascading Middle East Rosebud Cascade
GPS: 45.1508, -109.6820 Elevation: 7,385 feet

6.0 Footbridge at Rimrock Lake

6.4 View of Upper East Rosebud Cascade across Rimrock Lake
GPS: 45.1439, -109.6892 Elevation: 7,700 feet

6.5 View of tall unnamed waterfall on the right

7.1 Rainbow Lake
GPS: 45.1384, -109.6901 Elevation: 7,770 feet

7.8 Side trail on the left to campsites near Rainbow Lake. Keep right to continue route.

8.4 Scenic overlook of Rainbow Lake

9.1 Lake at Falls and view of Martin Falls
GPS: 45.1245, -109.7118 Elevation: 8,145 feet

9.6 Big Park Lake
GPS: 45.1256, -109.7214 Elevation: 8,200 feet

11.1 First view of Impasse Falls and Duggan Lake

11.5 Reach shore of Duggan Lake. Scramble to base of Impasse Falls or stay on trail to ridgetop view.

11.6 Base of Impasse Falls
GPS: 45.1175, -109.7407 Elevation: 8,805 feet

11.8 Ridgetop view

23.6 Arrive back at the trailhead.

99 Sentinel Falls and Calamity Falls

Located in the Absaroka-Beartooth Wilderness, Calamity Falls and Sentinel Falls are some of the easternmost of Montana's waterfalls. The trail follows West Fork Rock Creek, which parallels impressive ridges to the north and south that stand over 10,000 feet tall. Forest fires devastated the section of the drainage where the trail passes, creating a bizarre terrain of dead snags and exposed boulders. The unshaded trail can be very sunny, so try to pick a cooler time to take this hike. This is an easy walk the whole family can do in a few hours, and it's a good way to get a small taste of the majestic Beartooth Mountains.

See map on p. 358.
Stream: West Fork Rock Creek
Height: Sentinel Falls, 15 feet; Calamity Falls, 15 feet
Distance: 4.2 miles out and back
Elevation gain: 395 feet
Difficulty: Easy
Trail surface: Dirt and rock
Hiking time: 2-3 hours
Canine compatibility: Dogs are allowed
Seasons: June to Oct
County: Carbon

Land status: Wilderness area, national forest
Fees and permits: No fees required
Trail contact: Custer Gallatin National Forest, PO Box 130, 10 East Babcock Ave., Bozeman, MT 59771; (406) 587-6701; fs.usda.gov/main/custergallatin
Maps: *DeLorme Atlas and Gazetteer Montana* Page 85, E1; *USGS Quad* Sylvan Peak
Camping: Cascade Campground is located just before reaching the trailhead and has thirty heavily used sites for a fee. There is also a primitive campsite at the trailhead.

Finding the Trailhead: From Red Lodge, turn west onto West Fork Road, which begins 1.3 miles south of downtown on US 212. The road is well marked with signs for Red Mountain Ski Area. Drive 2.9 miles to a split in the road and then turn left onto West Fork Rock Creek Road #2071. Travel 10.1 miles to West Fork Rock Creek Trailhead at the end of the gravel road.
GPS: 45.1687, -109.4959 Elevation: 7,885 feet

The Hike

The hike begins amid a landscape of boulders and dead snags ravaged by the Cascade Fire of 2008. Senia Creek Trail merges immediately on the right, so keep left on West Fork Rock Creek Trail. After entering the Absaroka-Beartooth Wilderness, you soon reach an area of massive granite boulders. The underbrush is lush with bushes and flowers, and tiny pines and spruce are beginning to repopulate the forest. Dry heat–loving wild raspberries line the sides of the trail in the summer.

High peaks rise on both sides of the West Fork drainage and charred forests lead all the way up. Silver Run Plateau runs from east to west on the south side of the canyon. An adventurous hiker could probably find a way to scramble up to the top of the ridge to explore this alpine plateau that sits at over 10,000 feet. After about a

Sentinel Falls.

mile, you begin to border a patch of green forest. As you continue through talus fields and glacially deposited boulders, views appear to the northwest of the lower cliffs of the 11,050-foot Grass Mountain. The trail climbs more steadily, and then you come to a faint side trail. Turn left and follow the path toward the sound of Calamity Falls. Watch your step when you reach the rim of the narrow canyon, where water spills down with great force. The path leads to the edge of the falls, where you can sense the powerful movement of cascades ranging from 2 to 8 feet. If you're an advanced hiker, you can scramble to the base for a better view.

Make your way back to the main trail and turn left to explore the next waterfall.

Along the way, you drop to a wide, calm bend in the stream. This is a relaxing spot to rest between the two waterfalls or to take a break for swimming or fishing. Up ahead, you encounter a side trail on the left that enters the shady trees along the creek. You soon reach Sentinel Falls, which stair-steps down a 15-foot-tall ledge of bedrock in the stream. If you keep following the rough path over a few fallen logs, you can access the base of the falls for a full view.

To extend the hike, continue southwest on West Fork Rock Creek Trail. The path leads you deeper into the wilds of the Beartooth Mountains and beyond the destruction of the Cascade Fire. Locations such as Lake Mary and Sundance Lake offer a great backcountry camping experience. As with all hikes in the Greater Yellowstone Ecosystem, keep your bear spray handy for the slim possibility that you will need to deter an approaching grizzly.

Miles and Directions

0.0 West Fork Rock Creek Trailhead #1

0.05 Keep left at junction with Senia Creek Trail #13.

0.2 Enter Absaroka-Beartooth Wilderness.

1.5 Brink of Calamity Falls
GPS: 45.1616, -109.5213 Elevation: 8,250 feet

2.1 Base of Sentinel Falls
GPS: 45.1569, -109.5286 Elevation: 8,280 feet

4.2 Arrive back at the trailhead.

100 Silver Falls

The hike to Silver Falls is a stellar destination in itself or part of an extended trip into the Absaroka-Beartooth Wilderness. Except for the short side trail to the falls, the route follows Lake Fork Creek, which bisects the Silver and Hellroaring Plateaus of the Beartooth Mountains. Lake Fork Trail attracts families looking for an easy day-hike close to Red Lodge. It is also well loved by backpackers heading toward Lost Lake, Keyser Brown Lake, First and Second Rock Lakes, September Morn Lake, and Sundance Pass. Remember to carry bear spray when recreating in the Beartooth Mountains.

Stream: Silver Falls Creek
Height: About 50 feet
Distance: 3.0 miles out and back
Elevation gain: 590 feet
Difficulty: Easy to viewpoint, optional challenging scramble to base of falls
Trail surface: Dirt and rock
Hiking time: 2-3 hours
Canine compatibility: Dogs are allowed
Seasons: June to Oct
County: Carbon

Land status: Wilderness area, national forest
Fees and permits: No fees required
Trail contact: Custer Gallatin National Forest, PO Box 130, 10 East Babcock Ave., Bozeman, MT 59771; (406) 587-6701; fs.usda.gov/main/custergallatin
Maps: *DeLorme Atlas and Gazetteer Montana* Page 86, F2; *USGS Quad* Black Pyramid Mountain
Camping: There are some dispersed campsites along Lake Fork Road.

Finding the Trailhead: From the south end of Red Lodge, take US 212 south for about 9.5 miles. Turn right onto Lake Fork Road, #2346. Drive 1.7 miles to the trailhead at the end of the road.
GPS: 45.0790, -109.4116 Elevation: 7,140 feet

The Hike

You cross a pack bridge and begin to hike upstream along the south side of Lake Fork Creek. Healthy forests of lodgepole pine mixed with boulders of assorted sizes carpet the valley floor and slopes. Patches of aspen and willow appear along the stream banks. Lake Fork Creek gushes through the forest in a constant tumble of whitewater. After about a quarter mile you pass a sign marking entrance to the Absaroka-Beartooth Wilderness. Watch for raspberries and dwarf huckleberries that ripen in late July and August. As you follow the stream closely, look between the trees for views of craggy Tollman Point to the north. Gradually, the boulders along the sides of the trail get bigger, the creek cascades get taller, and the climb gets steeper.

An unmarked side trail appears on the left, shortly after the trail levels out again. Watch for it because this junction is easy to miss. Leave the main trail and hike another quarter mile up a steep, winding path toward the sound of Silver Falls Creek.

Silver Falls. Photo by Martha Gunsalam.

The trail leads you out of the trees and into a boulder field beneath a multicolored wall of rock with stunning views of the falls.

The final approach requires a moderately difficult scramble over large boulders and loose rock but there is a path to guide you. Stay to the left of the large boulders to find the trail. The path takes you right up next to the shower of water that plunges

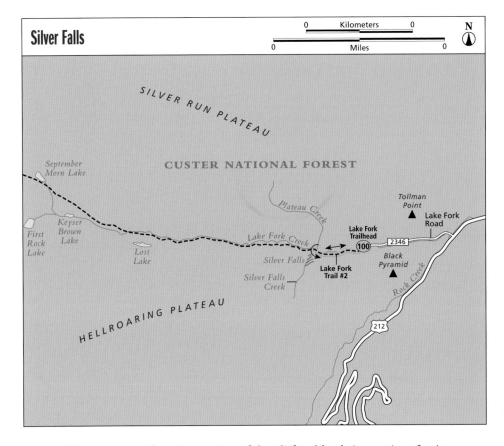

Silver Falls

Kilometers

Miles

N

SILVER RUN PLATEAU

September Morn Lake

CUSTER NATIONAL FOREST

Keyser Brown Lake

First Rock Lake

Lost Lake

Plateau Creek

Lake Fork Creek

Silver Falls

Silver Falls Creek

Lake Fork Trail #2

Lake Fork Trailhead

100

Tollman Point

Black Pyramid

Lake Fork Road

2346

Rock Creek

212

HELLROARING PLATEAU

vertically over an overhanging section of the cliff and lands in a series of stair-steps. Silver Falls Creek flows briskly down from Black Pyramid Mountain on its way to empty into Lake Fork Creek. From the waterfall area, enjoy the views across the drainage to the north. Look closely for a series of falls on Plateau Creek that plummet out of the east end of Silver Plateau.

To extend the hike, follow Lake Fork Trail to a number of scenic lakes on the way to Sundance Pass. You can also complete a 19-mile shuttle hike over the pass and down to West Fork Rock Creek Trailhead on the other side.

Miles and Directions

0.0 Lake Fork Trailhead, #2

0.3 Enter Absaroka-Beartooth Wilderness.

1.3 Unmarked side trail on left to Silver Falls
GPS: 45.0786, -109.4328 Elevation: 7,455 feet

2.1 Base of Silver Falls
GPS: 45.0758, -109.4345 Elevation: 7,730 feet

4.2 Arrive back at the trailhead.

THE TEN ESSENTIALS OF HIKING

American Hiking Society

American Hiking Society recommends you pack the "Ten Essentials" every time you head out for a hike. Whether you plan to be gone for a couple of hours or several months, make sure to pack these items. Become familiar with these items and know how to use them.

1. Appropriate Footwear
Happy feet make for pleasant hiking. Think about traction, support, and protection when selecting well-fitting shoes or boots.

2. Navigation
While phones and GPS units are handy, they aren't always reliable in the backcountry; consider carrying a paper map and compass as a backup and know how to use them.

3. Water (and a way to purify it)
As a guideline, plan for half a liter of water per hour in moderate temperatures/terrain. Carry enough water for your trip and know where and how to treat water while you're out on the trail.

4. Food
Pack calorie-dense foods to help fuel your hike, and carry an extra portion in case you are out longer than expected.

5. Rain Gear & Dry-Fast Layers
The weatherman is not always right. Dress in layers to adjust to changing weather and activity levels. Wear moisture-wicking cloths and carry a warm hat.

6. Safety Items (light, fire, and a whistle)
Have means to start an emergency fire, signal for help, and see the trail and your map in the dark.

7. First Aid Kit

Supplies to treat illness or injury are only as helpful as your knowledge of how to use them. Take a class to gain the skills needed to administer first aid and CPR.

8. Knife or Multi-Tool

With countless uses, a multi-tool can help with gear repair and first aid.

9. Sun Protection

Sunscreen, sunglasses, and sun-protective clothing should be used in every season regardless of temperature or cloud cover.

10. Shelter

Protection from the elements in the event you are injured or stranded is necessary. A lightweight, inexpensive space blanket is a great option.

Find other helpful resources at AmericanHiking.org/hiking-resources